IMAGES
of America

SACRAMENTO'S BOULEVARD PARK

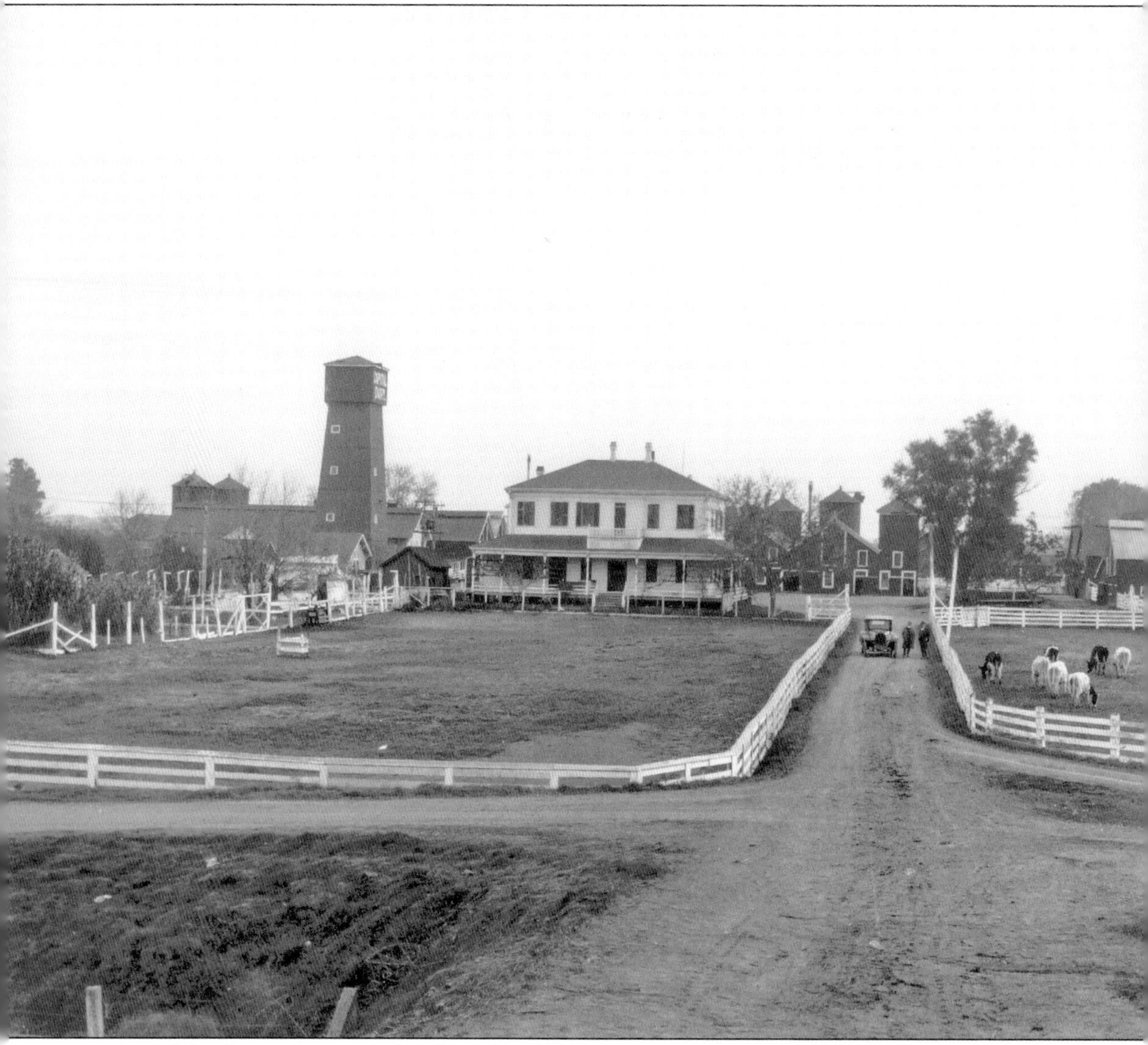

One of the things that made Boulevard Park unique during its early years was that it was home to founders, managers, and captains of business and industry. This peaceful early morning photograph was taken at the Meister family's Capital Dairy in the Elvas district. William Sexton, who lived in a Craftsman bungalow at 331 Twenty-first Street, was the general manager of the dairy for many years. It was located on land that is now bisected by the Business 80 Freeway as it leaves the downtown grid and heads toward Cal Expo. (Courtesy of SAMCC.)

On the Cover: The women in the carriage are employees of the Capital National Bank. They are dressed in period costume as they prepare to celebrate the Days of '49, a 1922 tribute to the California gold rush. The carriage is the bank's entry in the opening parade. Boulevard Park resident Alden Anderson was one of the founders and the president of the bank at that time. He is visible in this image on the extreme right with his back to the camera. During its early years, Boulevard Park was home to the founders, managers, and captains of business and industry. (Photograph courtesy of SAMCC)

IMAGES
of America

SACRAMENTO'S BOULEVARD PARK

Don Cox and Paula Boghosian

ARCADIA PUBLISHING

ISBN 978-0-7385-2955-4

Published by Arcadia Publishing
Charleston, South Carolina

Printed in the United States of America

Library of Congress Catalog Card Number: 2006923160

For all general information contact Arcadia Publishing at:
Telephone 843-853-2070
Fax 843-853-0044
E-mail sales@arcadiapublishing.com
For customer service and orders:
Toll-Free 1-888-313-2665

Visit us on the Internet at www.arcadiapublishing.com

This book is dedicated to the memory of Eugene Hepting.

Contents

ACKNOWLEDGMENTS

In particular, we would like to thank the employees of the Sacramento Museum and Archive Collection Center (SAMCC) who provided the bulk of historic photographs that appear in this book. We would also like to thank the staffs of the California Room of the California State Library, the Sacramento Room of the Sacramento Public Library, and the California State Railroad Museum. The above provided great assistance in the creation of this book. We would also like to acknowledge the contribution of Eugene Hepting and his extensive collection of photographs and memorabilia. He worked nights as a guard for the state treasurer, and so he had his days free. Hepting wandered about the central area, and the surrounding region, taking photographs of buildings and streetscapes. Any time he learned of the existence of a historical photograph, he would attempt to obtain a copy for his collection. The result of his efforts was a collection of thousands of images, clippings, and ephemera—all annotated with his knowledge and comments. All of us who work in the field of Sacramento history are deeply indebted to Eugene Hepting.

INTRODUCTION

For the purposes of this book, we defined Boulevard Park as the area that was designated as the Boulevard Park Historic District by the City of Sacramento. That survey included some additional houses on the south and southeast portion of the original development as designed by Wright and Kimbrough, such as some Victorian houses that predated the development.

Boulevard Park became a new community when the California State Fair moved its racetrack to a site on Stockton Boulevard. The Park Realty Company bought most of the land for proposed residential development. However, they turned the development over to one of the most market savvy real estate firms in Sacramento—Wright and Kimbrough. While most communities are defined by their institutions, such as schools, churches, parks, lodge halls, and business districts, Boulevard Park was designed to have none of these. In its initial brochure for the project, Wright and Kimbrough proudly proclaimed, "There can be no front fences in the entire tract. No stores, no saloons, no wash houses, no wood yards."

The entire tract was divided up into residential lots with wide, numbered streets and planted boulevard strips to create a park-like image. The architecture of its houses and the occupations and accomplishments of the people who lived there further distinguished the development. An egalitarian mixture of people of various income levels and professional achievements settled in the development, but this did not happen out of altruism or the mandates of urban planners. It was rather somewhat a result of the manner in which the lots were defined. The major factor was the manner in which the tract was divided into lots.

The four square block bounded by Twentieth to Twenty-second Streets and from F to H Streets had larger and more costly lots, and in the center of each block was a 100-foot by 140-foot community park. These blocks were reserved for residents that would not blanche at paying from $1,100 to $1,550 per lot. Wright and Kimbrough also required that no home costing less than $2,500 could be built on these blocks, while the average working man's home on other blocks would cost around $1,500.

In contrast, the location of the Southern Pacific Railroad tracks along the northern boundaries of the tract made the lots in that area less desirable and potentially more difficult to market. However, the shops of the Southern Pacific Railroad were not far, and hundreds of the people who worked there were skilled craftsmen who were well paid and had the money and desire to become homeowners.

Wright and Kimbrough responded by making those lots closest to the railroad berm large, 40 feet by 150 feet, and inexpensive, $275–$300, in order to make them more attractive. As one moved further away from the noise of the rail lines, the lots became smaller, 40 feet wide and from 70 feet to 110 feet deep, and priced from $375 to $725. In the middle of each block, from C Street to F Street, there were some large 40-foot by 160-foot lots.

When Wright and Kimbrough began selling lots in July 1905, the first buyers were speculators. As in Oak Park, only a handful of those purchasing lots in 1905 actually intended to build on them. Also as in Oak Park, this tended to slow down the development process. Some houses appeared by 1906, but the real flurry of building occurred in 1909–1915.

An added inducement to buying property in Boulevard Park was transportation. A new trolley line was announced for D Street, providing service from McKinley Park to downtown. It actually wound up on C Street and was operated by the Sacramento Northern Electric Railroad. The trolley line ended at the ticket office for the Northern Electric from which one could travel to most of the cities between Sacramento and Alameda in the northern part of the Sacramento Valley. For those residents on the south end of Boulevard Park, the J Street trolley was already operating. After Oak Park, Boulevard Park became Sacramento's second trolley car suburb.

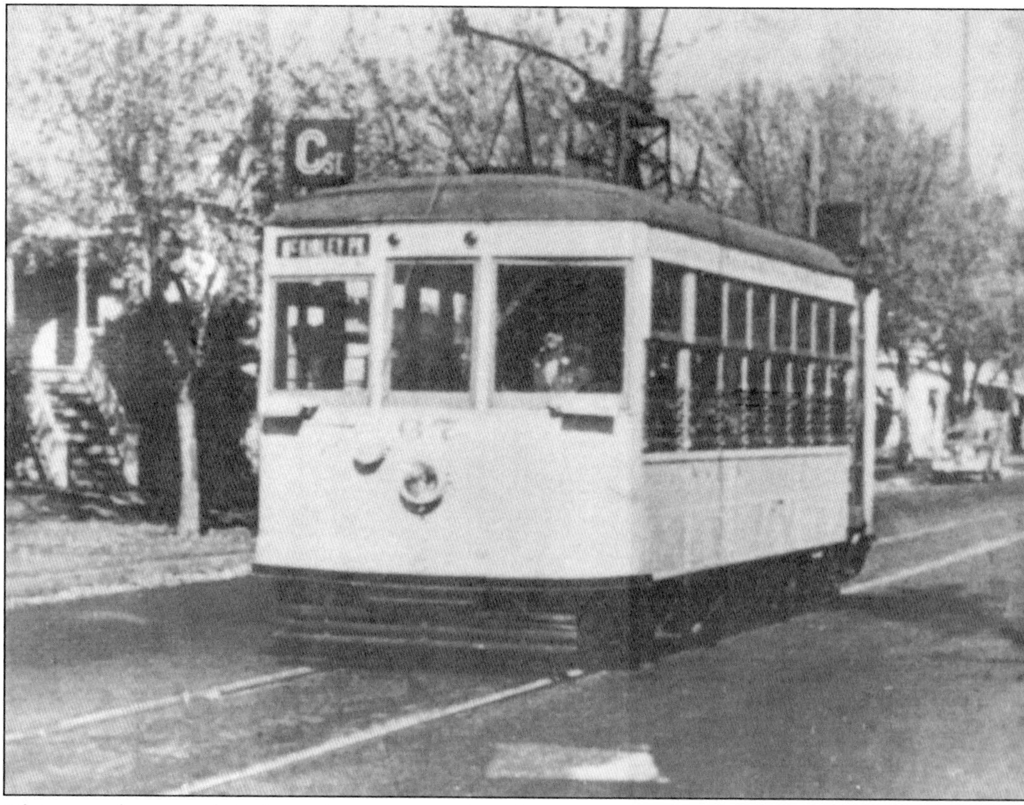

This rare photograph is the only one the authors have ever seen of the C Street trolley. (Courtesy of BPNA.)

One

From Horses to Hollywood

Who would've thought that a California trotting horse in the 1800s would take the first step toward the development of 20th-century motion pictures? The story begins in Sacramento. In response to the dominant regional agricultural industry, Sacramento became the permanent home for the state fair in 1859, and the legislature provided funds for construction of a half-mile trotting park between E and H Streets and Twentieth and Twenty-second Streets in 1860, later expanded to a mile for use by the fair and the community. Trotting was a popular sport at the time, and Leland Stanford, Crocker, and others, such as James Ben Ali Haggin, raced their personal trotting teams on the track. Haggin owned 44,000 acres just across the American River containing a world famous horse-breeding ranch. The Sacramento Wheelmen cyclists also raced at the track.

In 1872, Stanford made a casual bet with a friend that all four feet of a trotting horse in motion were raised off the ground at one time during its stride. To prove his theory, he engaged well-known photographer Eadweard Muybridge to photograph his famous trotter Occident moving at full speed. Muybridge developed a technique to speed up the camera shutter and catch the moment when all of Occident's feet were off the ground at once. Later, at Palo Alto, he continued to experiment by placing several cameras at distances around the track with threads connected to camera shutters that were tripped by the horse during several successive stages of its motion. Devices were fabricated to rotate the photos quickly, simulating the image of the animal in motion. In Palo Alto and other locations, he went on to perform many additional motion studies that led to the development of motion pictures.

Other key elements of the annual state fair were the numerous county exhibits, first housed in a pavilion at Sixth and M Streets, and by 1884, displayed in a new Agricultural Pavilion at the east end of the capitol grounds. The popularity of the fair necessitated a move and consolidation of exhibit halls and racetrack on Broadway. The Union Park track and land was sold to Park Realty in 1905 for development into the Boulevard Park residential community.

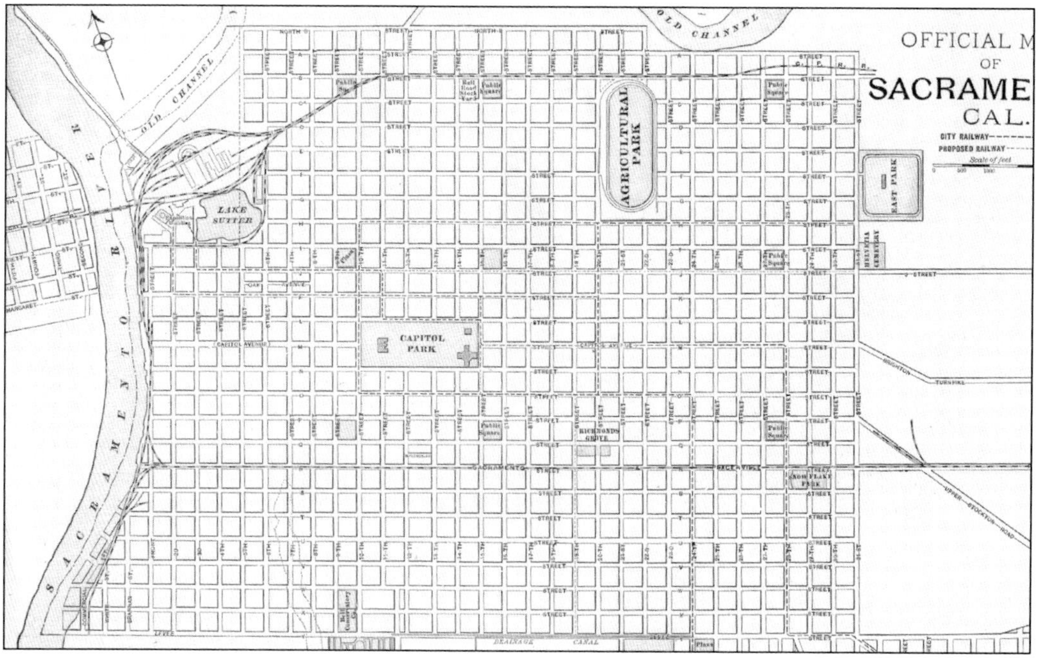

This *c.* 1900 map of Sacramento shows the State Fair Pavilion in Capitol Park and the location of the Agricultural Park and Union Park track, which would eventually become Boulevard Park in 1905. (Courtesy of Boulevard Park Neighborhood Association [BPNA].)

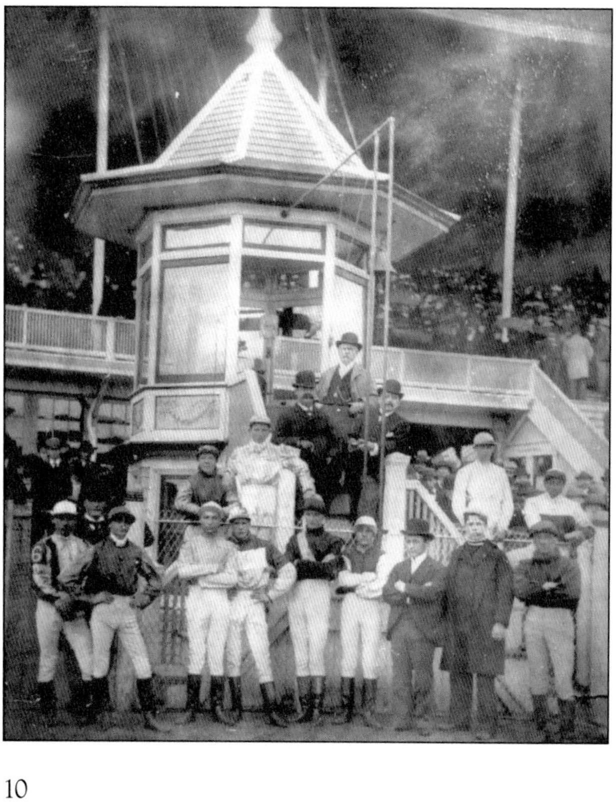

Some of the fastest horses in the world raced at Union Park. In this photograph, some of the jockeys and officials pose in front of the Starters Pavilion. Horse racing was very popular in Sacramento, and the grandstand was filled with spectators. (Courtesy of SAMCC.)

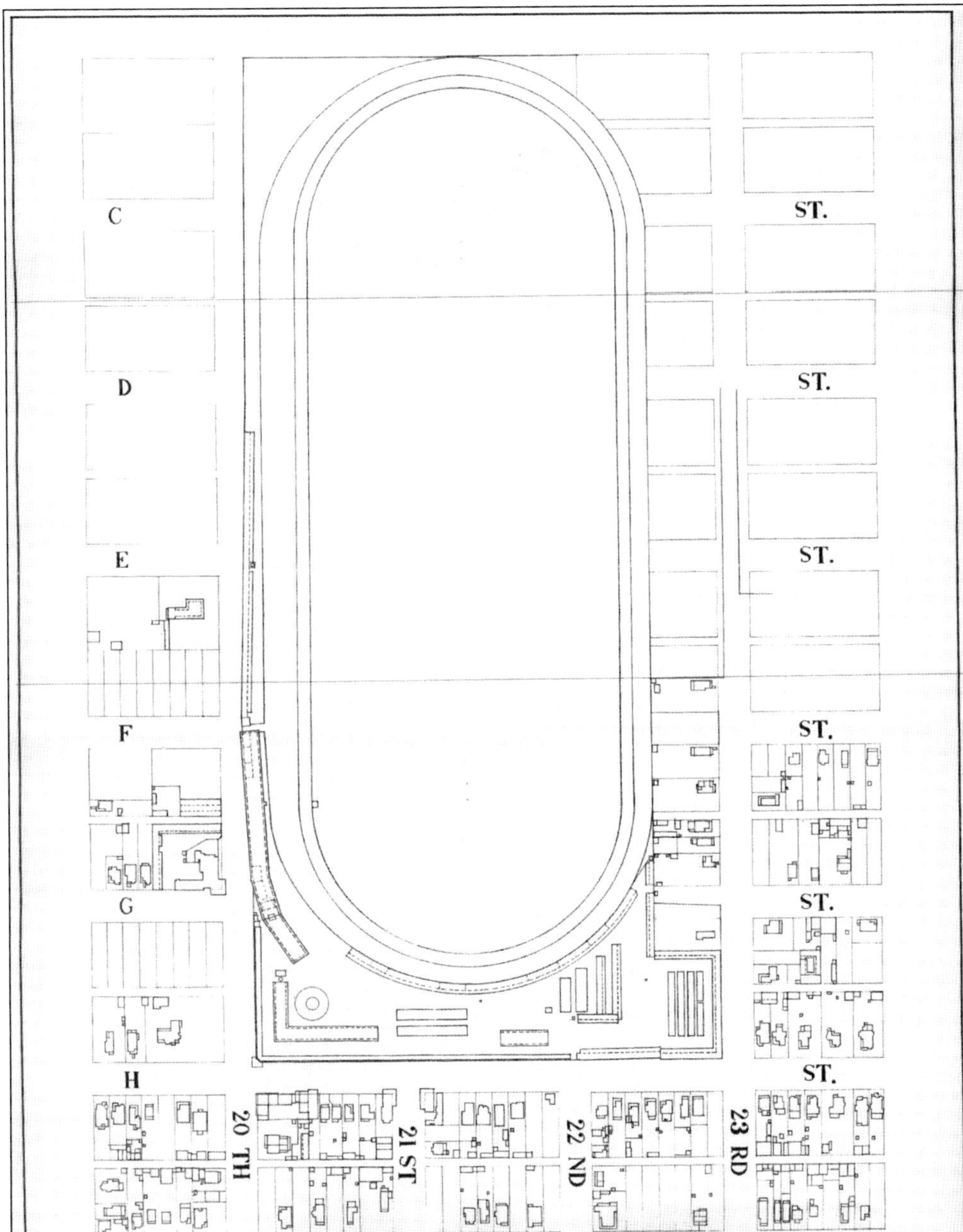

This drawing shows the location of the grandstand that ran along the west side of the track and into the southwest corner. The other buildings on the south end of the track were stables for the horses and other livestock. The entire compound was surrounded by an eight-foot-high brick wall. A handful of houses can be seen along the east side, and two of those houses are still in place at this time—600 and 620 Twenty-third Street. One of the first baseball games in California was reputed to have been played at this site. Home plate would have been in front of the stands in the southwest turn. (Courtesy of Edward J. Cox.)

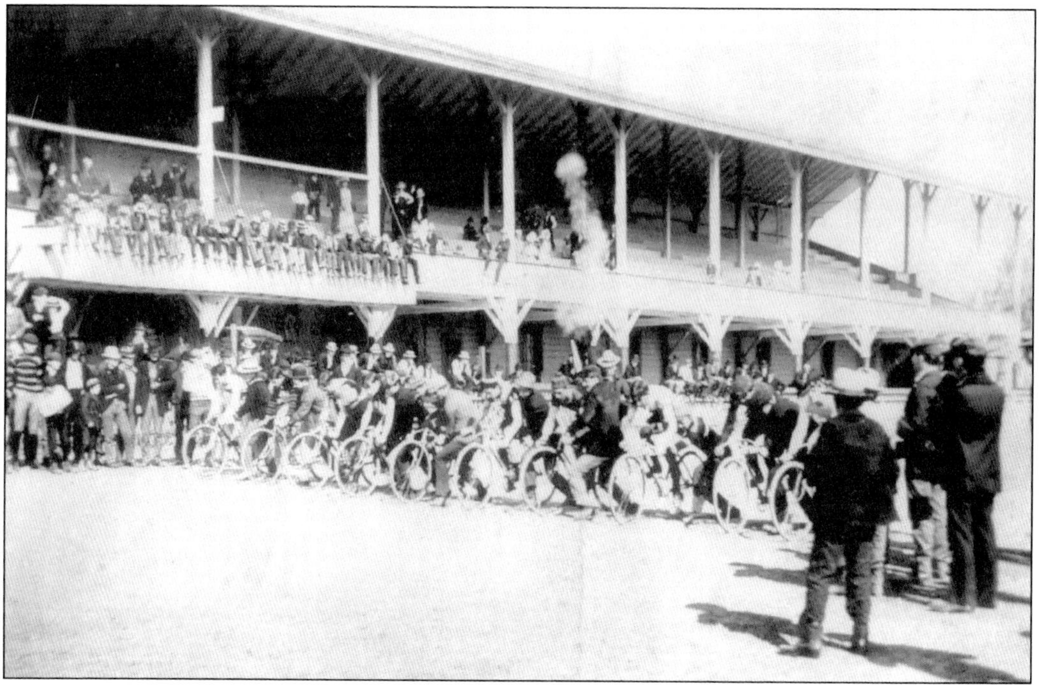

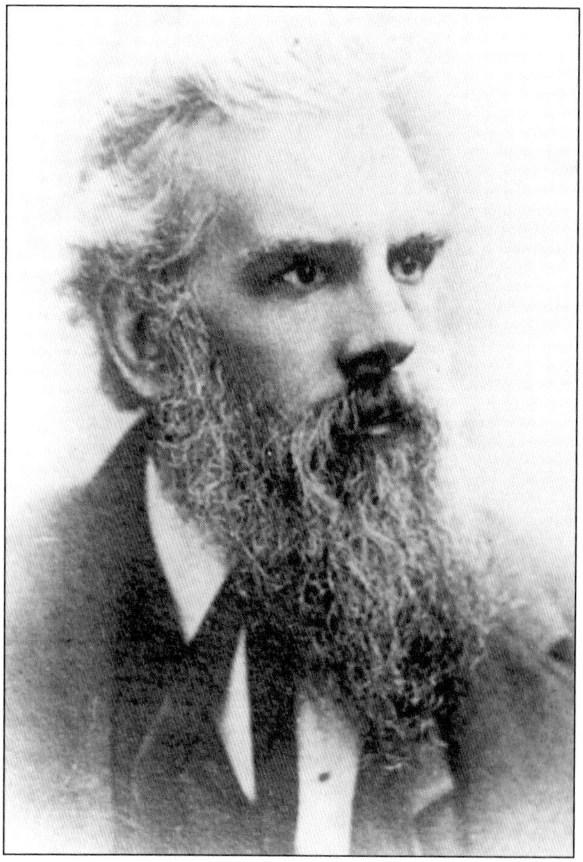

Horse racing was not the only event held at Union Park. In this photograph, the smoke from the starter's gun wafts above the heads of the Sacramento Wheelman. Eugene Hepting was one of the top racers for the wheelman at the beginning of the 20th century. Many of the historic pictures in this book, including this one, are from Hepting's collection. (Courtesy of SAMCC.)

Former California governor Leland Stanford had a disagreement with a friend. Stanford claimed that, at certain points in the stride of a galloping horse, all four of the horse's hooves would be off the ground. To prove his point, Stanford retained the services of photographer Eadweard Muybridge. This photograph of Muybridge was taken around the time of the experiments in 1872. (Courtesy of California State Library [CSL].)

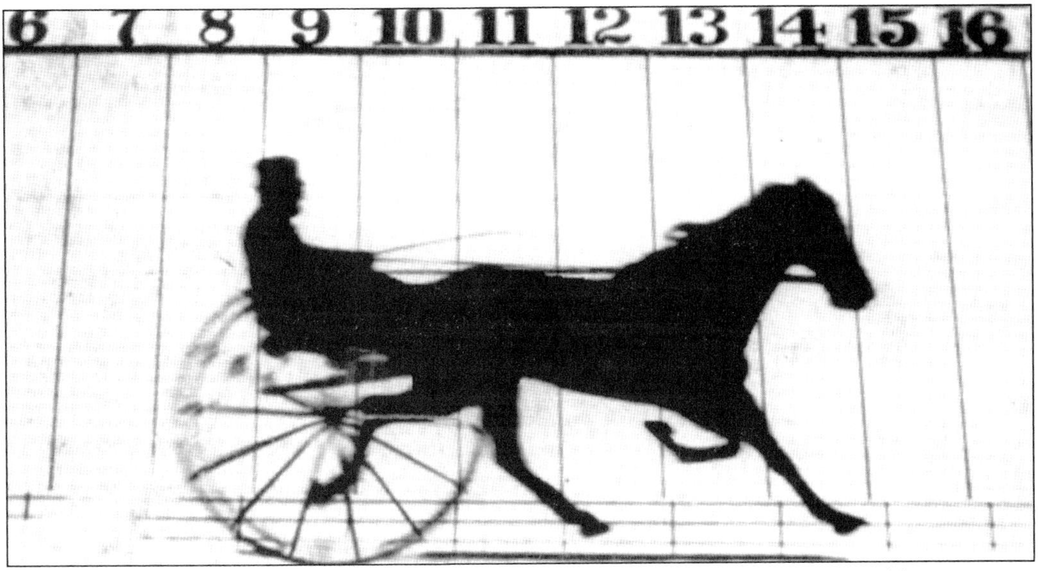

After some experimentation at Union Park Track, Muybridge, in May 1872, was able to create a photograph of Stanford's trotter Occident with all four hooves clearly off the ground. Some time later, Muybridge was able to convince Stanford to back the purchase of several cameras so that motion studies could be performed on horses and other creatures. (Courtesy of SAMCC.)

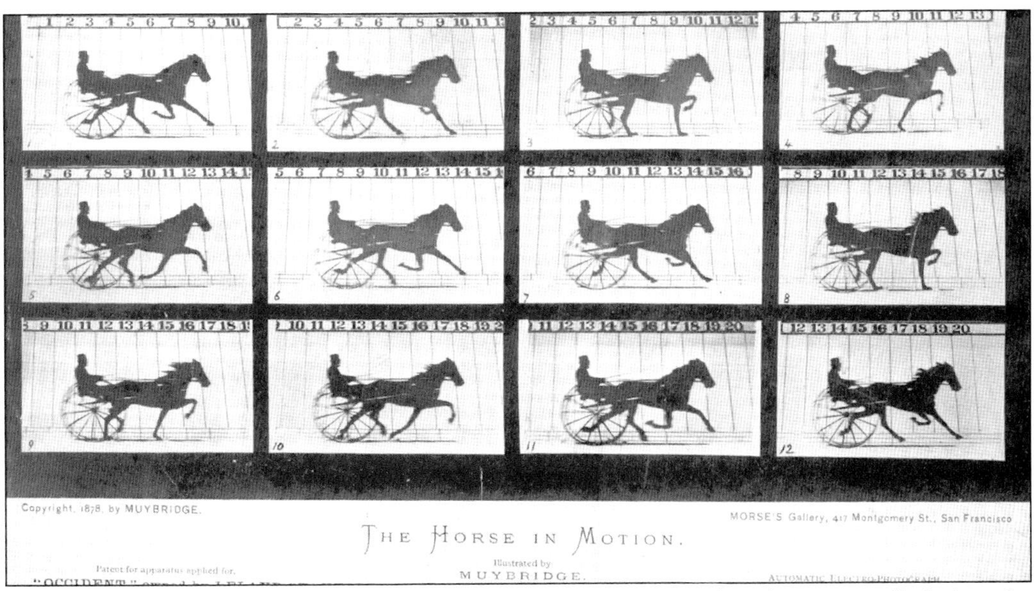

Eadweard Muybridge's motion studies on Stanford's ranch in Palo Alto eventually led to the development of the motion picture. However, the whole process started at Union Park, somewhere underneath Boulevard Park. (Courtesy of SAMCC.)

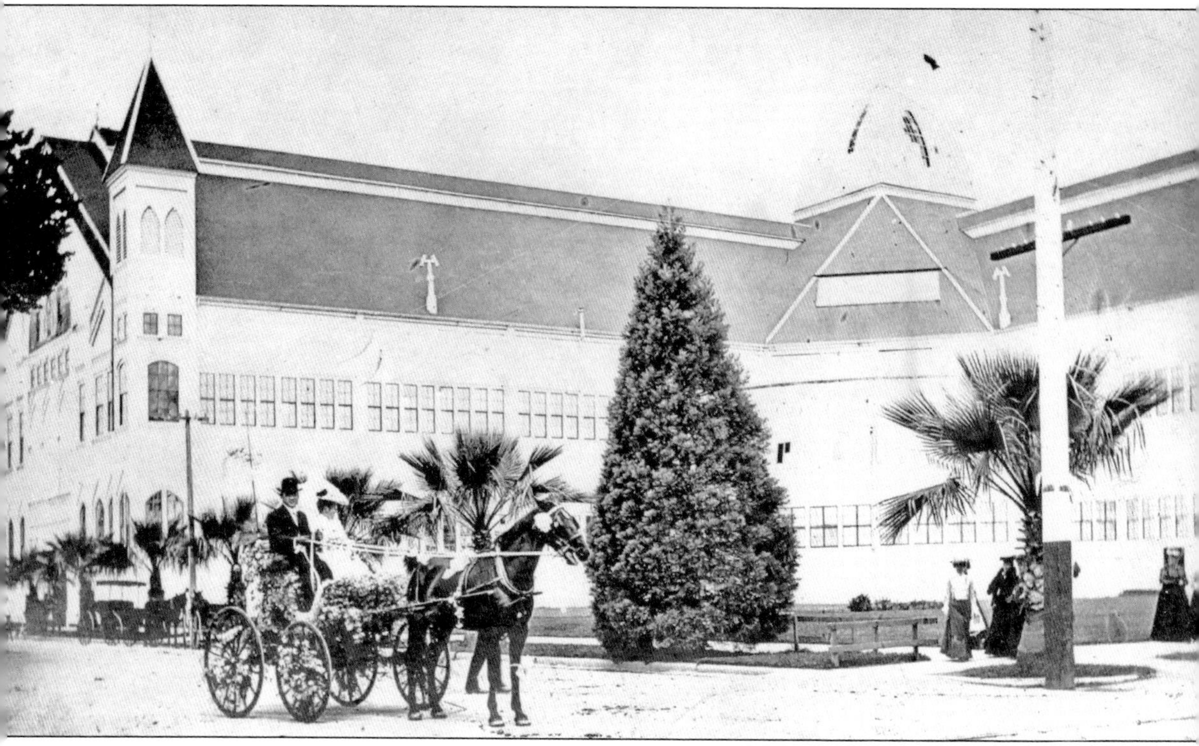

The need for the state fair to continue to grow created the momentum to buy a new site in Oak Park and to bring the racetrack and pavilion onto the same grounds. Photographed in the carriage in front of the old pavilion building is famed Sacramento furniture dealer John Bruener. This photograph was taken at one of the last state fairs to be held in the old pavilion before it was demolished. (Courtesy of SAMCC.)

Two

In the Beginning

In 1905, Park Realty purchased the Union Park and its land for the purpose of residential development as a neighborhood named Boulevard Park. The track was demolished early in 1905 and the land graded. The first lots sold that same year.

The development was promoted by the young real estate firm of Wright and Kimbrough, on the path to regional prominence in its field. Within one and a half months, 55 lots were sold. Sales strategies included transporting clients to view lots and houses by horse and carriage (later by auto), offering a discount if the house was constructed within a year and easy financial terms—generally 10 percent down, followed by low monthly payments.

Wright and Kimbrough had their own architectural design department and provided house plans with customized features to clients as well. They also constructed houses on speculation and advertised them in the newspapers with sketches, floor plans, and photographs.

Wider streets were constructed down Twenty-first and Twenty-second Streets in order to provide planted medians and create boulevards with a park-like image.

The development was attractive to both wealthy leaders of the community and the working class. Residents included bank presidents and business leaders as well as railroad workers, policemen, and carpenters. Not far from Boulevard Park were the shops of the Southern Pacific Railroad. Thousands of railyard workers there were skilled craftsmen who were well paid and eager to become home owners. An added inducement to buying in Boulevard Park was the new trolley line on C Street, operated by the Sacramento Northern Electric Railroad, which also ran cars from Chico to Alameda. After Oak Park, Boulevard Park became Sacramento's second trolley car suburb.

Most of the houses in Boulevard Park were built between 1905 and 1915.

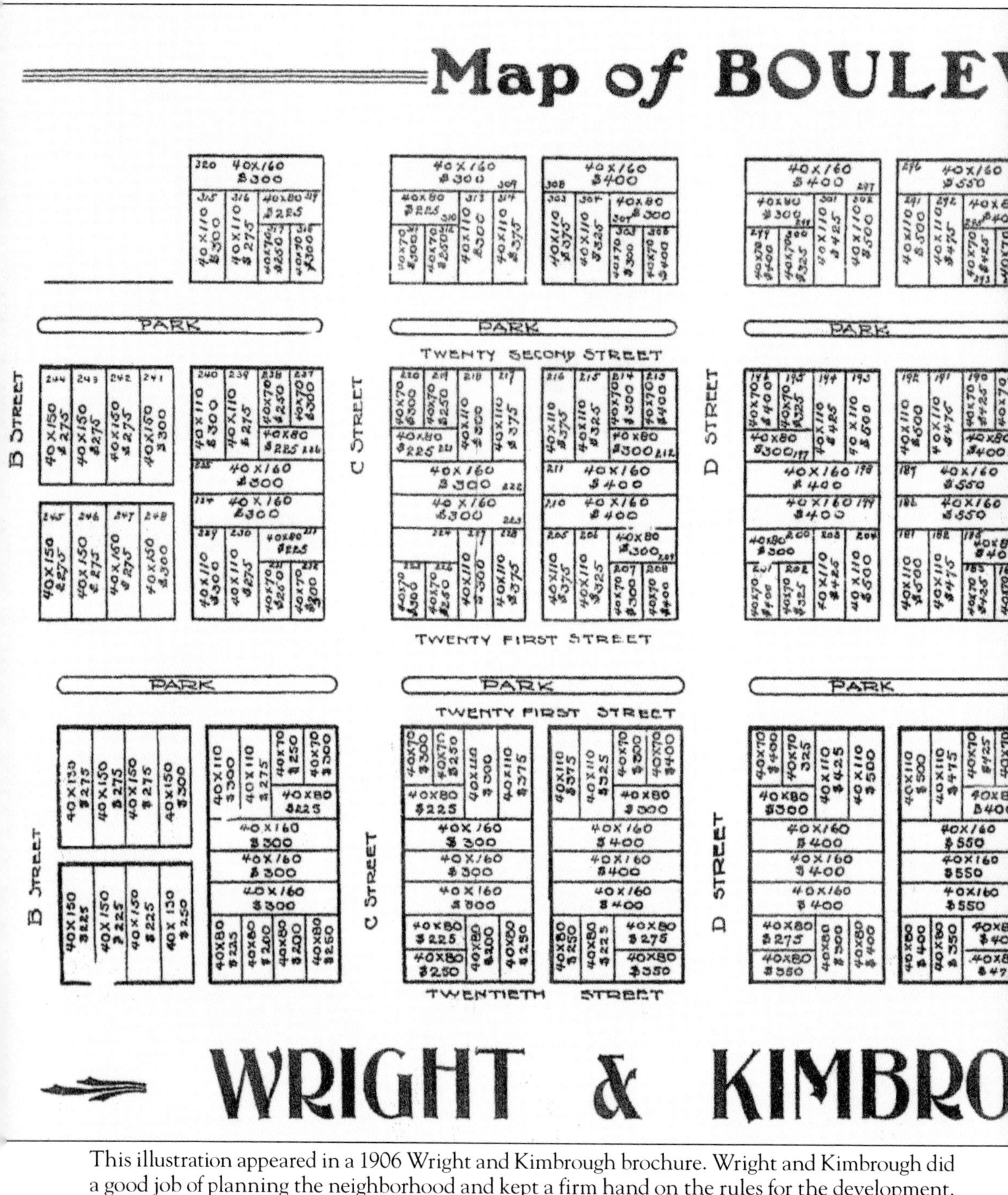

This illustration appeared in a 1906 Wright and Kimbrough brochure. Wright and Kimbrough did a good job of planning the neighborhood and kept a firm hand on the rules for the development. They established uniform setbacks and they promised, "There can be no front fences in the entire

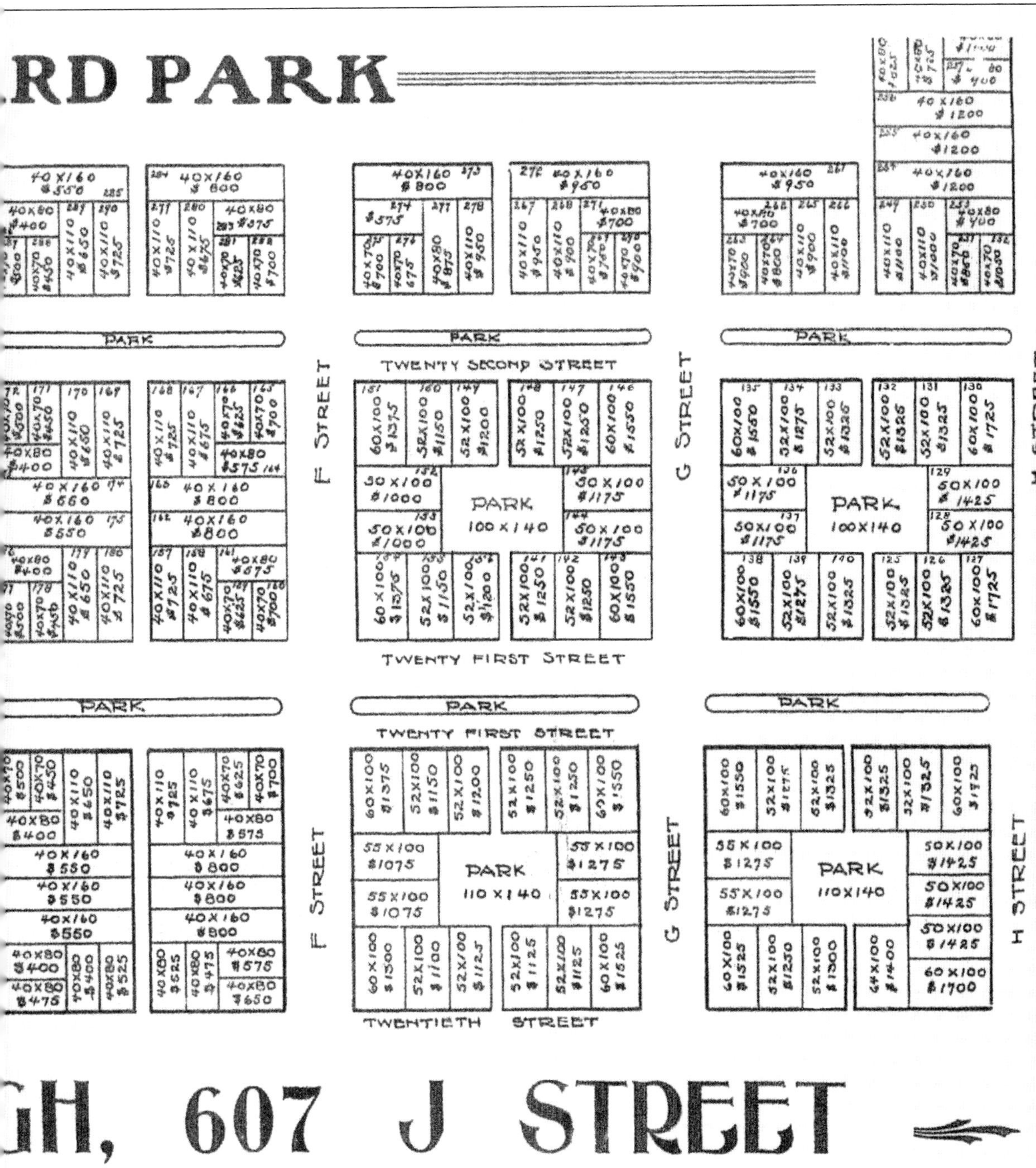

tract. No stores, no saloons, no wash houses, no wood yards." They left out the part about no churches and no schools. They also restricted the price of homes on the four blocks with park centers to a minimum of $2,500 and up. (Courtesy of BPNA.)

EVENING BEE: WEDNESDAY, JULY 19, 1905

Watch Boulevard Park Grow

35 lots were sold Monday morning, the greater number being on the Twenty-first Street Boulevard.

To Mr. Henry C. Stevens, an electrician with the Cen. Cal. Electric Co., will doubtless fall the honor of having the first home in Boulevard Park, we having signed a contract with him Monday evening for the erection of a handsome 5-room cottage on lot 69; though Mr. Arthur E. Miller, the well-known attorney, may dispute honors with Mr. Stevens, as he is rushing his plans for an elegant 2-story home on lot 6, and it will doubtless be a close race to see which will be the first to occupy a home on the Boulevard.

We take this occasion to say that A CEMENT WALK GOES WITH EVERY LOT. Owing, perhaps, to the fact that cement walks were not laid, many beautiful lots on Twentieth Street were overlooked.

To appreciate the cheapness of the lots let us give you a few comparisons. Lot 35, on the corner of Twentieth and F Streets, is priced at $650, with over $100 worth of cement walk on it. We sold the corner of Eighteenth and F 4 months ago, without any sidewalk, the same size lot, for $950.

Lot 83, on Twentieth and D, with strong probability of a car line in a year, and over $100 worth of cement work, is priced at $350. Just one block away, on Nineteenth and D, $500 is the very lowest price for same size lot, without sidewalk.

Buy one of these and it will be worth 50 per cent. more in one year.

WRIGHT & KIMBROUGH, 607 J Street

Wright and Kimbrough put teasers in their newspaper advertisements for several days before opening sales on July 17, 1905. This advertisement appeared two days later announcing the sale of 35 lots on the first day. They also make it sound like Henry Stevens and Arthur Miller were locked into an incredible duel to see who could occupy the first house in Boulevard Park. Take the time to read the advertisement because Wright and Kimbrough lay the hype on thick.

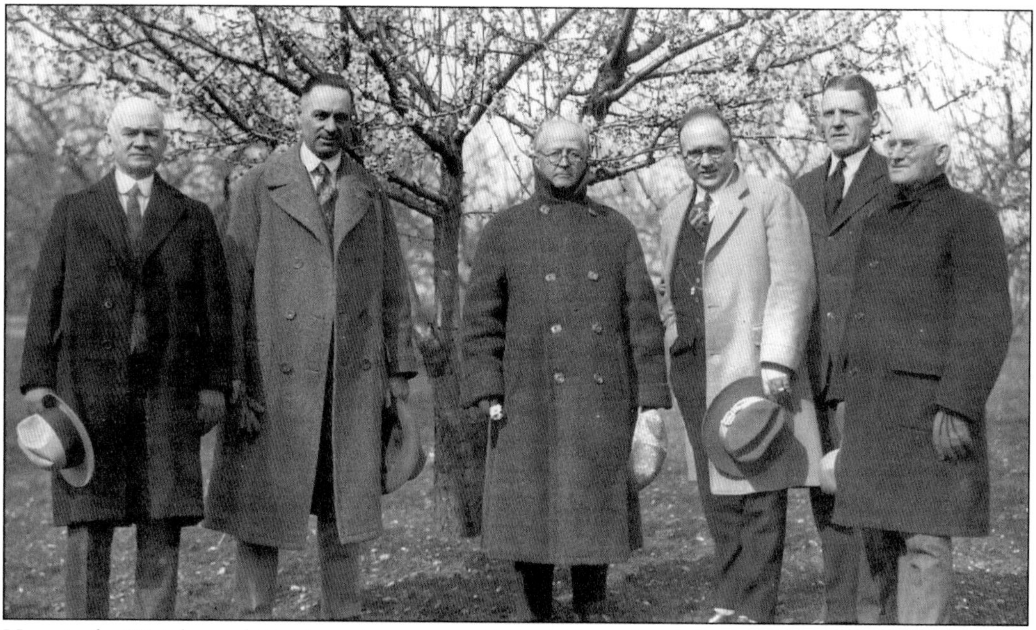

Here is the Wright and Kimbrough team, c. 1930. Although no identification accompanied the photograph, the authors have deduced that, pictured, from left to right, are Howard Kimbrough (?), A. Russell Galloway Jr., Charles E. Wright, William C. Wright, unidentified, and also possibly Howard Kimbrough. Galloway put together the package that brought Julia Morgan to Sacramento to work with Elizabeth Glide on the Public Market. (Courtesy of Wright and Kimbrough.)

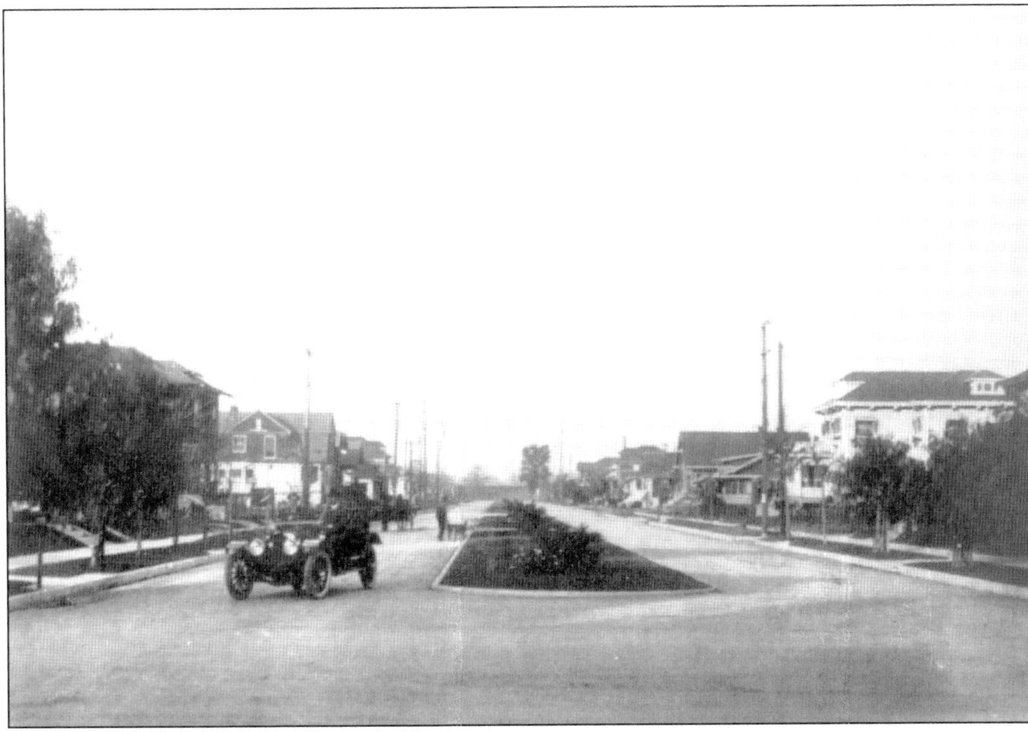

This c. 1910 photograph of Twenty-first Street is one of the earliest historic photographs of Boulevard Park. (Courtesy of BPNA.)

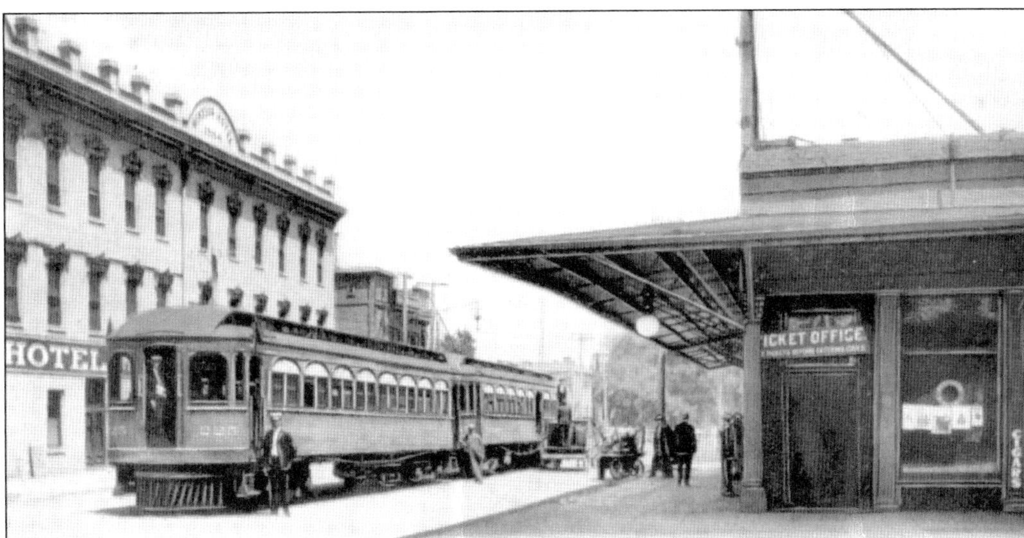

The Sacramento Northern Railroad put a trolley car line down C Street, connecting their downtown depot with McKinley Park. Regular trolley car service allowed people to move out of the central area and into neighborhoods like Boulevard Park. From the Sacramento Northern depot, one could make a connection to the Bay Area or up the valley as far as Chico. (Courtesy of SAMCC.)

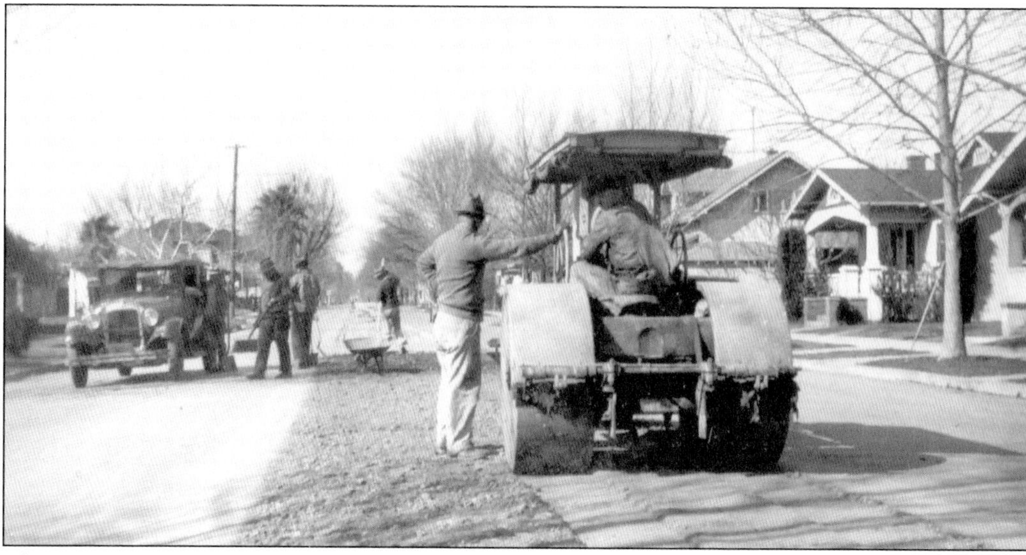

This Hepting photograph depicts the removal of boulevard strips from the middle of I Street in 1937. (Courtesy of SAMCC.)

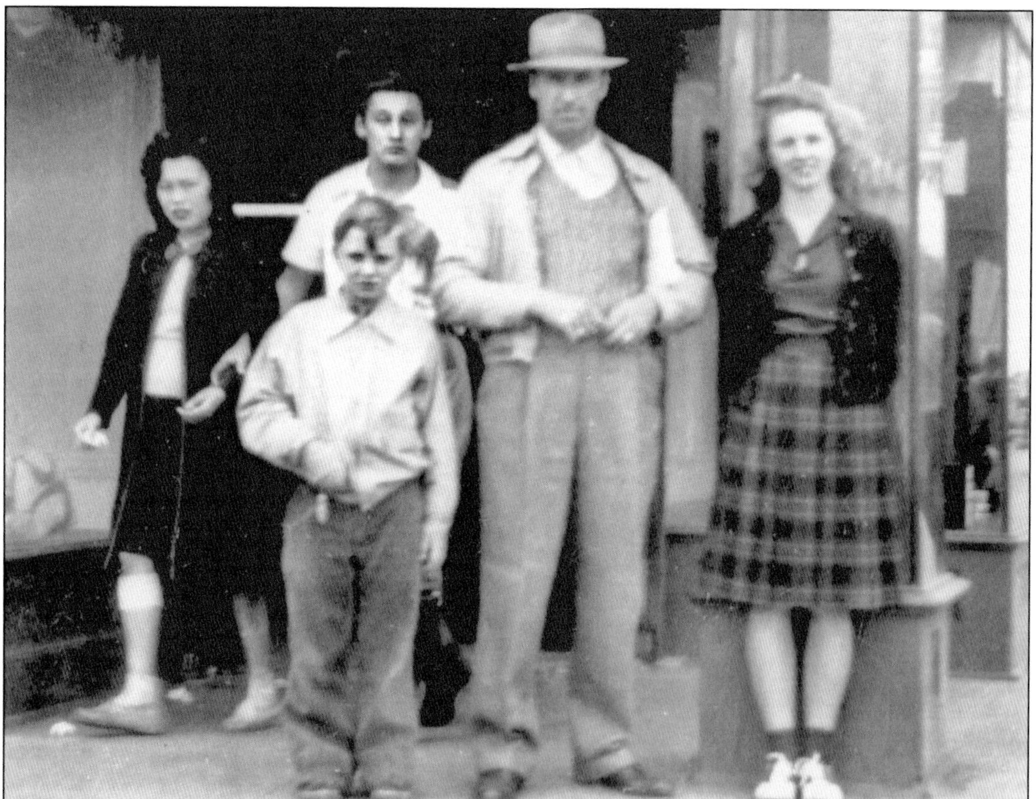

In 1942, a Japanese friend of Eugene Hepting was having a closeout sale at his store because he was being removed to an internment camp. The boy in front is unidentified and the rest, from left to right, are unidentified; Ernest Hepting, who served in the Marine Corps in World War II; Eugene Hepting; and unidentified. (Courtesy of SAMCC.)

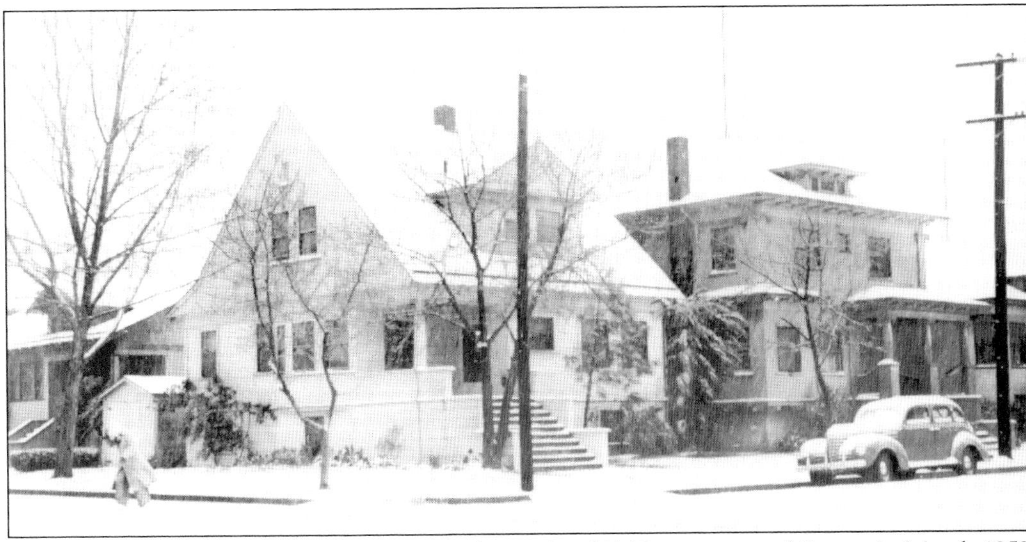

This photograph shows the Hepting house, located at 501 Twenty-second Street, in March 1952. The Hepting family occupied the house for about 30 years. (Courtesy of SAMCC.)

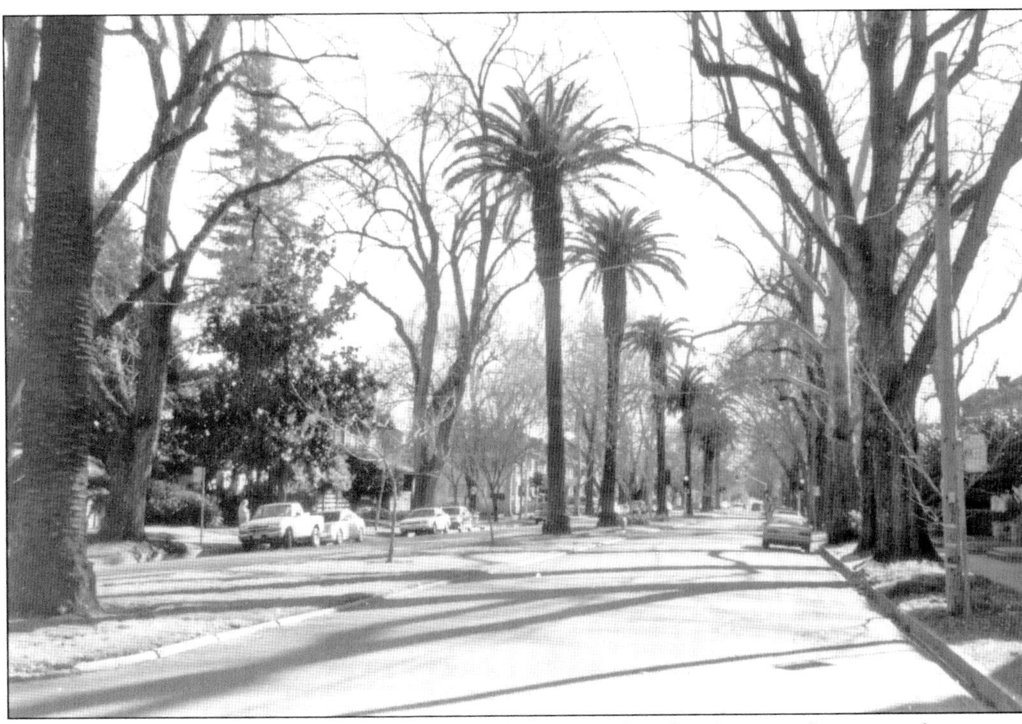

When the name Boulevard Park is mentioned to people who do not often visit the central area, they usually do not recognize the name. However, when the planted median strips are mentioned, a light of recognition quickly goes off. These stately palm trees have matured nicely and make Boulevard Park one of Sacramento's most distinctive neighborhoods. (Photograph by Paula Boghosian.)

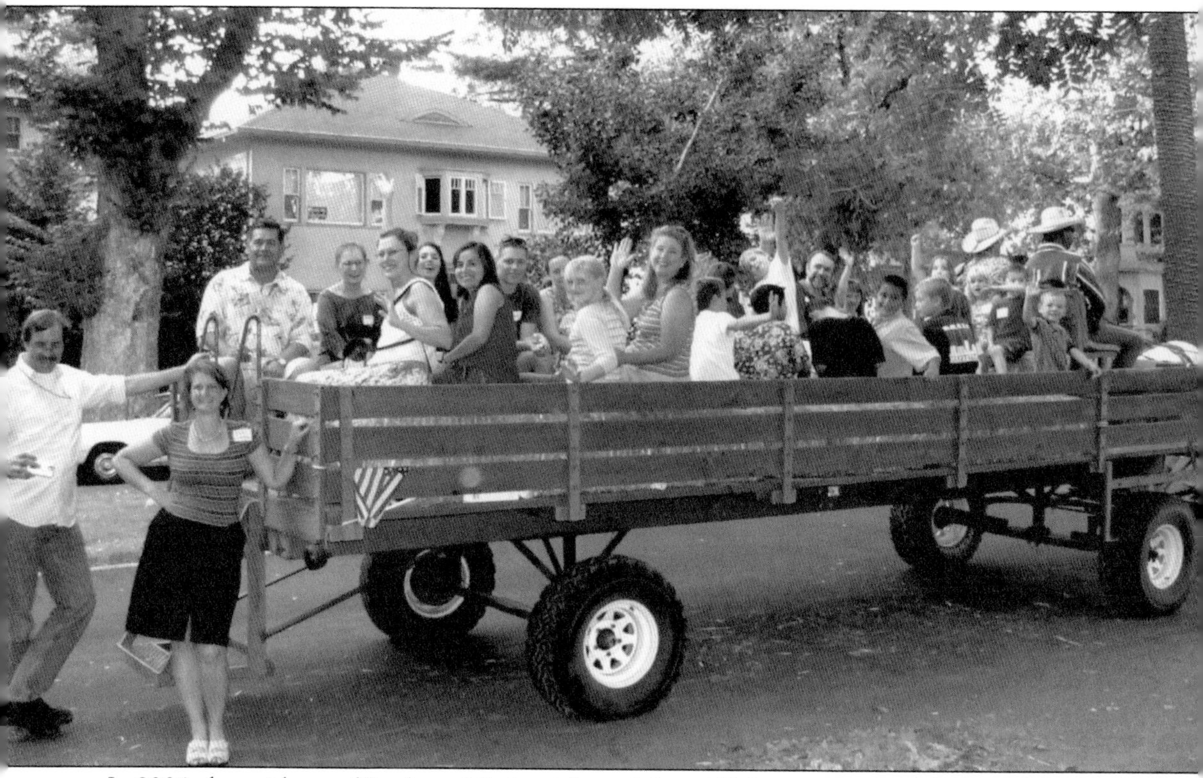

In 2004, the residents of Boulevard Park celebrated their 100th anniversary. (Photograph courtesy of BPNA.)

Three

Architecture and Lifestyles

Boulevard Park has a special character—it is distinguished by both its park-like image with planted medians and its buildings. The substantial majority of houses were constructed between 1905 and 1920. While several different architectural styles are represented within the park, there is a consistency of character, scale, materials, and image that reflects the continuity of construction. The City of Sacramento has identified Boulevard Park as a Historic District due to its visual design integrity and unique character.

A few structures within the park were built while the Union Park racetrack was still in place, between 1870 and 1905. In general, the oldest houses in the park were influenced by Italianate design, popular during the mid-1870s and 1880s. Typically they have two-story angled bays, decorative balustrades, brackets beneath the cornice eave, a shallow hip roof, and shiplap siding. In 1890, Queen Anne styles emerged, identified by different siding surfaces on the first and second stories, delicate spindle work, turns of balusters, made possible by the invention of the lathe, and sometimes "witch hat" towers. Houses designed after the track was gone used styles that were popular between 1905 and about 1920. Architectural design progressed to Colonial and Classical Revivals, with simple forms and details that reflected either Colonial houses or classical Greek design. Prairie School themes began to influence and combine with other styles, and Craftsman design, with its use of natural materials and rustic qualities, became popular. There are a few 1920s period revival designs with English or Spanish Colonial Revival themes. While styles are generally identified by a set of particular attributes, most of the houses are a combination of aspects of other styles as well.

Boulevard Park has a lifestyle of its own, formed by its visual character and the common interests of the residents that create a sense of community. While the predominance of park residents live in single-family houses, a number of them often share the same large house or live in flats and apartments, with lots of neighborly interaction. The park's proximity to downtown was important when it was first settled, since downtown Sacramento had most of what anyone wanted or needed, including employment, and one could walk or take the trolley. The lifestyle was relaxed, friendly, and efficient, and still is.

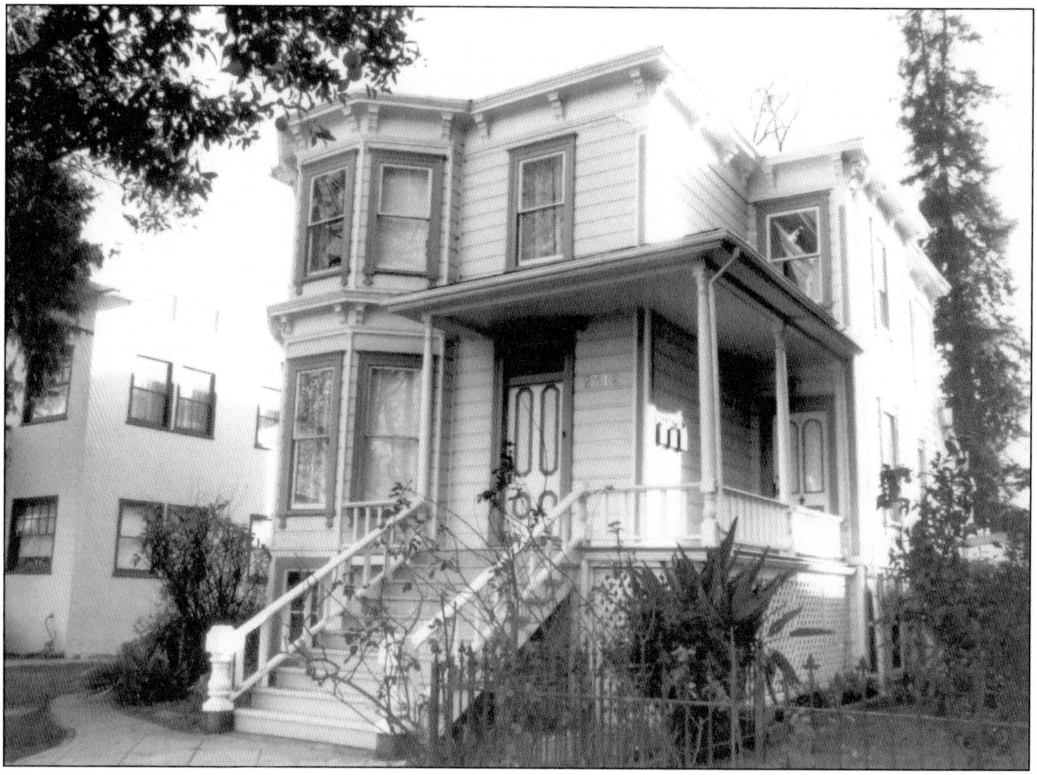

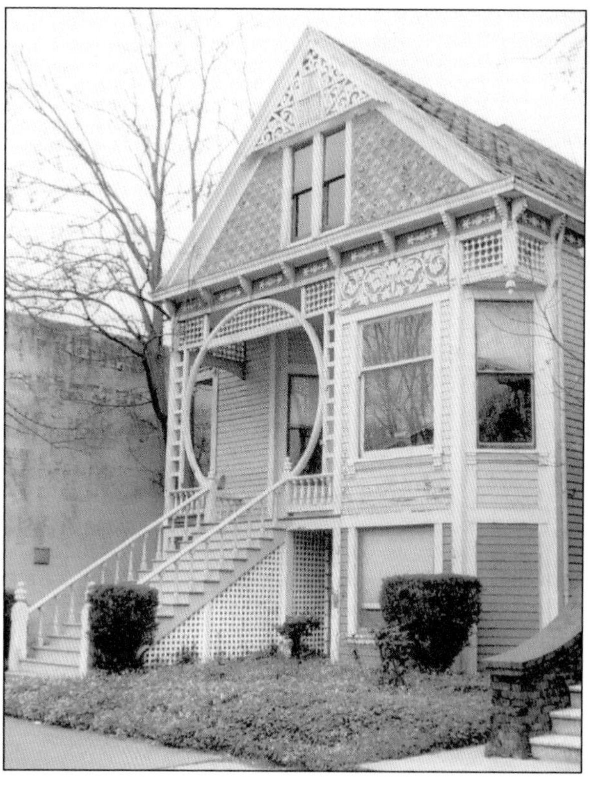

The building at 2312 H Street reflects an Italianate style popular during the late 1870s and 1880s. Its L-shaped porch, angled two-story bay, and shallow hip roof are common to the style in Sacramento. Some versions of the style have wood quoins to resemble stonework along the corners of the building and decorative wood shapes in the frieze. Richard Withington, proprietor of the Capitol Soap Company, lived there in 1881.

This Queen Anne–style house at 2011 I Street is characterized by the decorative porch with its dramatic circular pattern, the ornamental bargeboard in the gable end, applied floral pattern to the frieze above the window, and the use of different textures in the gable end and the siding. The spools and floral patterns give the house a lacy look, perhaps the work of David Menear, a carpenter and house mover who lived here from 1897 to about 1938.

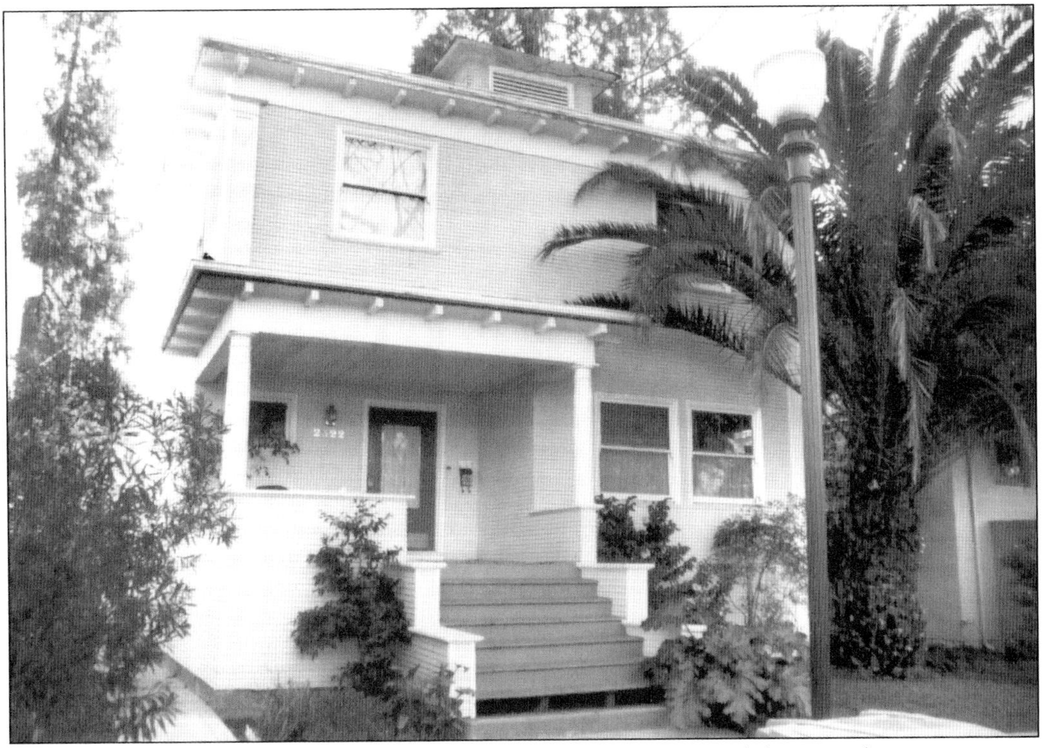

The beginning of the 20th century saw much simpler architectural forms and ornamentation in reaction to 19th-century excesses. There were fewer applied wood shapes, dormers projected from rooftops, porches were often supported by columns, and Colonial American design images were employed. This Colonial Revival house at 2322 I Street was built in 1908 by fireman Walter Van Gelder. The vernacular term foursquare is sometimes used to describe the cube-like forms of some of these houses.

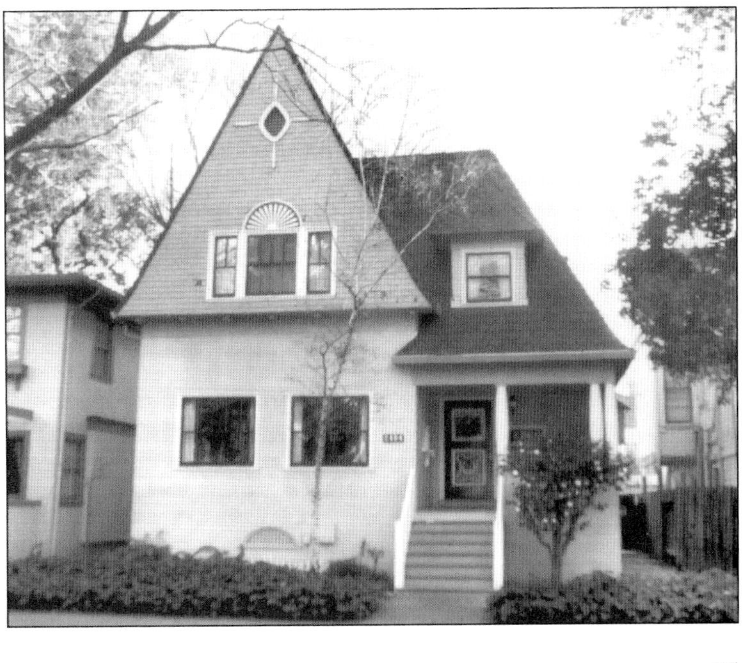

Other versions of Colonial Revival styling included houses with gambrel roofs or steeply gabled roofs and detailing reflecting the Colonial period. This 1900 house at 2404 H Street has a decorative end gable, with windows that display a Palladian form but have a radial wooden arch rather than glass. The vent above it is dramatized by sunburst shapes. Dwight Moulton, deputy state controller, lived here.

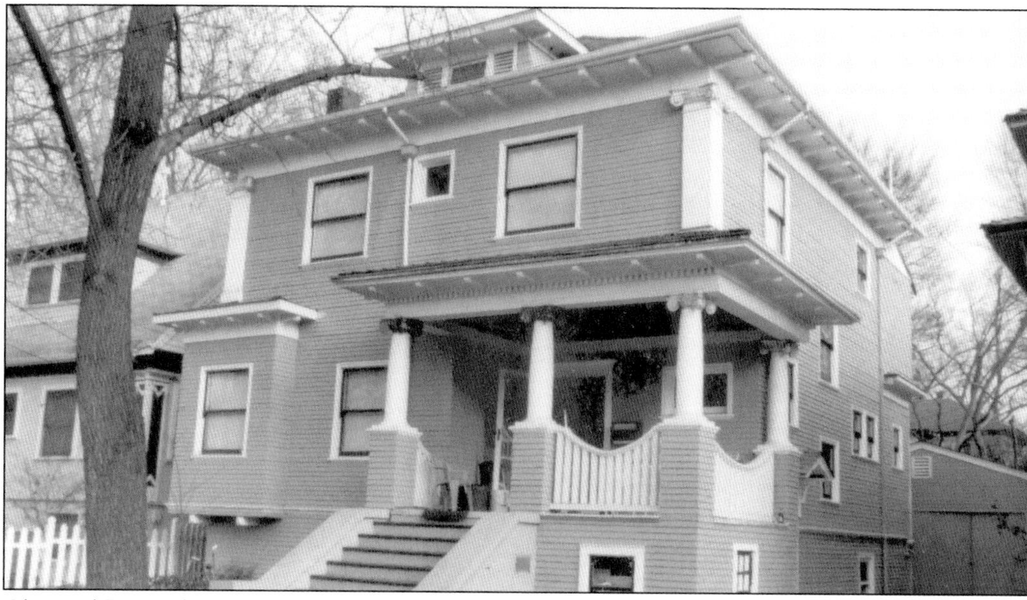

Classical Revival styles were often related to Colonial Revival designs with the use of similar building forms and columns. Classical Revival versions borrowed details like dentil patterns, fluted pilasters, posts or columns, and decorative capitals from classical Greek architecture. There are dentils in the porch frieze and exaggerated scroll shapes in the column and corner pilaster capitals. Matthew Gallagher, sales manager at Swanston and Son, lived here at 505 Twenty-second Street from 1924 to 1947.

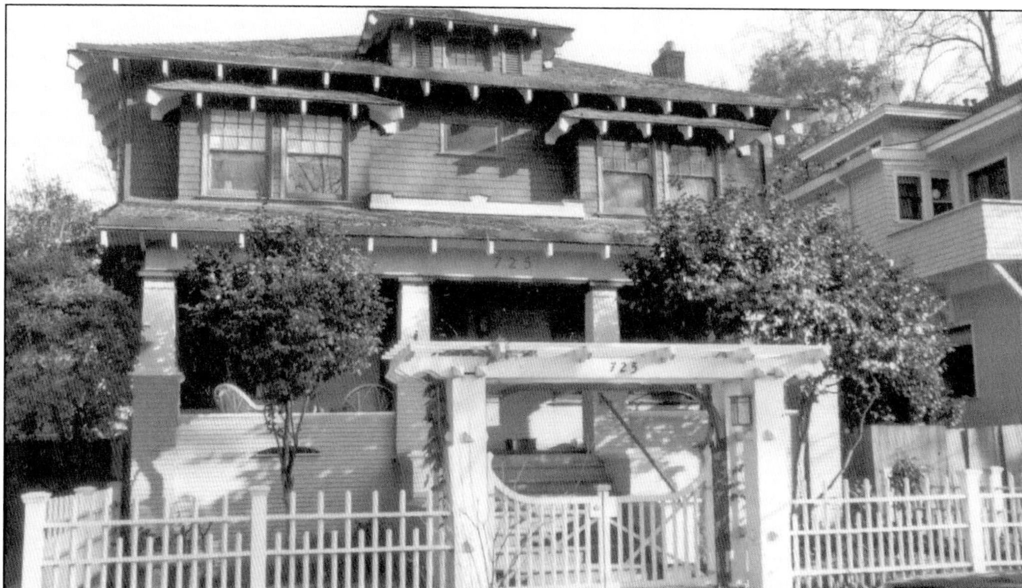

The Louise Groth home at 725 Twenty-first Street is a fine example of a two-story Craftsman house, a style very popular during this era and often expressed in bungalow form. Battered porch posts, roof forms, full-width porch, and exposed rafter tails reflect the style. Louise Groth had it built in 1910 when she was 61 years old. Her mother, Mrs. Pesron, daughters Emma and Bertha, and cousin Blanch Beau moved in with her. (Photograph by Paula Boghosian.)

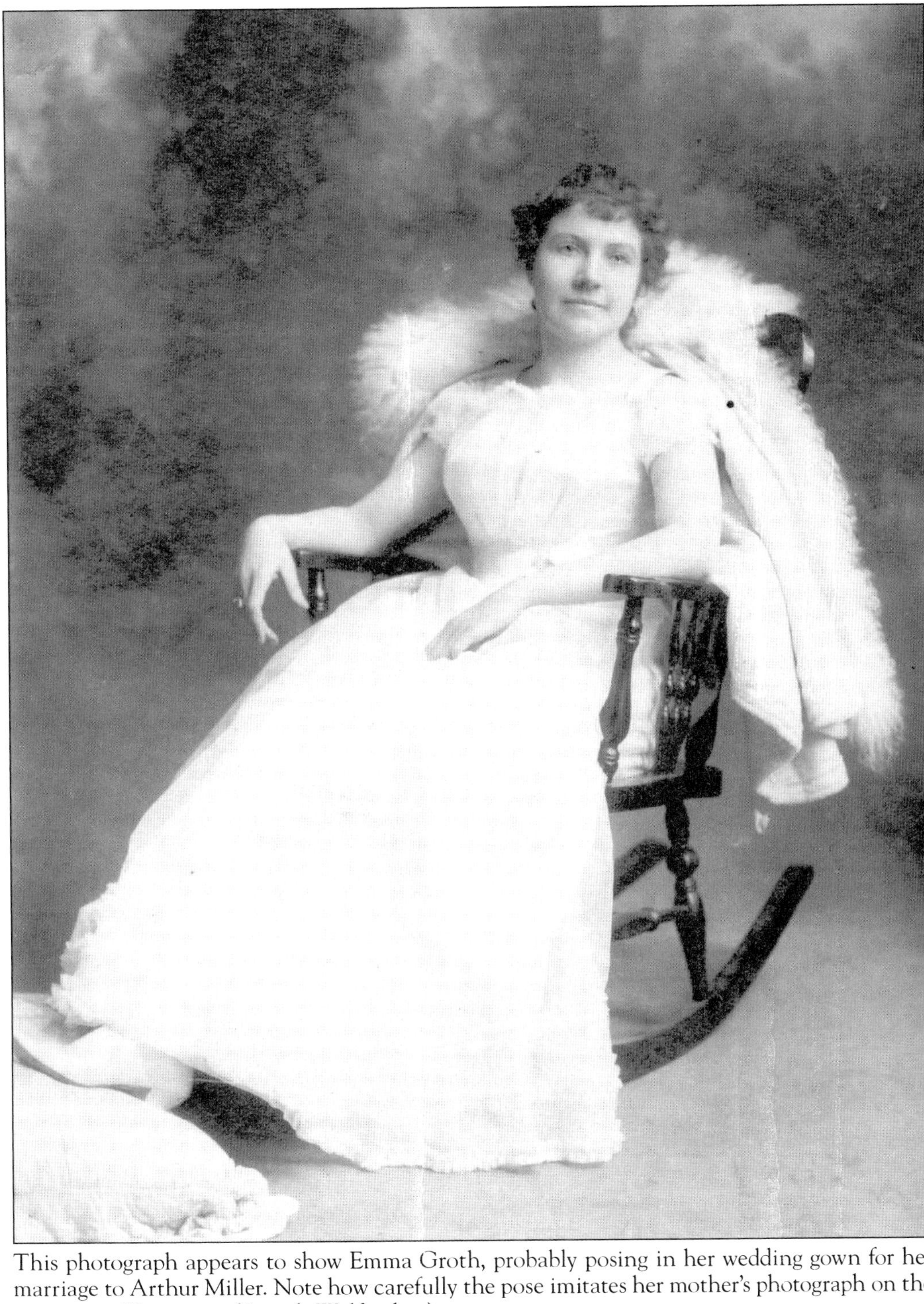

This photograph appears to show Emma Groth, probably posing in her wedding gown for her marriage to Arthur Miller. Note how carefully the pose imitates her mother's photograph on the next page. (Courtesy of Joseph Wolfenden.)

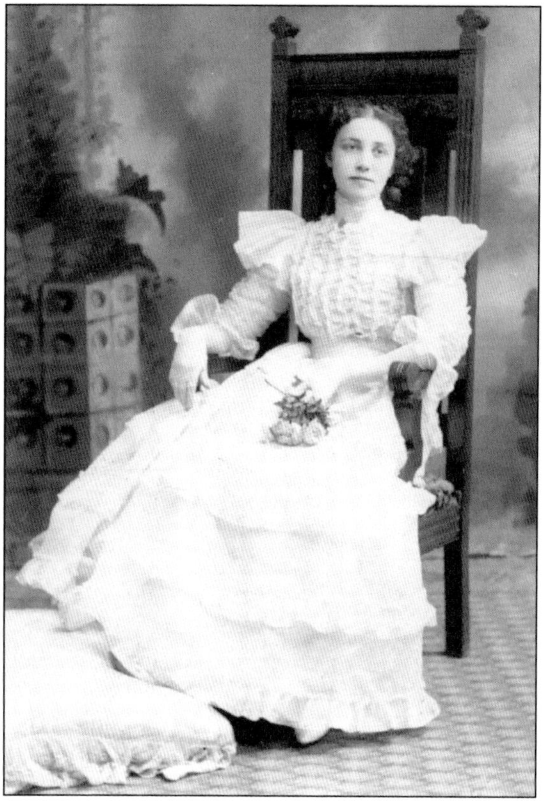

Louise Groth strikes an attractive pose in what is probably her wedding dress. This photograph dates to around 1870. Louise came to Sacramento in 1860 when she was 11 years old. Her husband, James H. Groth, served on the Sacramento Board of Supervisors from 1870 to 1874. He died in 1895, leaving her with a large real estate portfolio. (Courtesy of Joseph Wolfenden.)

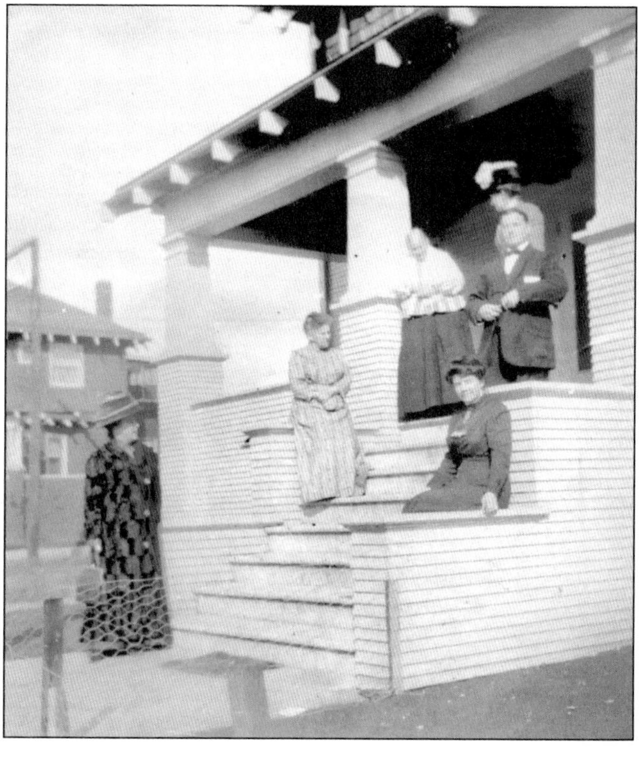

The Groth-Miller family poses in front of their house, *c.* 1915. Pictured, from left to right, are (first row) unidentified (probably one of the daughters), Louise Groth, her cousin Blanche Beau, and Arthur Miller; (second row) Louise's mother, Mrs. Pesron, and unidentified (probably one of her daughters). (Courtesy of Joseph Wolfenden.)

Louise Groth's daughter Emma was married for the second time to the attorney who secured her divorce from her first husband. Pictured here is Arthur Miller, whom Emma married in 1915. Miller lived across the street at 730 Twenty-first Street. After the wedding, he moved into the Groth house. (Courtesy of CSL.)

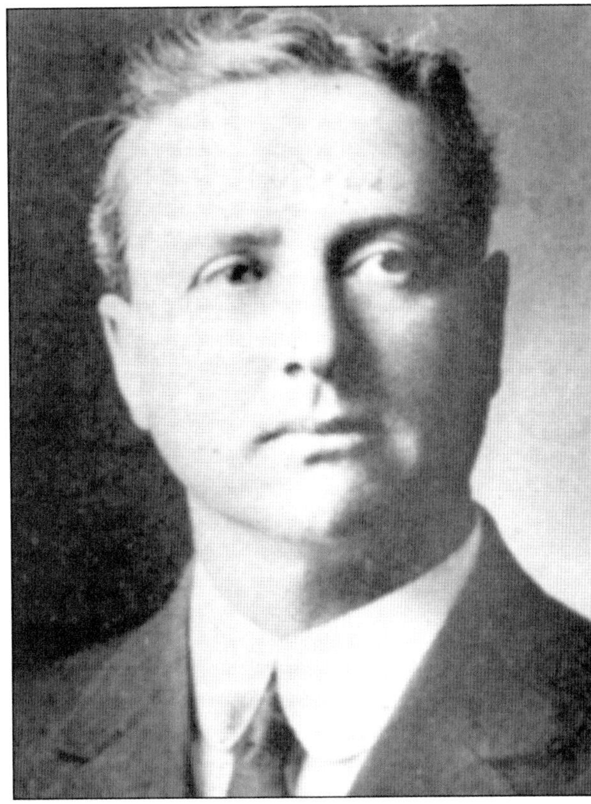

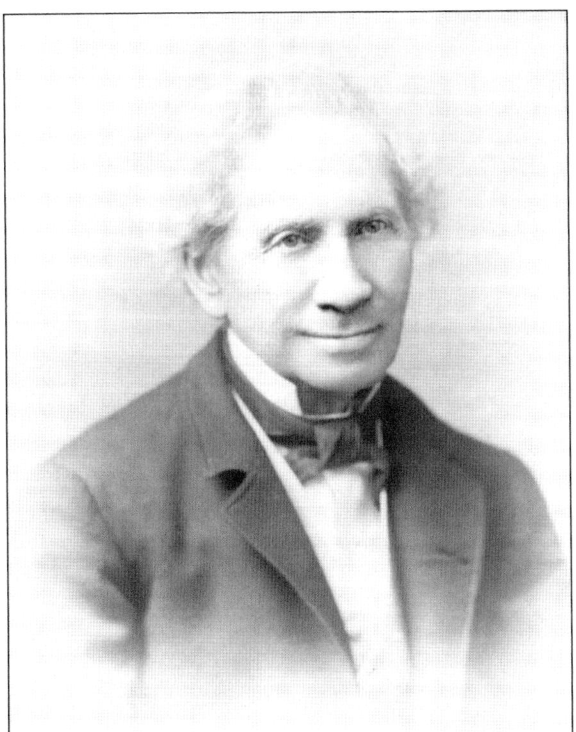

Louise Groth's father, Leon Andre Pesron, was one of the Sacramento area's first asparagus farmers. Asparagus was an important crop for Sacramento in the early 20th century. (Courtesy of Joseph Wolfenden.)

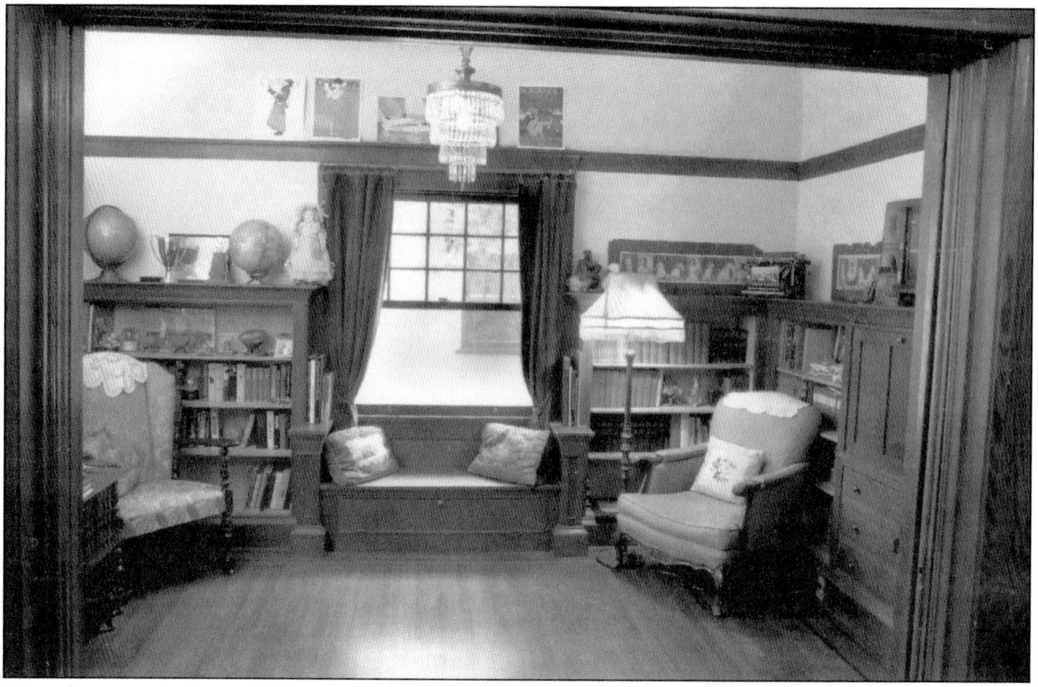

This photograph shows the study in the Groth house. There are hardwood floors, built-in cabinets, bookshelves, and a window seat. Located near the front door, this study is probably where most of the business of the household took place. (Courtesy of Joseph Wolfenden.)

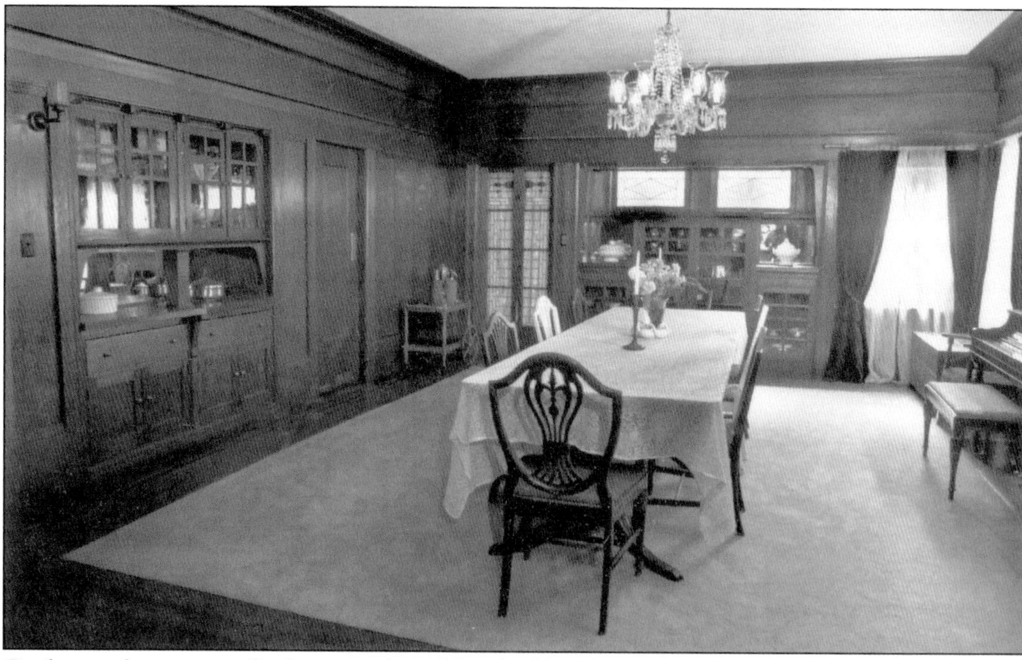

Craftsman houses usually feature a lot of finished hardwood. Here in the Groth's dining room are hardwood floors, built-in wood cabinets with glass fronts, and an elegant chandelier. What is unusual about this dining room is that instead of the more typical wood wainscoting, the finished hardwood goes all the way to the ceiling. (Courtesy of Joseph Wolfenden.)

Enjoying the roses in the backyard is Blanch Beau. Her mother died when she was one, and she was sent to Sacramento to live with the Pesron family. (Courtesy of Joseph Wolfenden.)

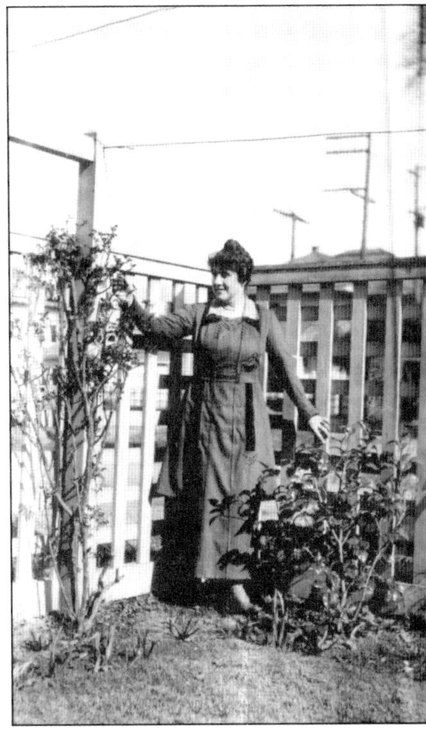

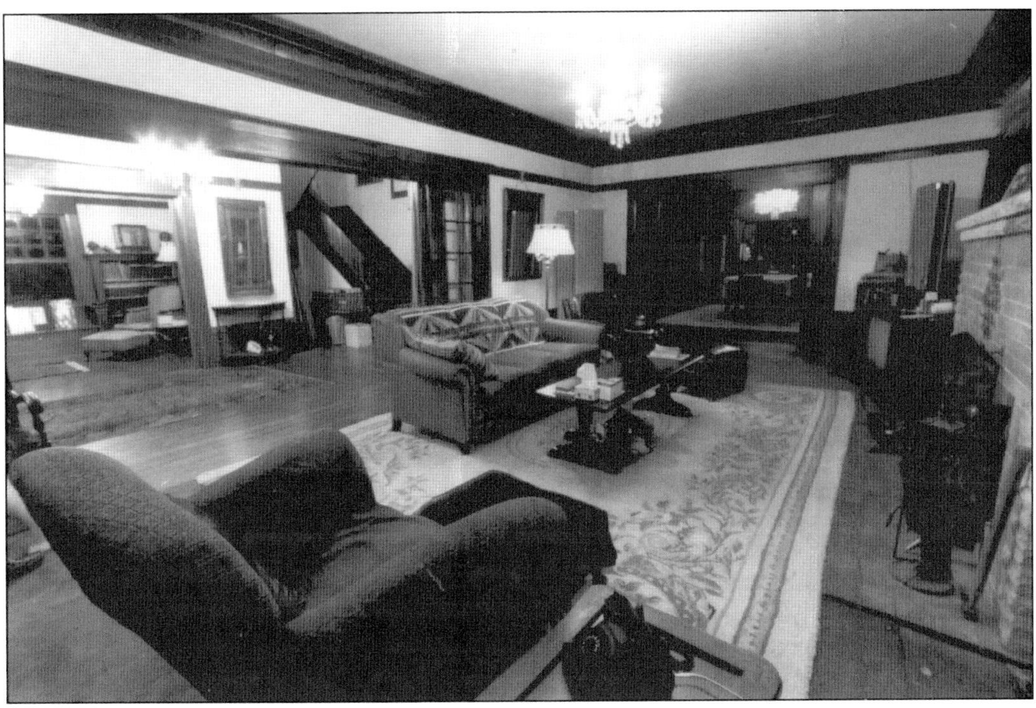

The spacious parlor has hardwood floors, a huge fireplace, and a chandelier. A pair of finished wooden pocket doors can be rolled out to separate the parlor from the dining room. Craftsman houses are generally more open spatially than Victorian-era interiors. (Courtesy of Joseph Wolfenden.)

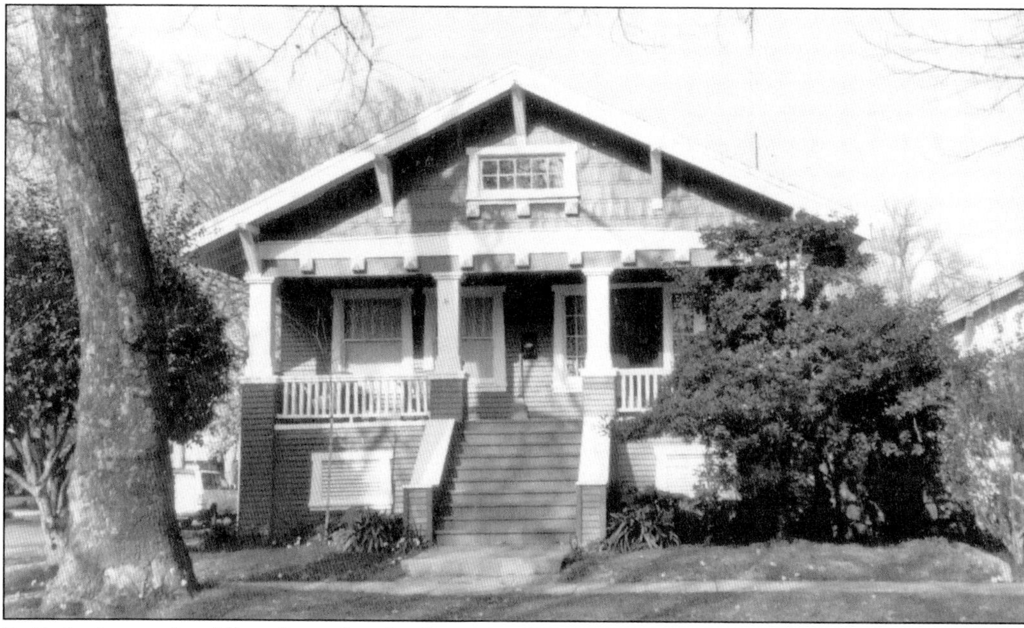

Built for bartender Albert Lincoln, this house at 2301 D Street is a good example of a Craftsman bungalow. The style embraced natural materials, such as wood, river rock, clinker brick (which looked as if a fiery natural force had created it), windows with divided pane patterns, and leaded glass. The style was a reaction to the Industrial Revolution and its factory-produced products, reflecting a desire to return to handcrafted, more individualistic artistic works.

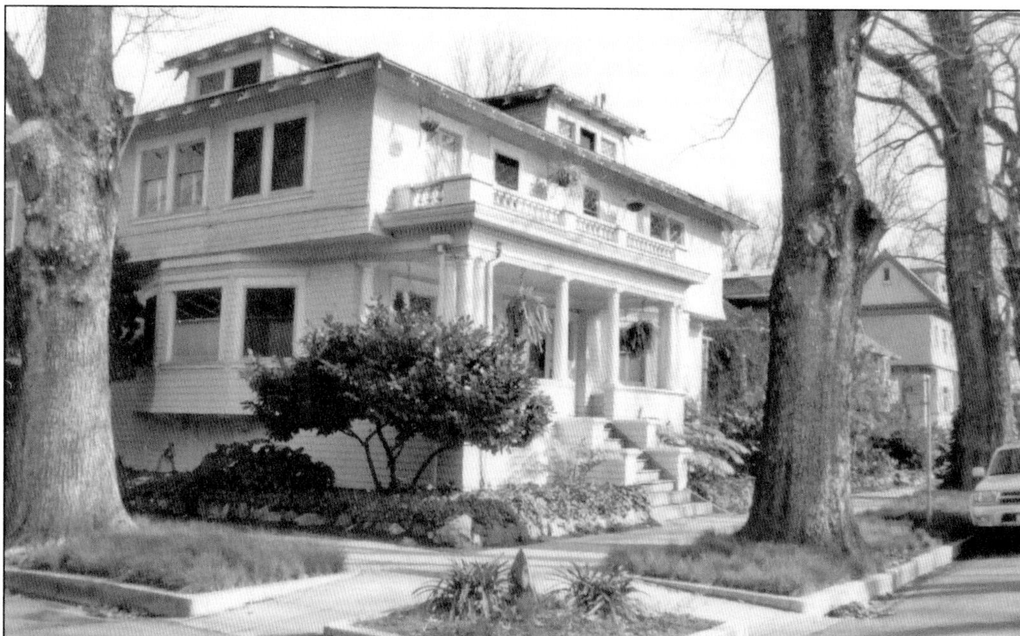

The architectural influences of 1900–1915 included Prairie School design themes, originating in the Midwest largely by Frank Lloyd Wright. Broad, horizontal roof and porch forms are characteristics of the style. This house at 2201 H Street combines Prairie School influences and Classic Revival design.

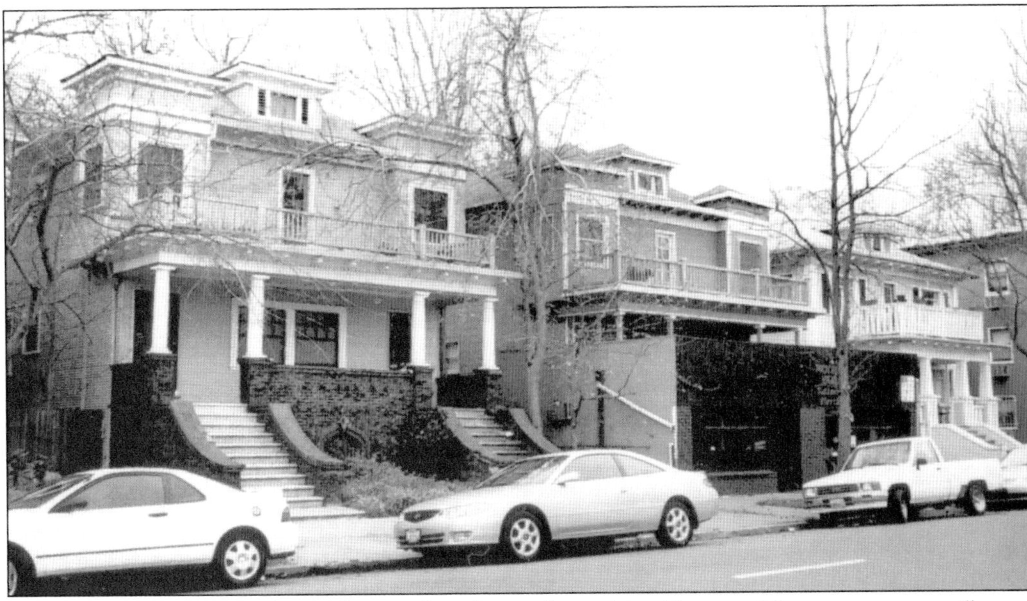

Boulevard Park also contained several multi-residential buildings, with apartments or flats to accommodate the many employees of downtown businesses, local government workers, and some blue collar employees. While these buildings at 2013–2015 I Street were built as duplexes, some originally single-family house owners have created ground floor apartments for tenants.

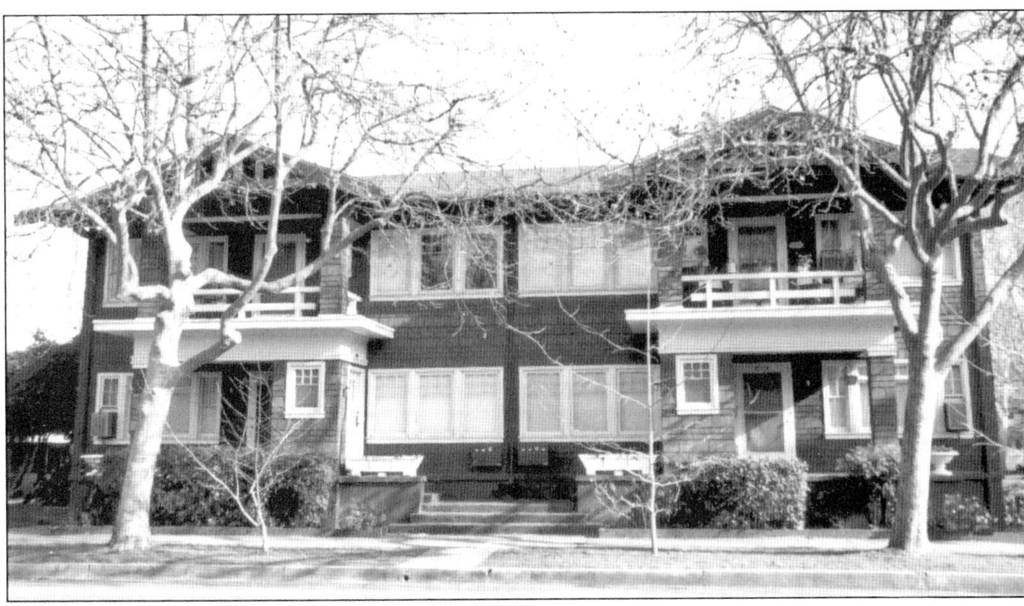

This Craftsman-inspired multi-residential design at 627–631 Twenty-third Street housed primarily single employees of various businesses, government positions, and perhaps railyard workers with access to employment by foot or trolley during the early 1900s.

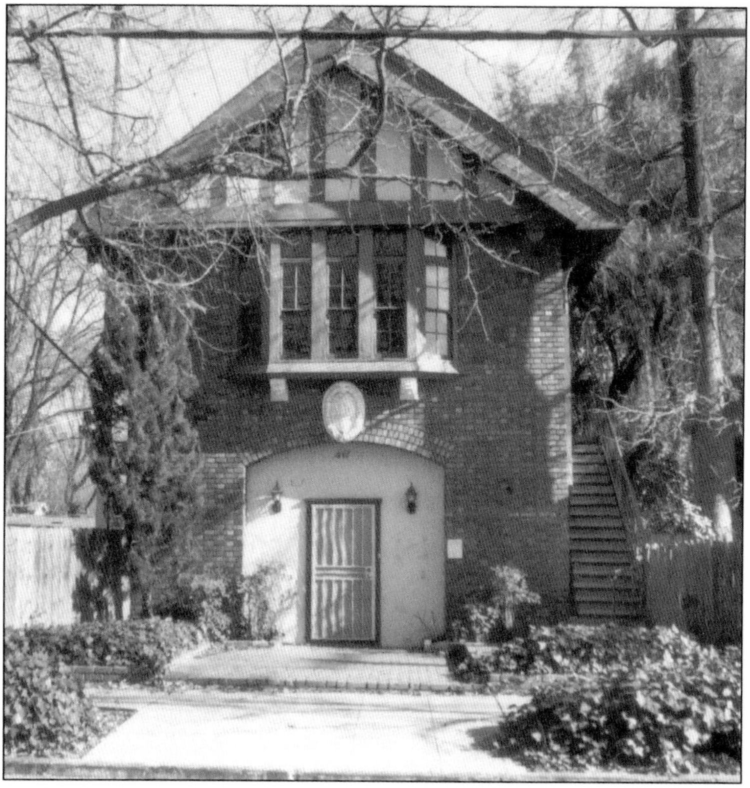

This firehouse at 417 Twentieth Street was the only public structure in Boulevard Park. When it was retired from public use, an architect created an office in the building. It reflects English design influences in its half-timbered gable end and the projecting windowed bay, probably part of the room firemen used for sleep or recreation. The fire engine access opening has been enclosed.

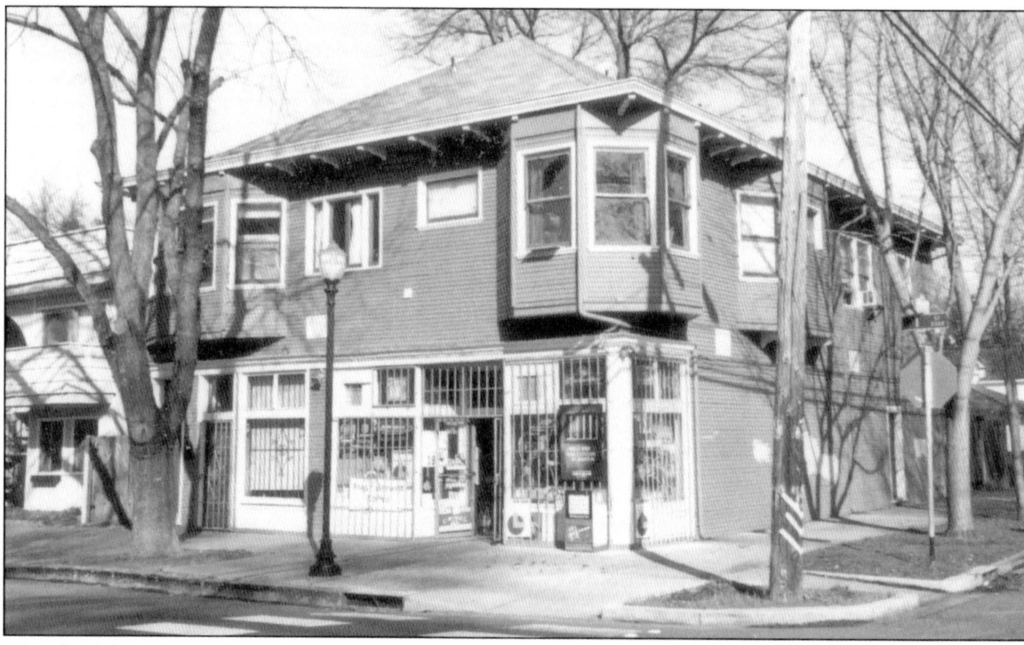

This building at 2331 I Street reflects the ubiquitous use of corner buildings within an urban neighborhood as markets on the ground floor with residential units above. The "corner" market has been an important element of city living for many years. Elizabeth and John Hogan constructed this building in 1909 and operated it as a grocery for about 40 years while living upstairs.

Four

The Land of Fruit and Nuts

Since the gold rush, agriculture has been a key component of the evolution of the Sacramento Valley and California. The enormous influx of immigrants to the California gold fields in 1849, generated a large market for supplies to feed them. Before that time, there were no towns with stable food sources, virtually no farms, no railroad transportation, and few roads for wagons to supply the hoards of people that descended upon the gold fields. Some observed potential profit from providing supplies, and others, discouraged after the "easy" gold was gone, turned to ranching and farming to survive. The Sacramento Valley proved a very rich resource for that activity, and wheat and grain soon became as important products as gold had been. The northern wheat fields supplied countries around the world for several years, until it became unprofitable. Fruit trees and orchards then became a viable and profitable substitute for grains.

Always vulnerable to vagaries of weather, transportation fees, and the market, farmers began to develop cooperative associations to work for changed banking policies, diminished transport fees, and marketing strategies. In 1901, the California Fresh Fruit Exchange was established, providing fruit growers with methods of getting fruit to market at the best possible price. Other cooperatives were established. By 1910, practically all of the deciduous fruit of the state was shipped through Sacramento, 85 percent of it grown within an 85-mile radius. State government created agencies, departments, and commissions to manage and oversee various agricultural operations throughout the state.

The development of the railroads, and the agricultural production it supported, played a key role in the growth of the state. Railroads delivered agricultural products, and canneries were established to accommodate produce that was not shipped fresh. Soon valley products were traveling around the world. Canneries and irrigation restructured the face of the valley between 1890 and 1910. At the height of the industry, two of the largest canneries in the world were said to have been in Sacramento.

A number of managers and executives of agricultural associations, as well as farmers, grocers, butchers, ranchers, and those associated with canneries, wineries, and other agriculturally related occupations, were represented strongly in the Boulevard Park community.

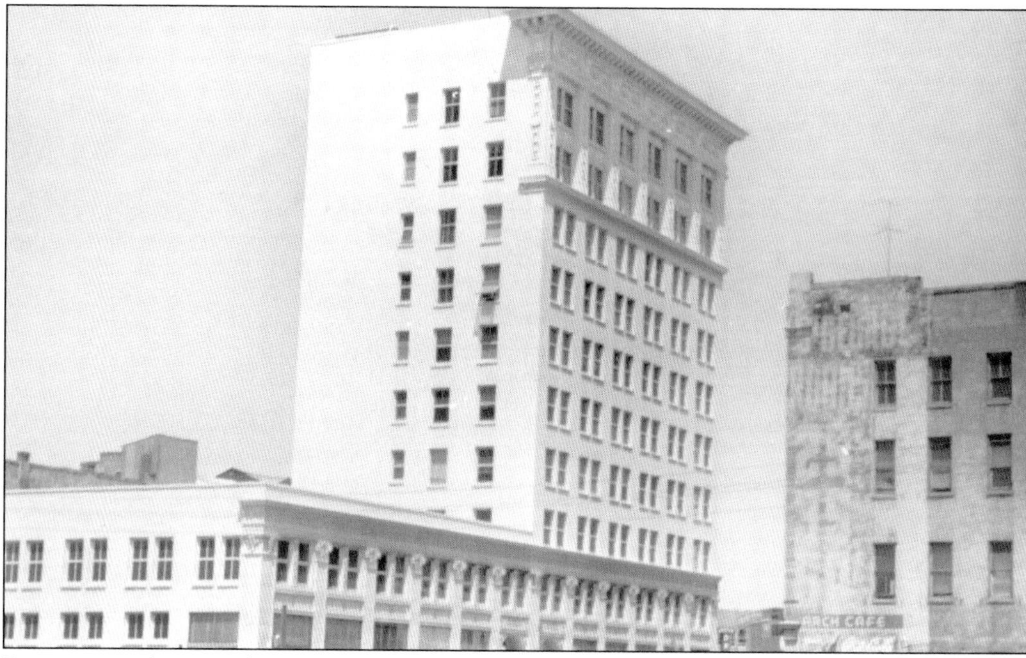

During its early years, the California Fruit Exchange had Charles Kaiser design this 1914 building at 1006 Fourth Street, and they located their offices there. It was built by the Ransome Concrete Company. When it was constructed, it was the tallest building in Sacramento and was the first poured concrete building in this city. (Courtesy of SAMCC.)

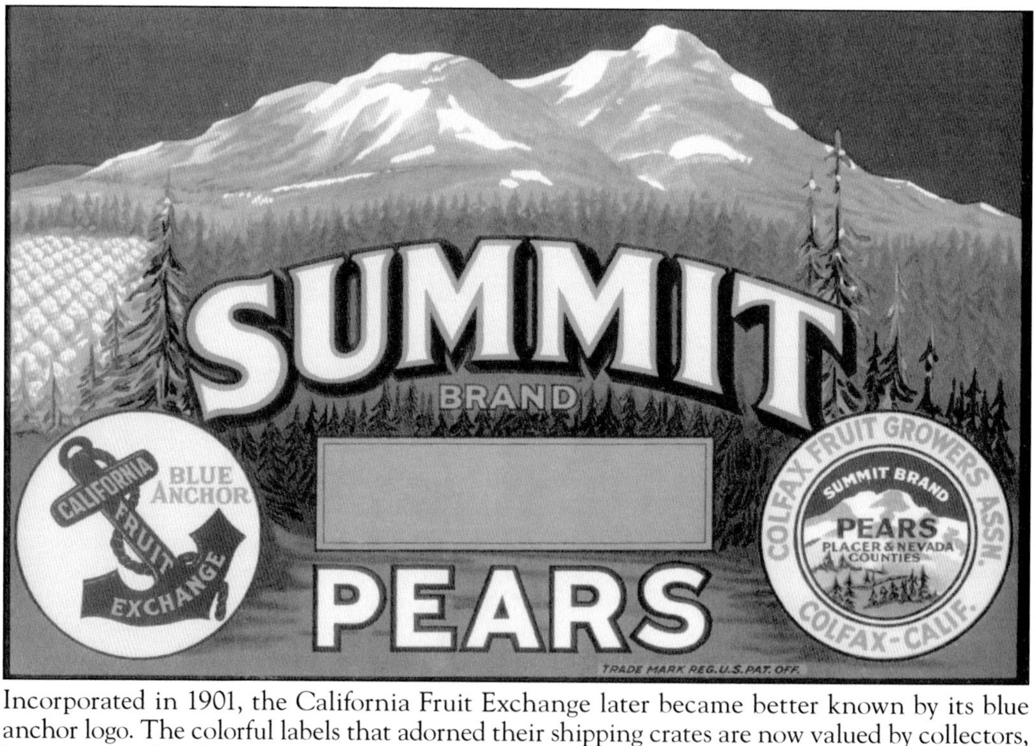

Incorporated in 1901, the California Fruit Exchange later became better known by its blue anchor logo. The colorful labels that adorned their shipping crates are now valued by collectors, historians, and archivists. (Courtesy of SAMCC.)

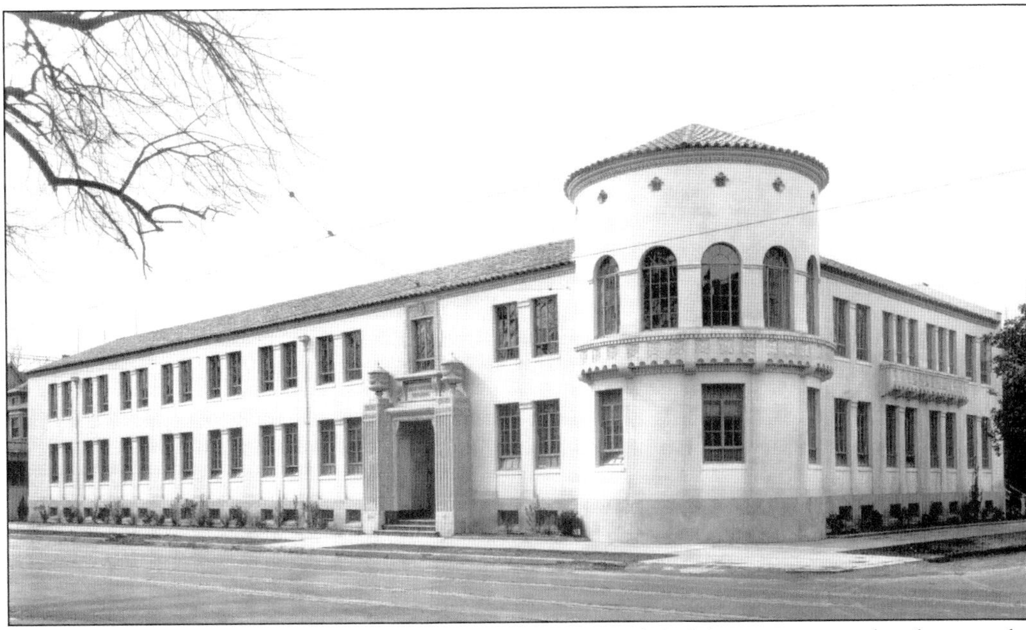

Originally the California Fruit Exchange only represented California growers, but later it also represented growers and growers associations all over the world. The growth of the organization forced the exchange to build a new, larger headquarters building at Tenth and N Streets, now known as the Blue Anchor Building. This 1932 Spanish Colonial Revival–style building was the design of architects Starks and Flanders. (Courtesy of SAMCC.)

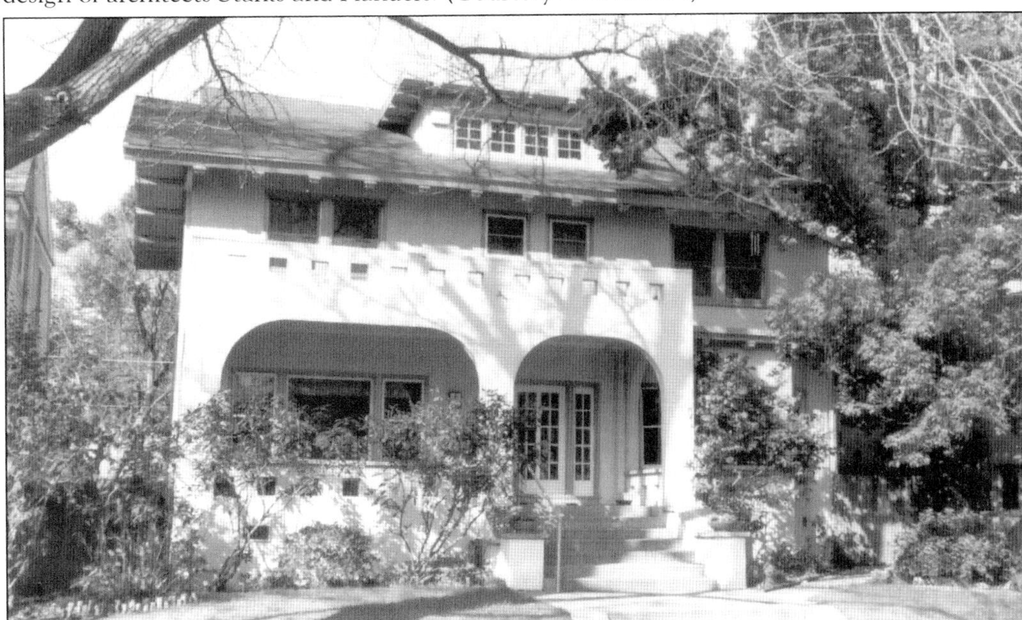

Thomas W. Madeley was one of the founders of the California Fruit Exchange and served as its corporate secretary and cashier. Alice and Thomas Madeley had this house at 610 Twenty-second Street built for them in 1912. It remained in possession of the Madeley family for over 40 years, until Alice died in 1953. (Photograph by Paula Boghosian.)

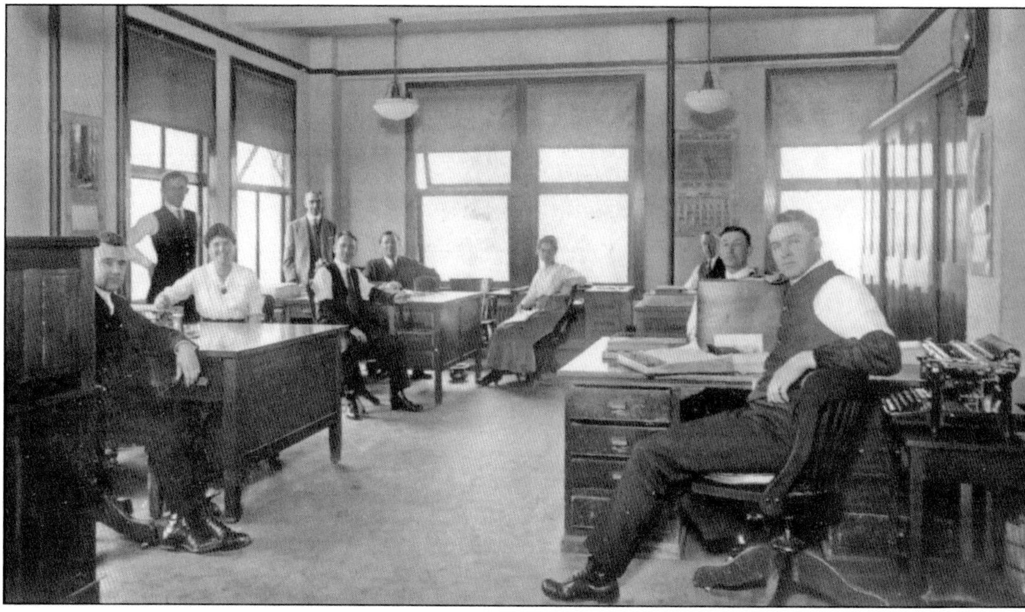

The men and women of the Pacific Fruit Exchange pose in their office around 1905. Scott Ennis of the Ennis-Brown Company was one of the founders of the Pacific Fruit Exchange. Willson Walker (614 Twenty-second Street) was the corporate secretary and later the manager of the Pacific Fruit Exchange.

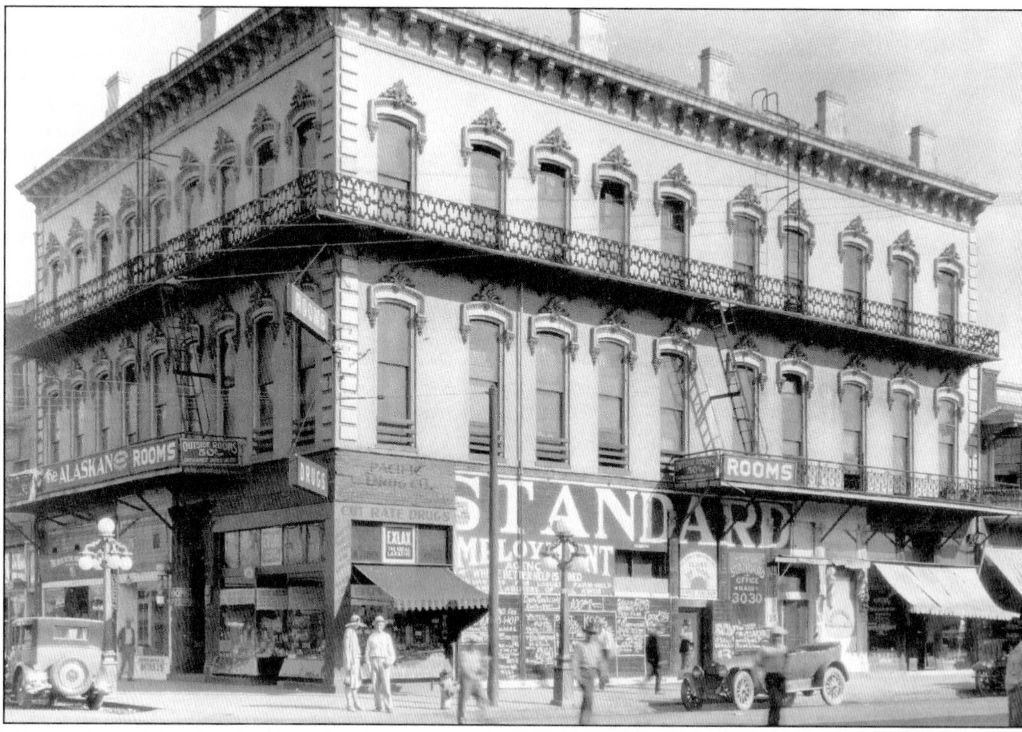

The offices of the Pacific Fruit Exchange were located on the upper floors of this Old Sacramento building seen in a c. 1925 photograph. It still exists on the southeast corner of Second and K Streets.

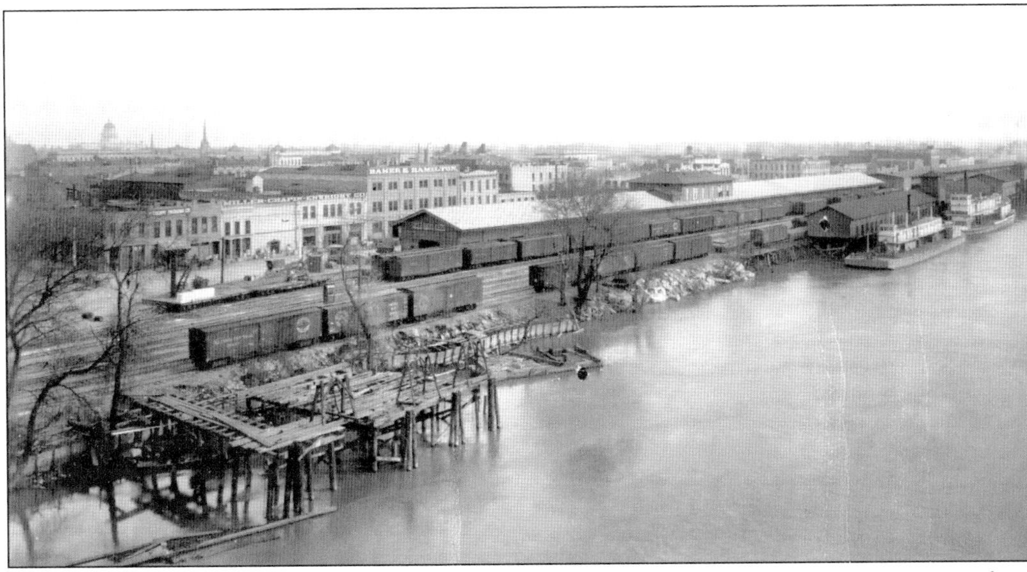

Virtually all of the deciduous fruit in California found its way through the Sacramento waterfront and into the eastern markets. The brick warehouses of the wholesalers who supplied Sacramento's markets lined Front Street.

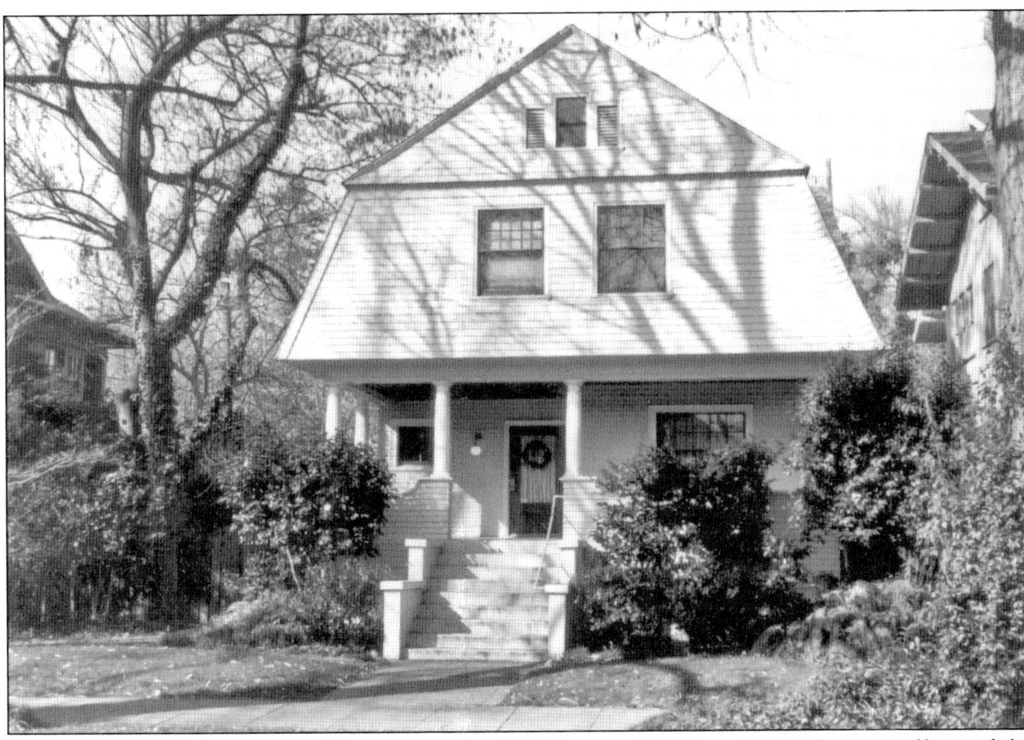

Located at 614 Twenty-second Street was the 1911 home of Willson C. Walker, an officer of the Pacific Fruit Exchange. It is next door to the Thomas Madeley house, who was one of the founders of the California Fruit Exchange.

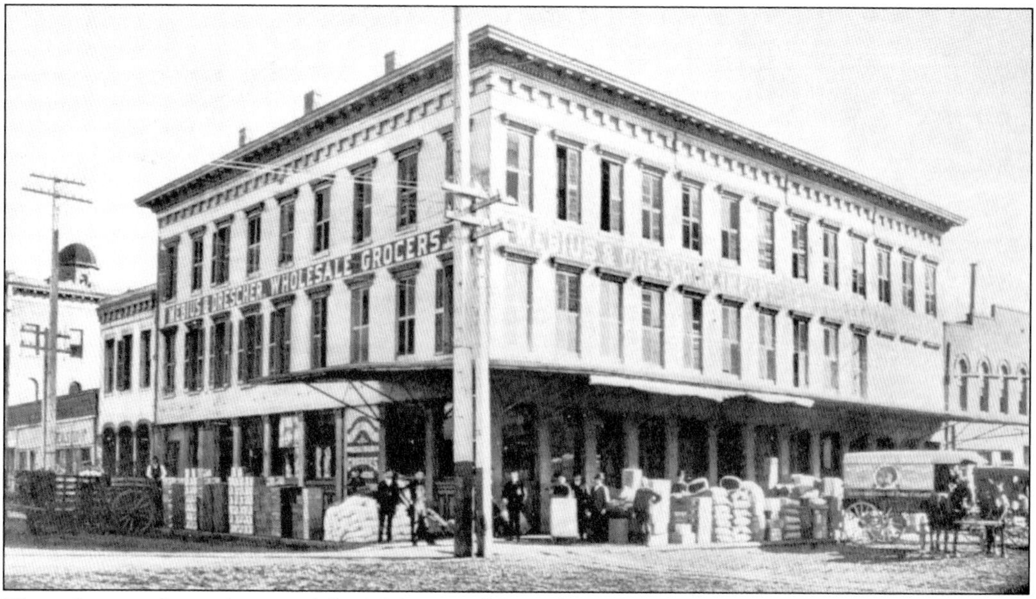

The substantial warehouse of the Mebius and Drescher wholesale grocery company was located at Front and K Streets. H. Bernard Drescher, the president of Mebius and Drescher, was on the executive committee and board of directors of the Red and White organization of independent grocers. He served four terms as district vice president of the American Wholesale Grocer's Association. (Courtesy of SAMCC.)

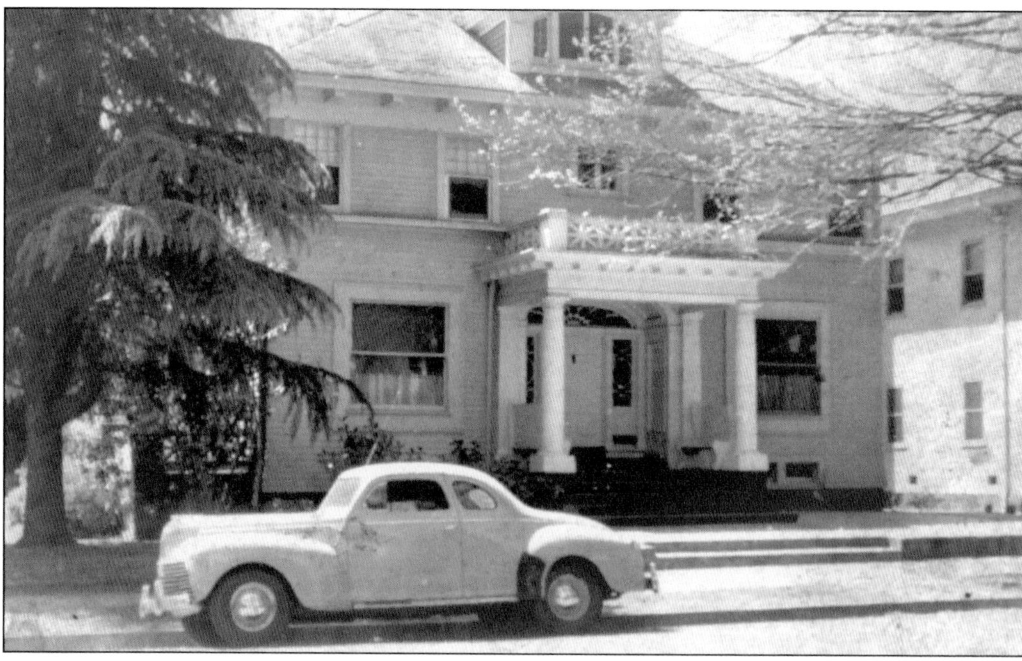

The home of H. Bernard Drescher at 2120 G Street was built in 1912. He and his wife, who was an avid horsewoman, lived there for 28 years. He was a director of the California Western States Life Insurance Company, the Capital National Bank, and the president and director of the Buffalo Brewing Company. His maternal grandfather settled here before the discovery of gold in 1848. (Photograph courtesy of BPNA.)

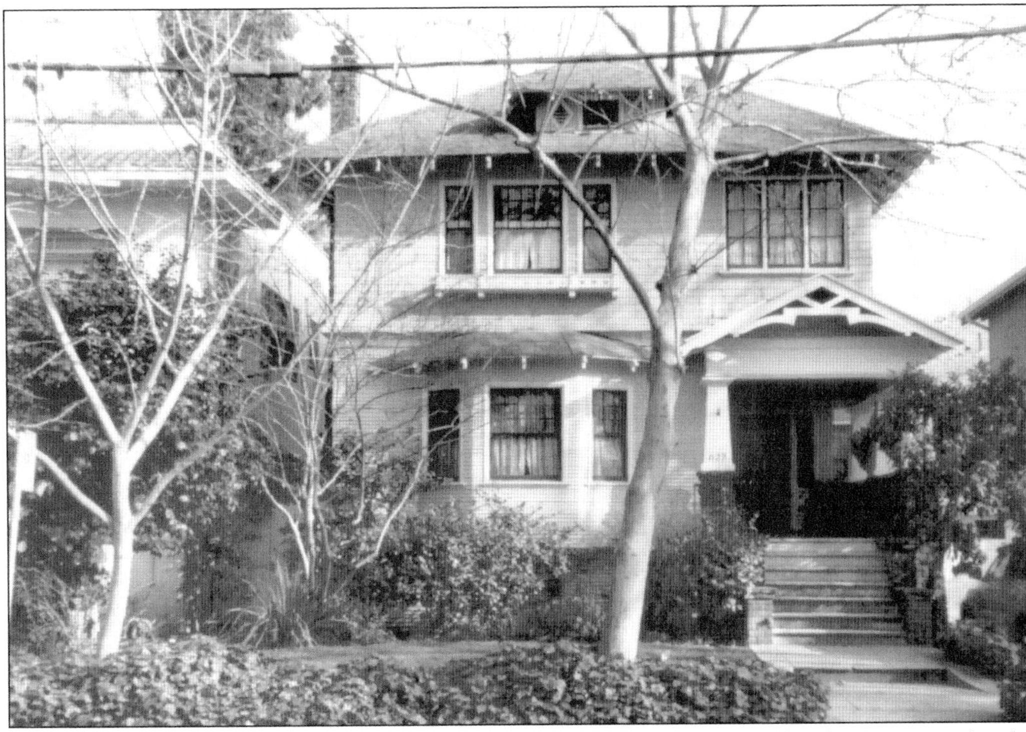

This 1910 house, 627 Twenty-second Street, was built for William Pritchard, a manager for the Ennis-Brown Company. Another Ennis Brown manager, Mallory Enos, also lived in Boulevard Park at 814 Twenty-third Street. The house was occupied in the late 1920s and 1930s by John and Fredericka Ochsner, who owned the Ochsner or Sun Building at 717 K Street. (Photograph by Paula Boghosian.)

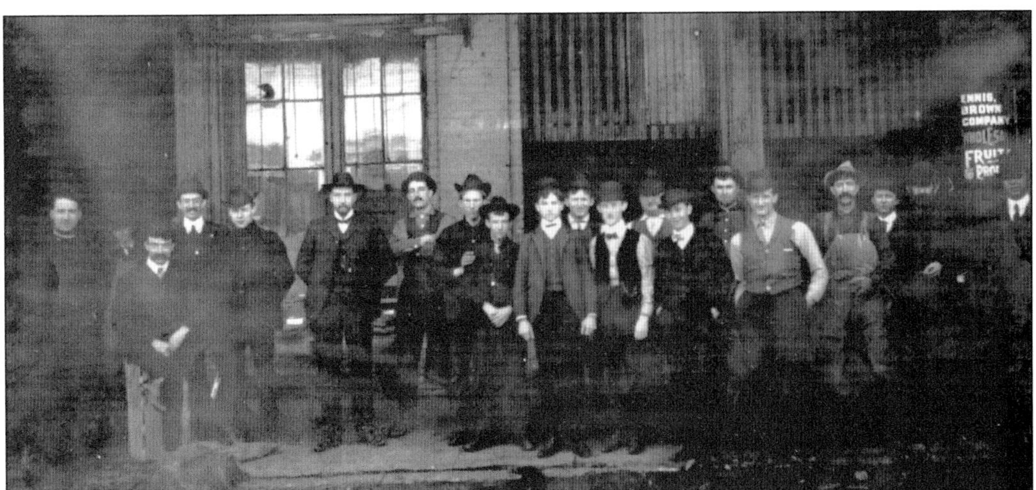

These men pose in front of the warehouse of wholesale fruit and produce for the Ennis-Brown Company. Three men were identified in this c. 1910 photograph: the man seated on the left is Scott F. Ennis, the man in front of the windows with the "Van Dyke" beard is Edward S. Brown, and the man at the extreme right is William Pritchard. (Courtesy of SAMCC.)

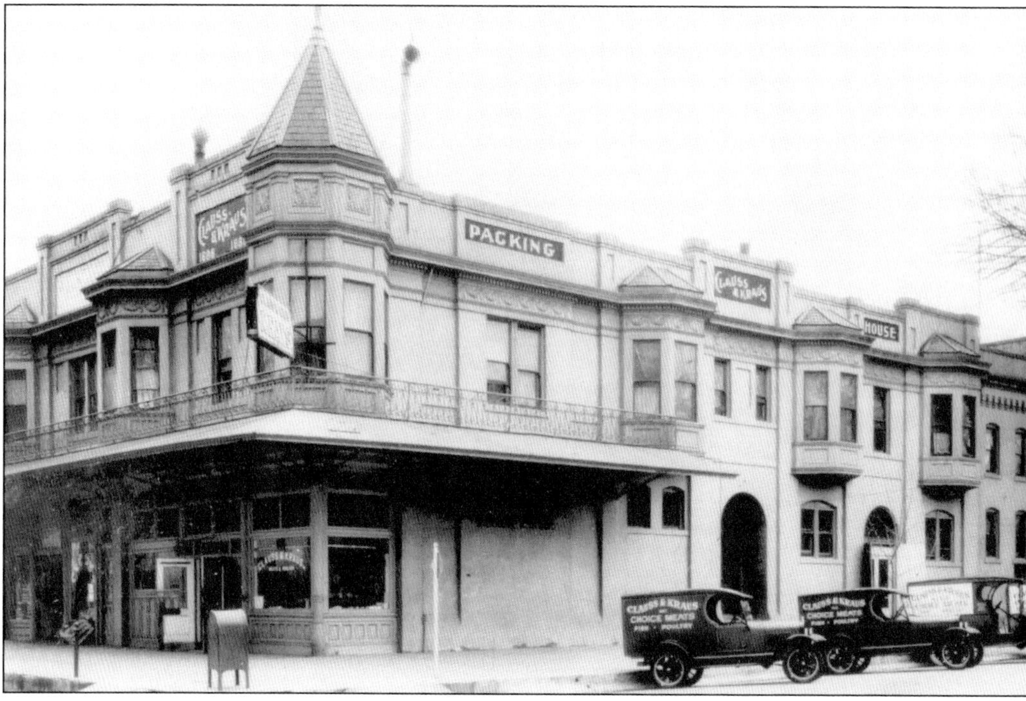

John Clauss, of Clauss and Kraus, was a Boulevard Park resident. His meatpacking business and retail store were located in this building at Seventeenth and I Streets. Clauss remained active in the business until the day he died in 1943, having served 55 years as the company's president. The building was renovated in the 1980s and now serves as an office building. (Courtesy of SAMCC.)

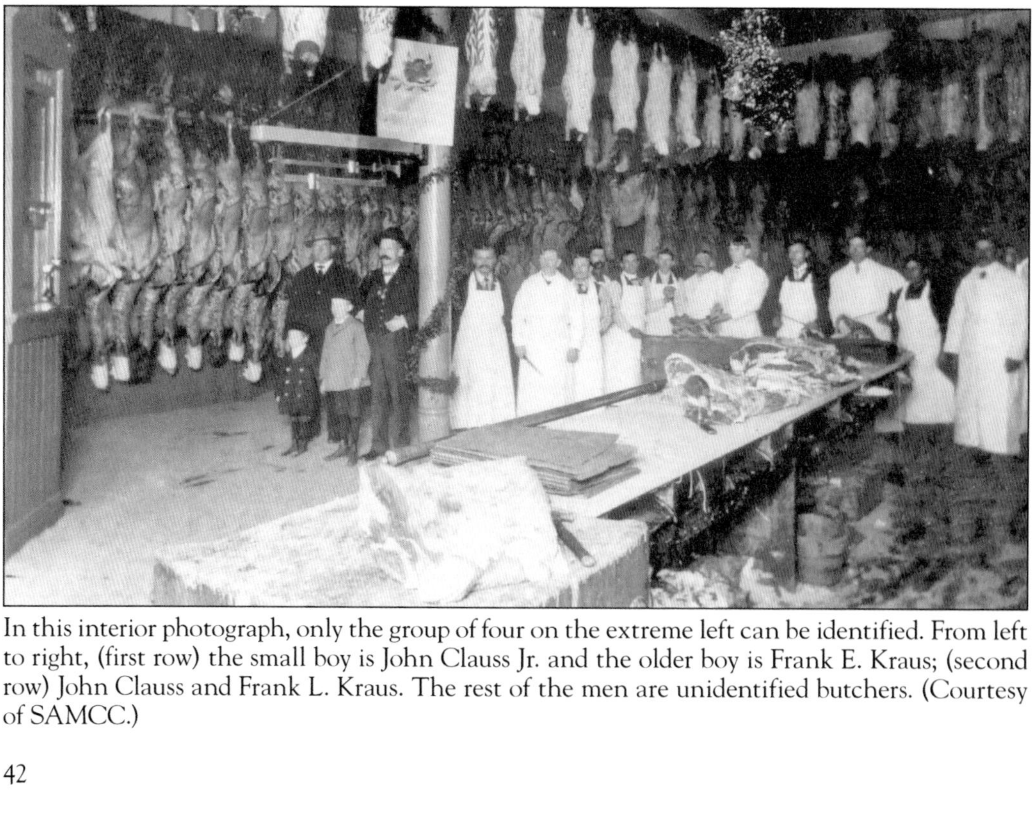

In this interior photograph, only the group of four on the extreme left can be identified. From left to right, (first row) the small boy is John Clauss Jr. and the older boy is Frank E. Kraus; (second row) John Clauss and Frank L. Kraus. The rest of the men are unidentified butchers. (Courtesy of SAMCC.)

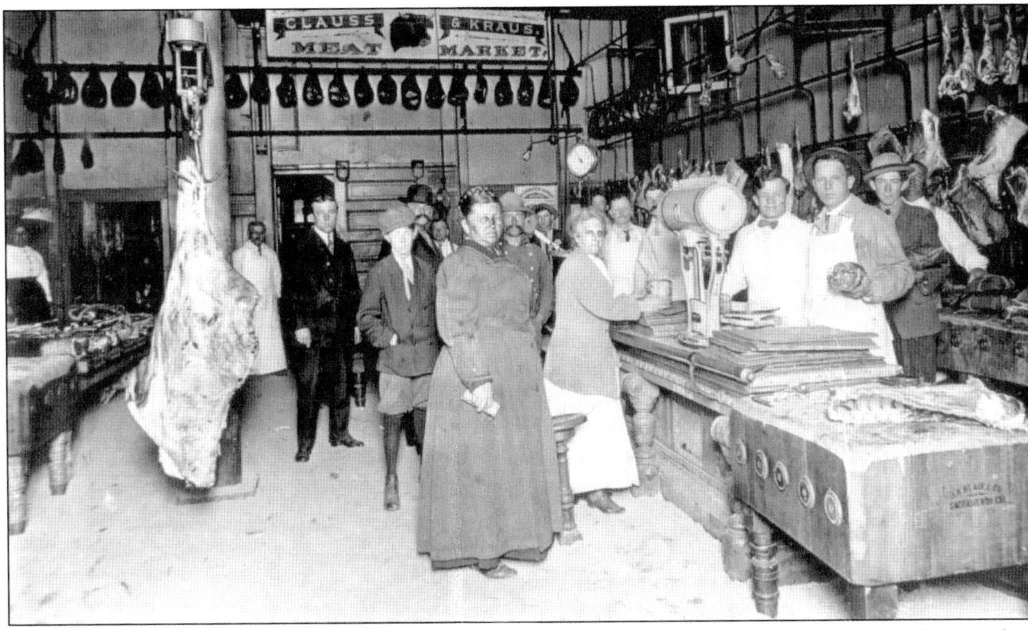

This *c*. 1900 photograph shows the interior of the Clauss and Kraus retail meat market. Before refrigeration, the meat was hung on hooks around the perimeter of the market. When a customer ordered some meat, a large hunk would be taken down, moved to the cutting block at lower right, and the portion ordered would be hacked off to the customer's satisfaction. (Courtesy of SAMCC.)

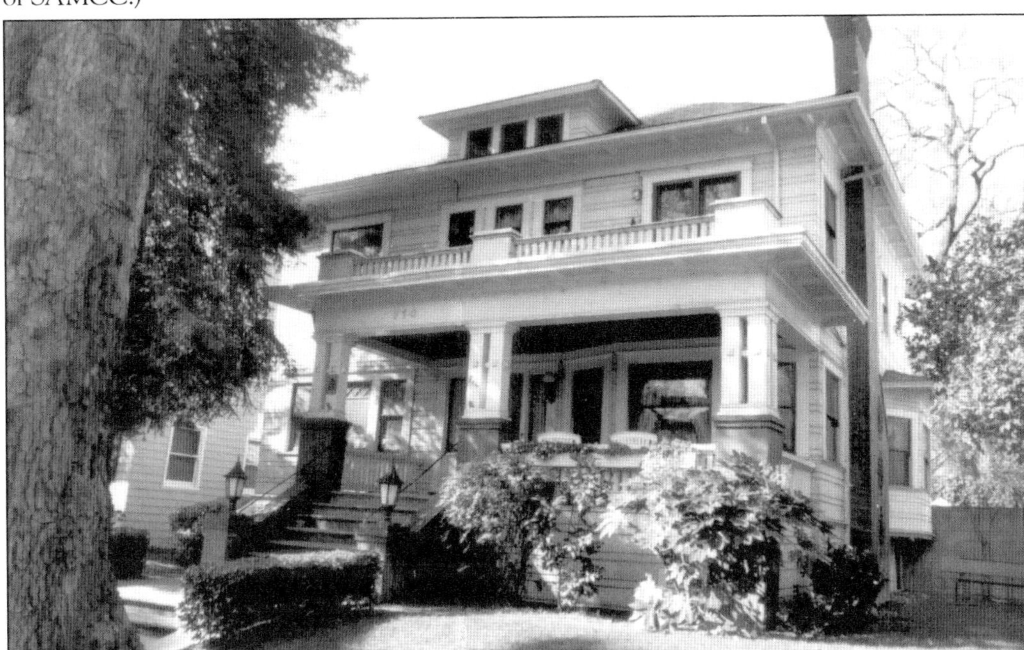

This house was built for local attorney Robertson McKisick in 1910. By 1920, it was the home of Rosa and John Clauss, and it would remain in the possession of the family for about 40 years. John Clauss was one of the founders of the Del Paso Country Club. He also served for many years on the board of directors for the Crocker Art Museum. (Photograph by Paula Boghosian.)

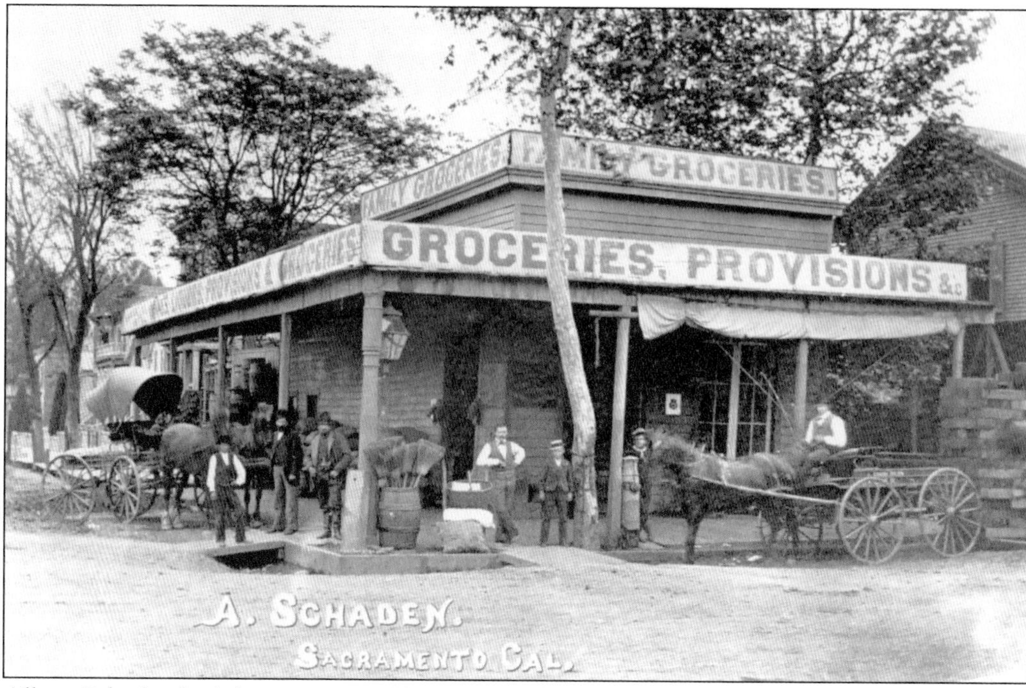

Albert Schaden had this grocery at 201 M Street (now Capitol Avenue), his brother John had a grocery at Fourth and M Streets, and his uncle Herman Winter (2324 H Street) was also a well-known grocer. (Courtesy of SAMCC.)

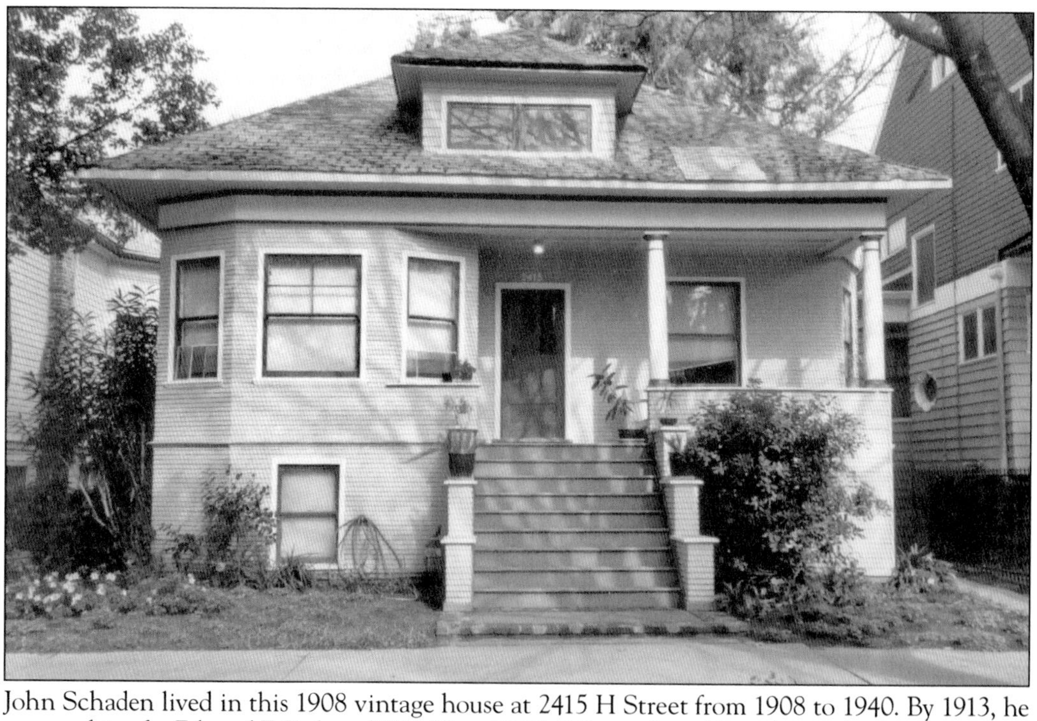

John Schaden lived in this 1908 vintage house at 2415 H Street from 1908 to 1940. By 1913, he was working for Edward F. Dalton (2430 H and 2131 F Streets), and later he worked as a traveling salesman for Lindley and Company wholesale grocers. (Photograph by Paula Boghosian.)

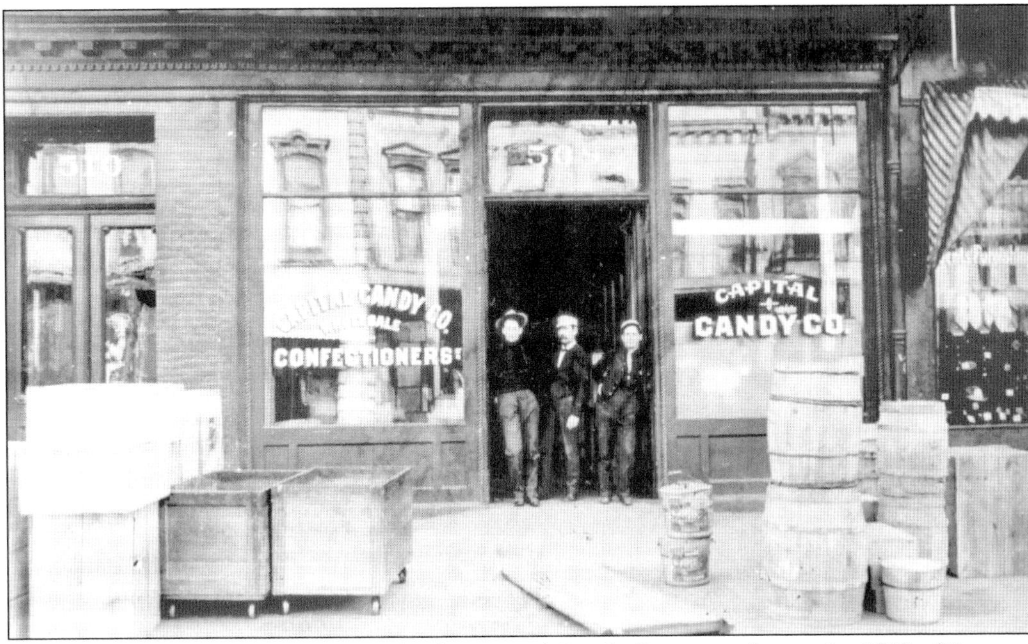

John Schaden worked as a salesman for the Capital Candy Company during the 1920s. (Courtesy of SAMCC.)

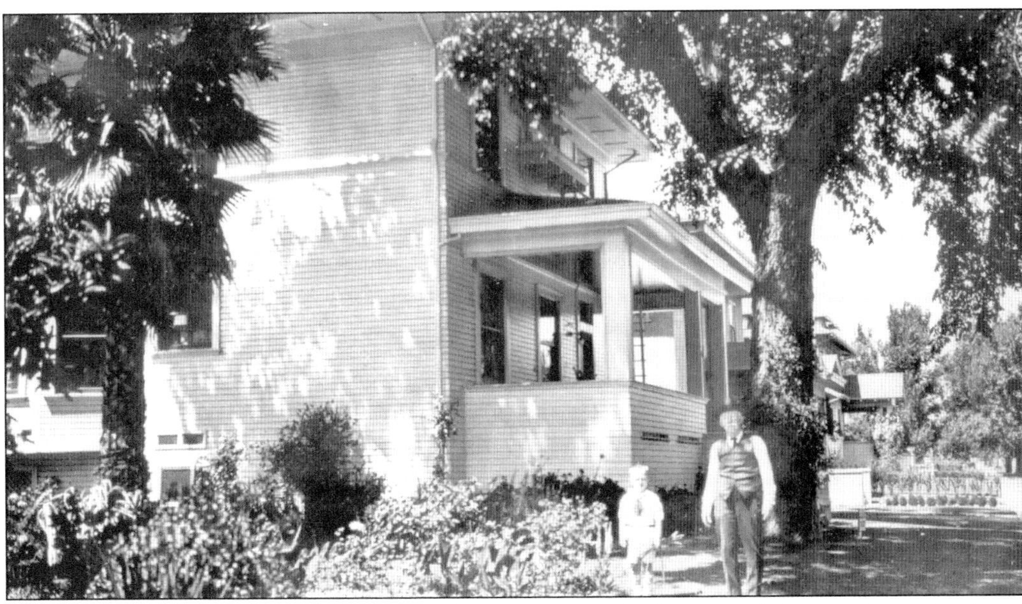
John Lund appears in this photograph with a small boy. Elizabeth and John Lund had this house at 716 Twenty-second Street built for them in 1908. John Lund and Son Grocers was located at the corner of Fourth Avenue and Broadway in Oak Park. Anne Lund lives in the house at the present time. (Courtesy of Anne Lund.)

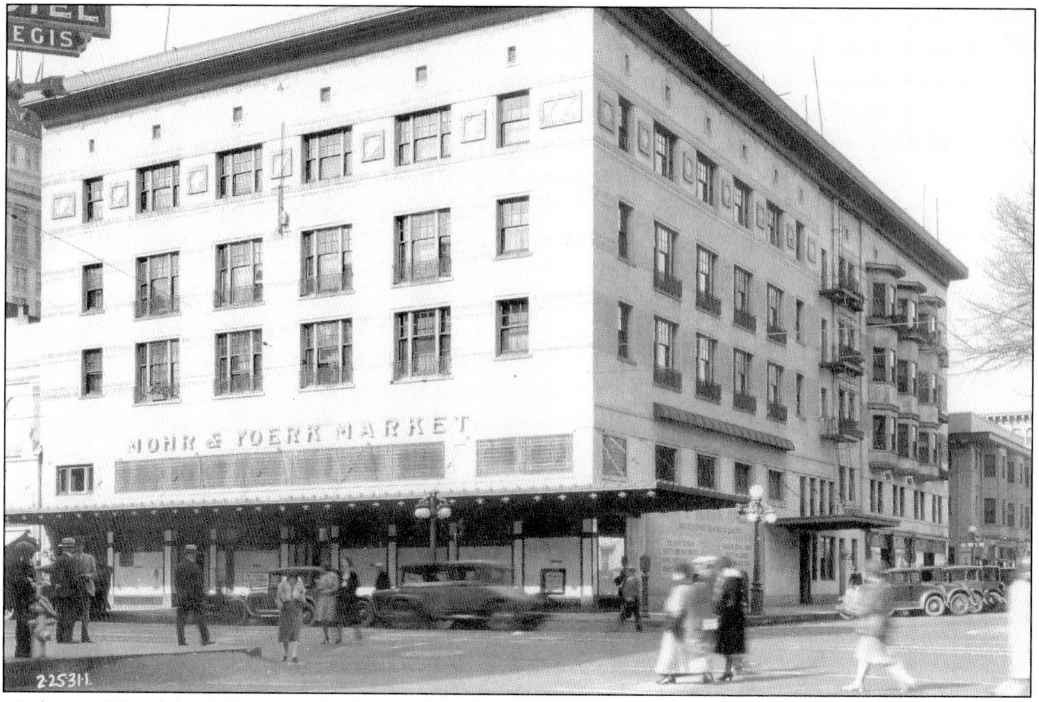

Mohr and Yoerk had their market located in the ground floor of this 1910 building at the northwest corner of Eleventh and K Streets. Louis Schwoerer (724 Twenty-first Street) was the corporate secretary of that company. The building was recently renovated and now houses the Pyramid Alehouse. (Courtesy of SAMCC.)

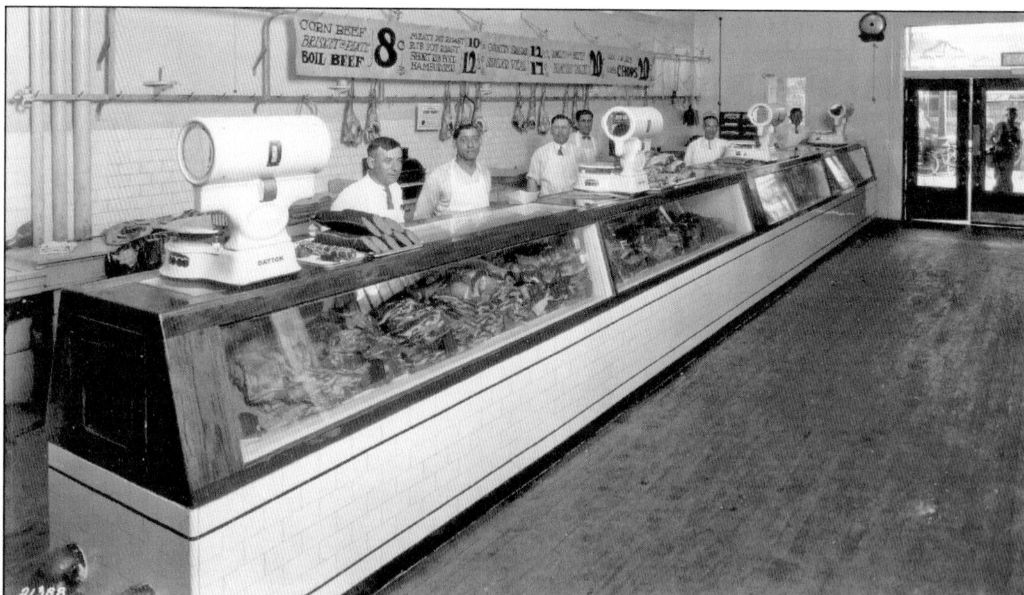

This is a 1920s photograph of the interior of the Mohr and Yoerk Market. Compare this to the photograph at the top of page 43 of the Clauss and Kraus market, taken just 20 years earlier. At the extreme lower left of the photograph note the pipes penetrating the base of the display case. These were some of the first refrigerated display cases in Sacramento. (Courtesy of SAMCC.)

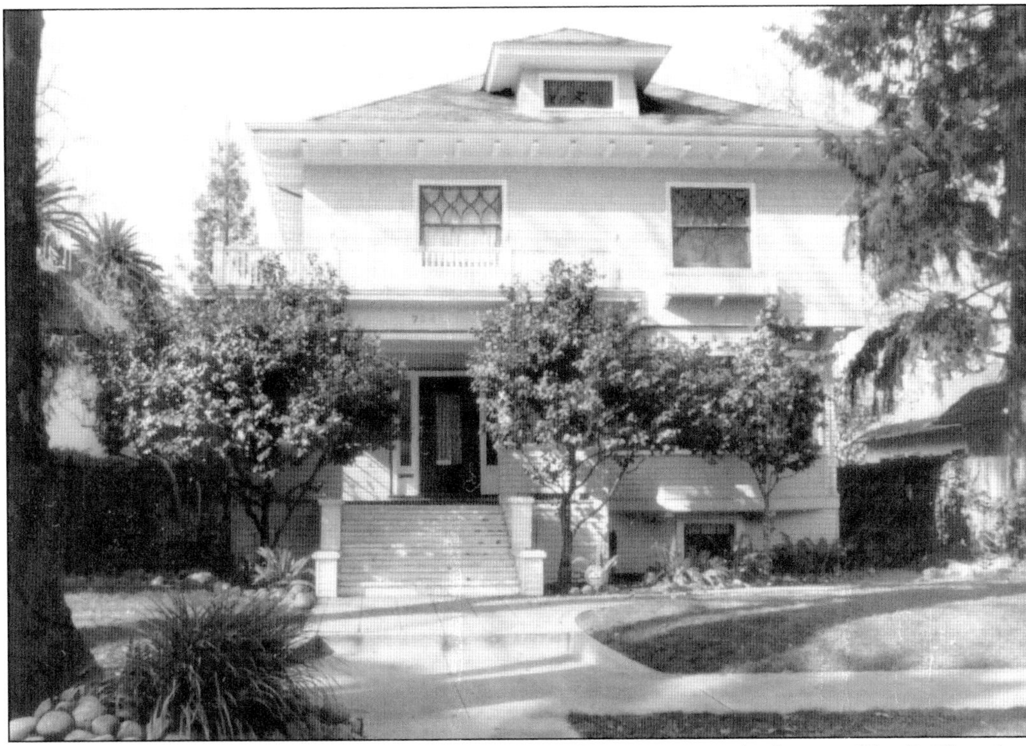

This house was built in 1908 for Louis Schwoerer, but by 1917, it was the home of Dr. E. Theodore Rulison, who lived there for about 20 years. (Photograph by Paula Boghosian.)

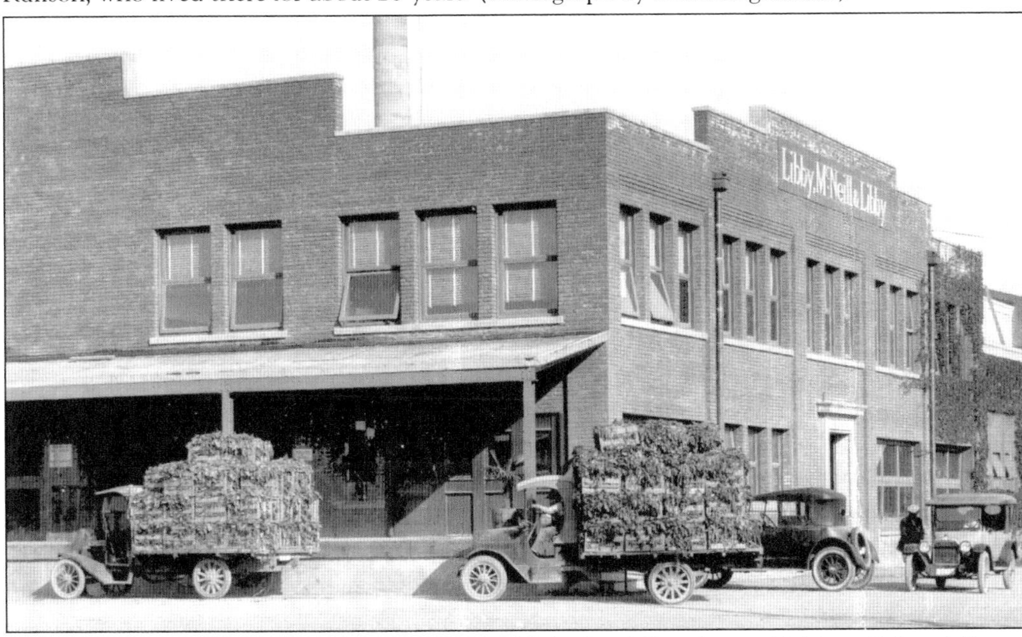

The Libby, McNeil, and Libby Cannery was established at Alhambra and M (now Folsom) Streets in 1912. Improvements in canning machinery and methods made large-scale plants like this one possible and, by the 1920s, they provided thousands of Sacramentans with jobs. Nick Vander Putten (2008 D Street) was a machinist at this plant. (Courtesy of SAMCC.)

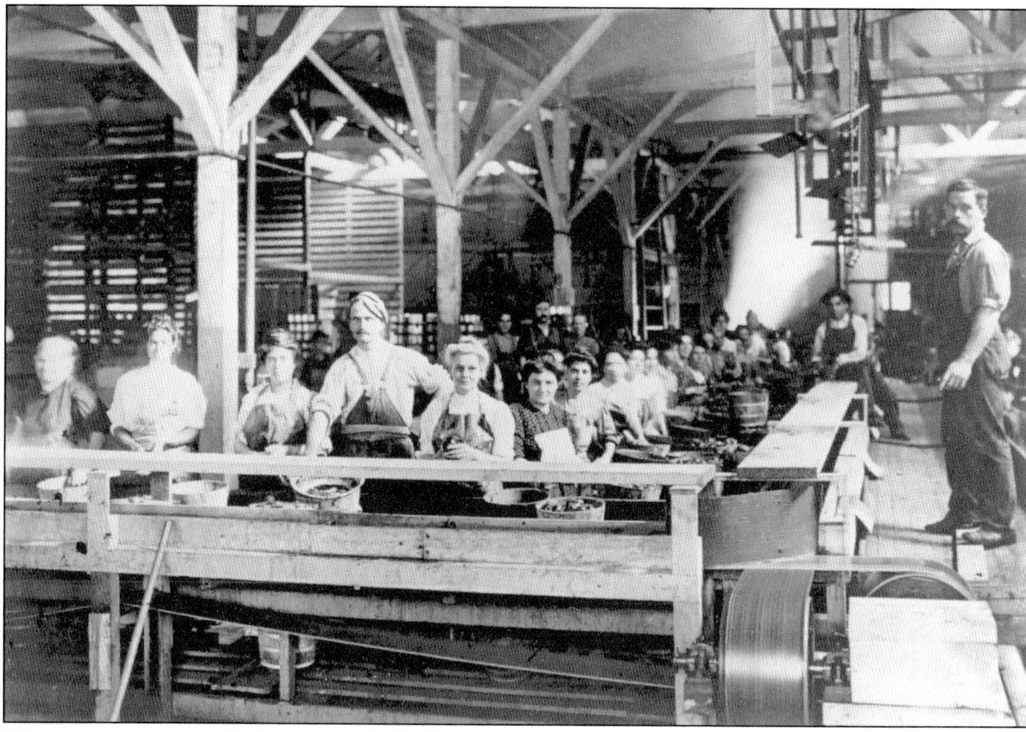

The canneries provided many unskilled immigrants, particularly women, with jobs. The extra income they produced for their families allowed some to save enough money to purchase homes and become part of the middle class. A number of the smaller homes in the north end of Boulevard Park were purchased in just this manner. (Courtesy of SAMCC.)

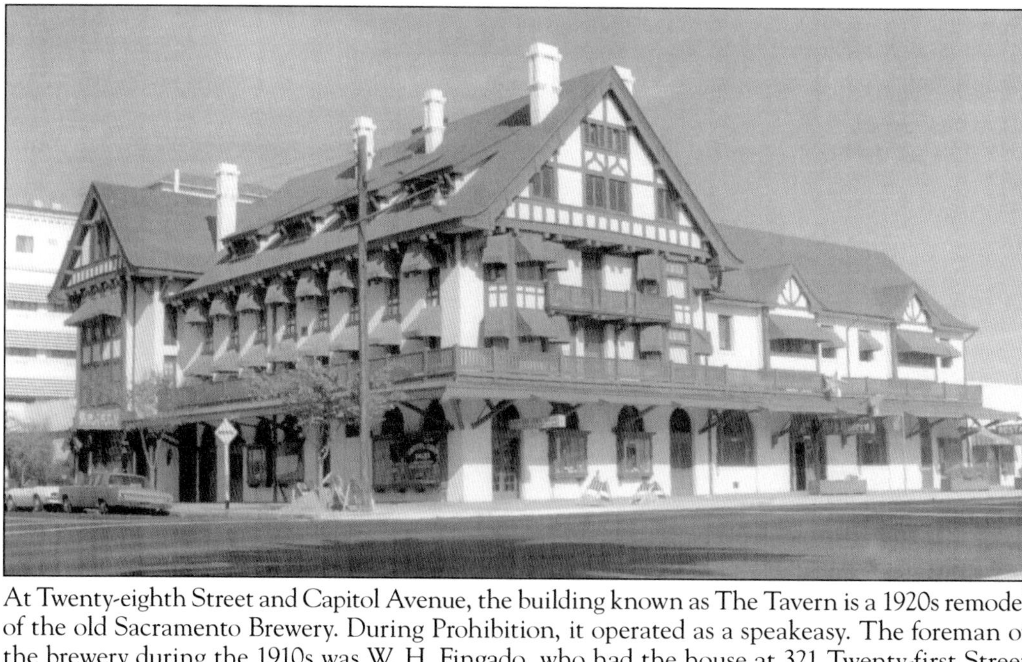

At Twenty-eighth Street and Capitol Avenue, the building known as The Tavern is a 1920s remodel of the old Sacramento Brewery. During Prohibition, it operated as a speakeasy. The foreman of the brewery during the 1910s was W. H. Fingado, who had the house at 321 Twenty-first Street built for him in 1913. (Courtesy of SAMCC.)

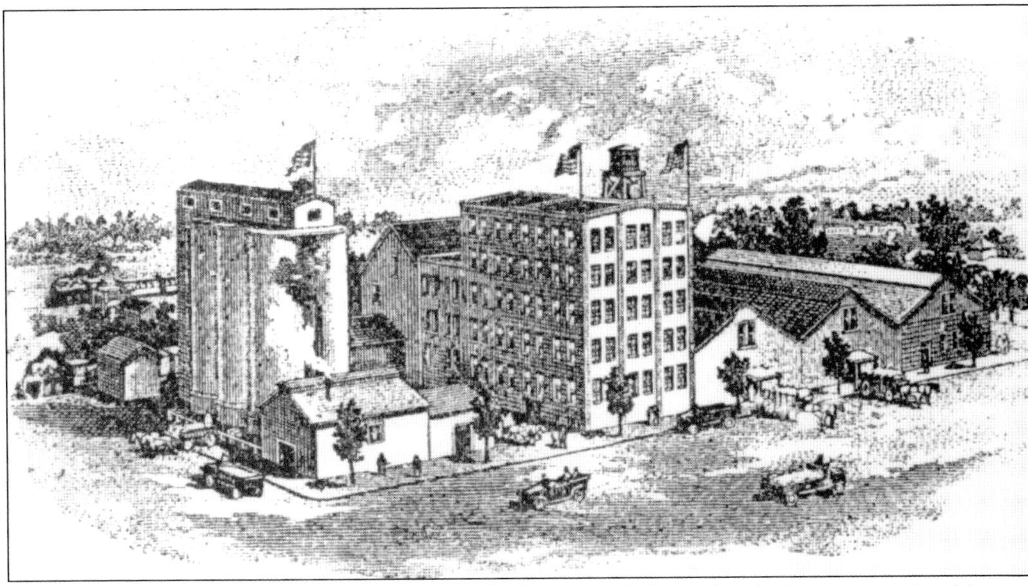

Emil E. Mattinson, who had a house built for him in 1910 at 2111 D Street, was bookkeeper for the old Phoenix Mill pictured in this illustration. The Phoenix Mill was later sold to Globe Mills. The old Globe Mills plant is currently undergoing renovation and will become a residential complex. (Courtesy of SAMCC.)

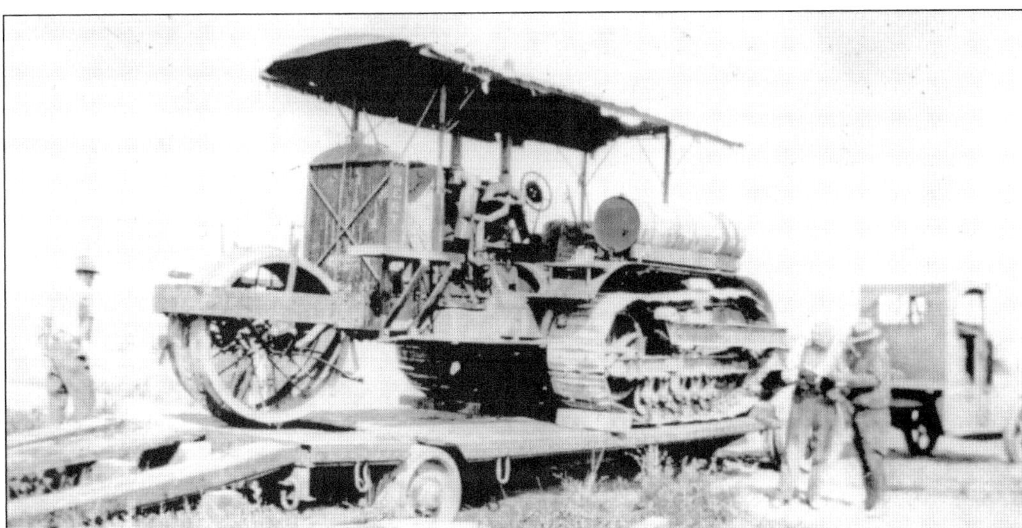

The Best tractor was one of the developments at the beginning of the 20th century that revolutionized farming. During the 1920s, Robert A. Bowden, of the R. A. Bowden Company, was a distributor of Best Tracklayer Tractors. He lived at 620 Twenty-second Street. In 1925, C. L. Best and Benjamin Holt, both of Stockton, merged their companies and became known as the Caterpillar Tractor Company. (Courtesy of SAMCC.)

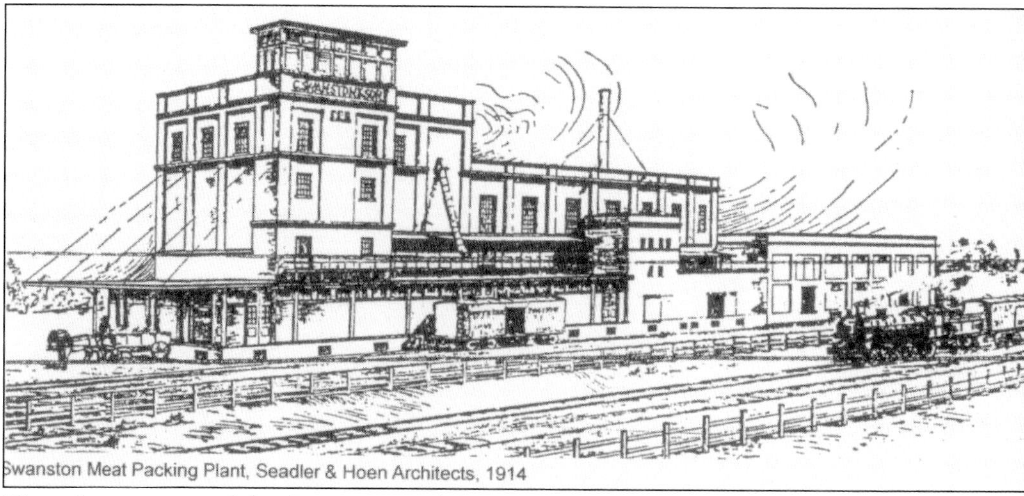

The sales manager of the Swanston and Son meatpacking plant was Mathew Gallagher, who lived at 505 Twenty-second Street. Regional Transit's Watt Avenue North light rail line passes through Swanston Station, which is the site of the old plant, just north of Arden Way. The plant was designed by Seadler and Hoen and was built in 1914. (Courtesy of the *Sacramento Bee*.)

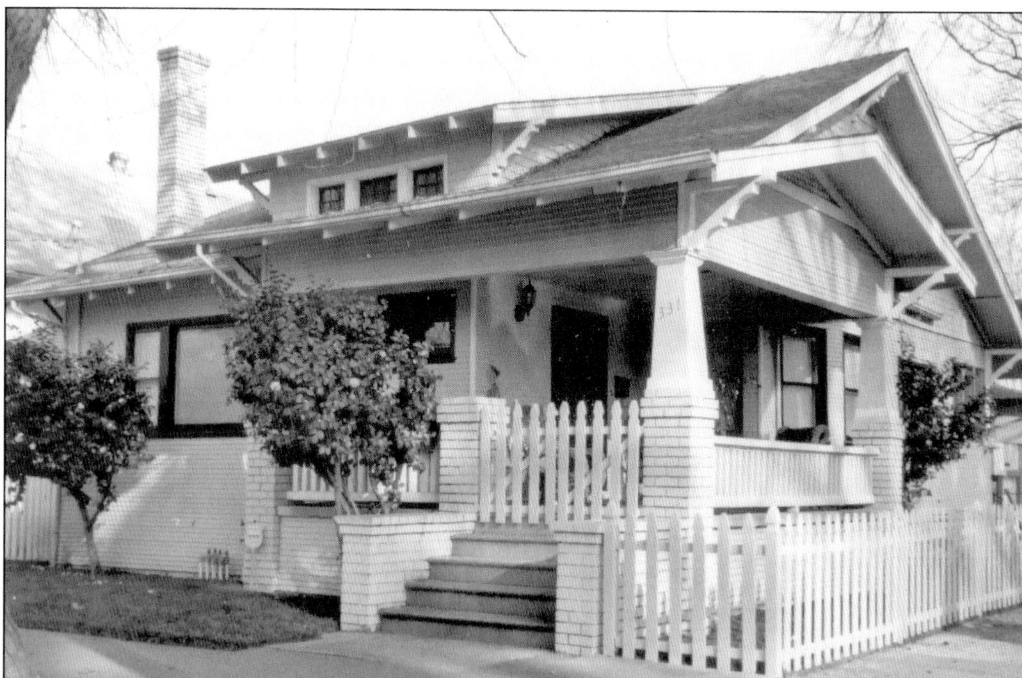

William H. Sexton, the general manager of the Capital Dairy, lived in this charming Craftsman bungalow at 331 Twenty-first Street for about 20 years.

Five

RAILROADS

The transcontinental railroad began construction in 1863 and was completed in 1869. In 1867, Central Pacific (CP) established its shops to repair and maintain their rolling stock in Sacramento. Later CP would see the need to manufacture their own locomotives and cars at the shops. The presence of the shops had a tremendous impact on the Sacramento economy. Thousands of well-paying, full-time jobs were created. In 1927, chamber of commerce statistics showed that railroad repair and construction employed an average of 4,378 people with a payroll of $10,064,293. That was 48 percent of the entire industrial payroll in Sacramento in 1927. The average SP (the name was changed from Central Pacific to Southern Pacific in the 1890s) job paid about $2,300 annually. A good single-story house at that time might cost about $1,500 and a two-story house about $2,500. The average for other industrial jobs was $1,570.

Southern Pacific found out early on that locomotives made in the east were not powerful enough to pull a long train over the Sierra Nevada. So they built their own locomotives here in the Sacramento shops. A. J. Stevens, who is memorialized with a statue in Chavez Park, was the head of the shops in those days. Stevens and others who worked in the shops had dozens of United States patents in their names.

Here at the Central Pacific shops, they manufactured cars for freight, passengers, dining, refrigeration, tankers, and cabooses. They also made the crockery and flatware for the dining cars, embellished with their logo, as well as the upholstery in passenger cars.

Draftsmen would execute mechanical drawings of the parts that were needed. Skilled carpenters, called pattern makers, would translate the drawings into exact-size wood models. These models would then be used in the forge shops to make the molds in wet sand, which would then accept the molten metal such as silver, copper, tin, iron, and steel. After the metal cooled, the parts would be taken to the machine shop for deburring, drilling of holes, cutting for bolt threads, etc. After parts were prepared, they then needed to go to the boiler shop, erecting shop (locomotives), or car shop. Once a piece of rolling stock had been assembled, it may have needed upholstery, cabinetry, and painting or finishing.

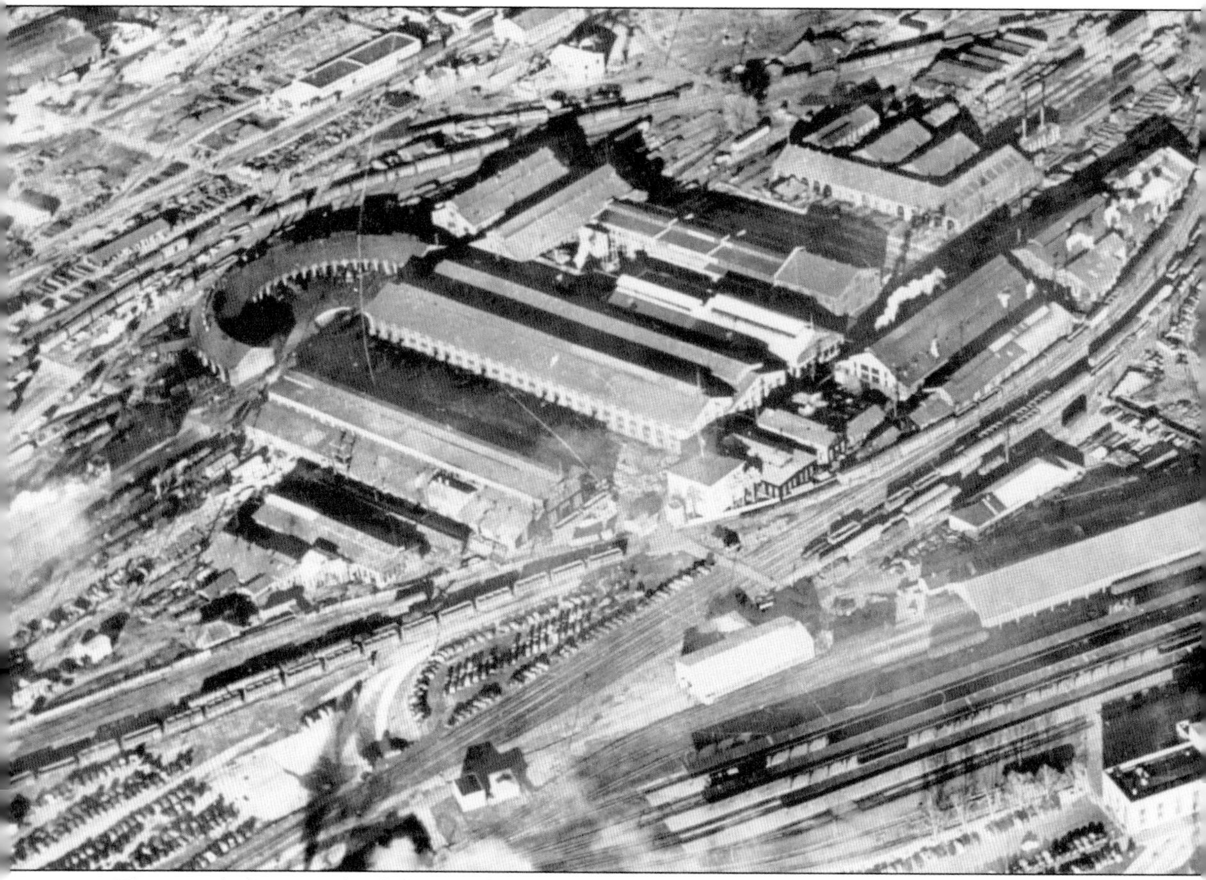

This aerial photograph of the Southern Pacific (SP) Railroad shops shows only the central area. There were other shops, storehouses, and mills scattered all over the 238-acre site. Portions of some of the older brick buildings go back to the late 1860s, before the intercontinental railroad was completed. (Courtesy of SAMCC.)

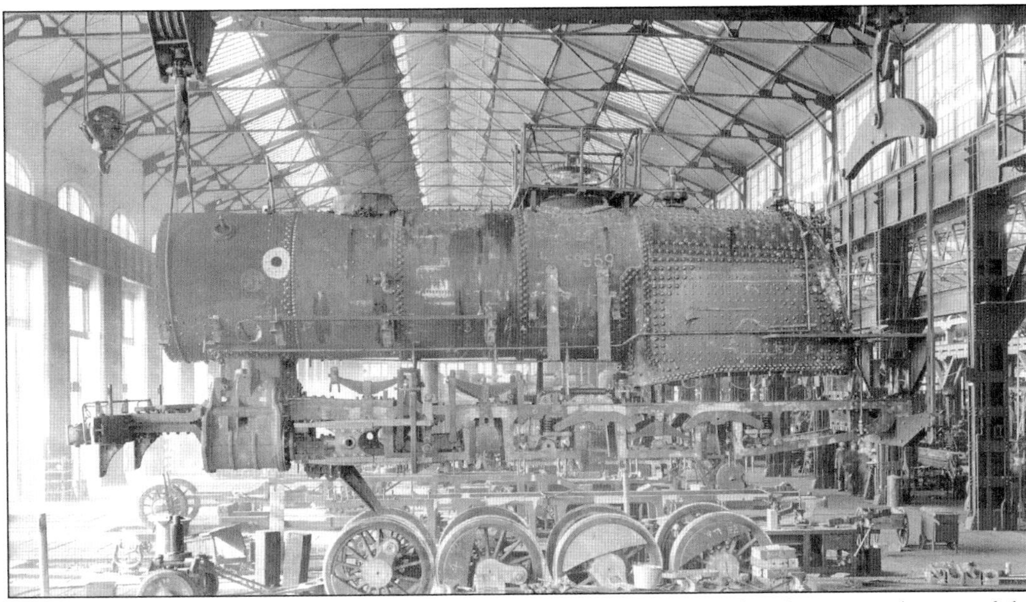

Locomotives were built here in the massive erecting shop. The overhead crane at the top of the photograph was capable of picking up and moving a locomotive. This shop was about 520 feet by 180 feet and had stations for the simultaneous construction of 25 locomotives. The machine shop was located beyond the wall at the right. The north half of the machine shop was built in 1867. (Courtesy of SAMCC.)

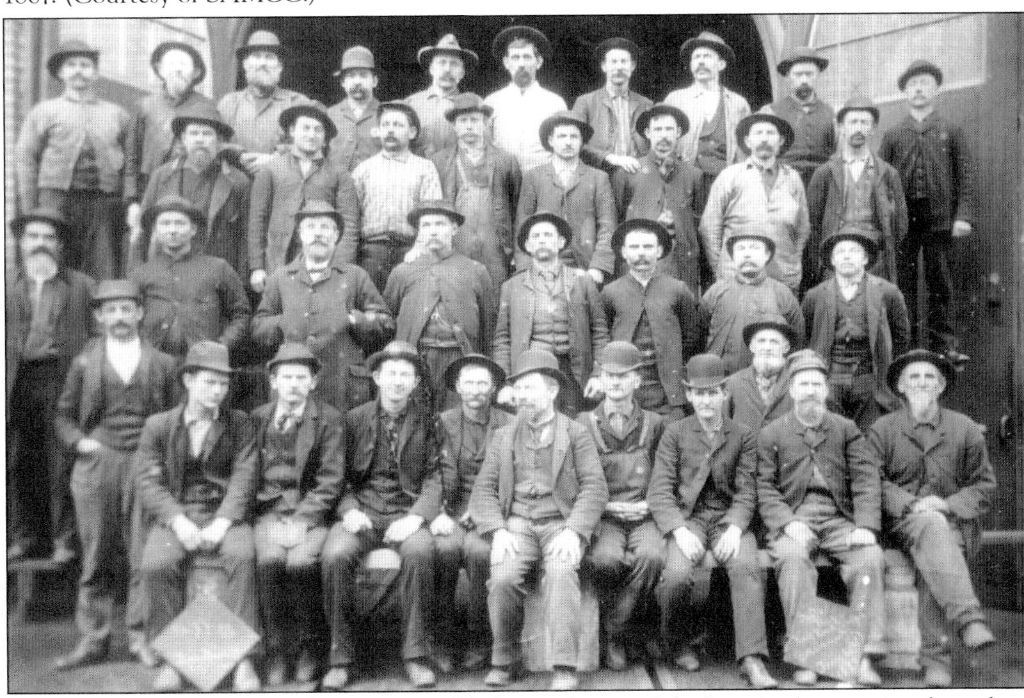

This photograph of the machinists, assembled outside one of the bays in the erecting shop, dates to the 1890s. To build locomotives, and all the other cars and parts that were required to meet the needs of a major railroad, took thousands of well-paid, highly skilled workers. Many of them lived in Boulevard Park. (Courtesy of SAMCC.)

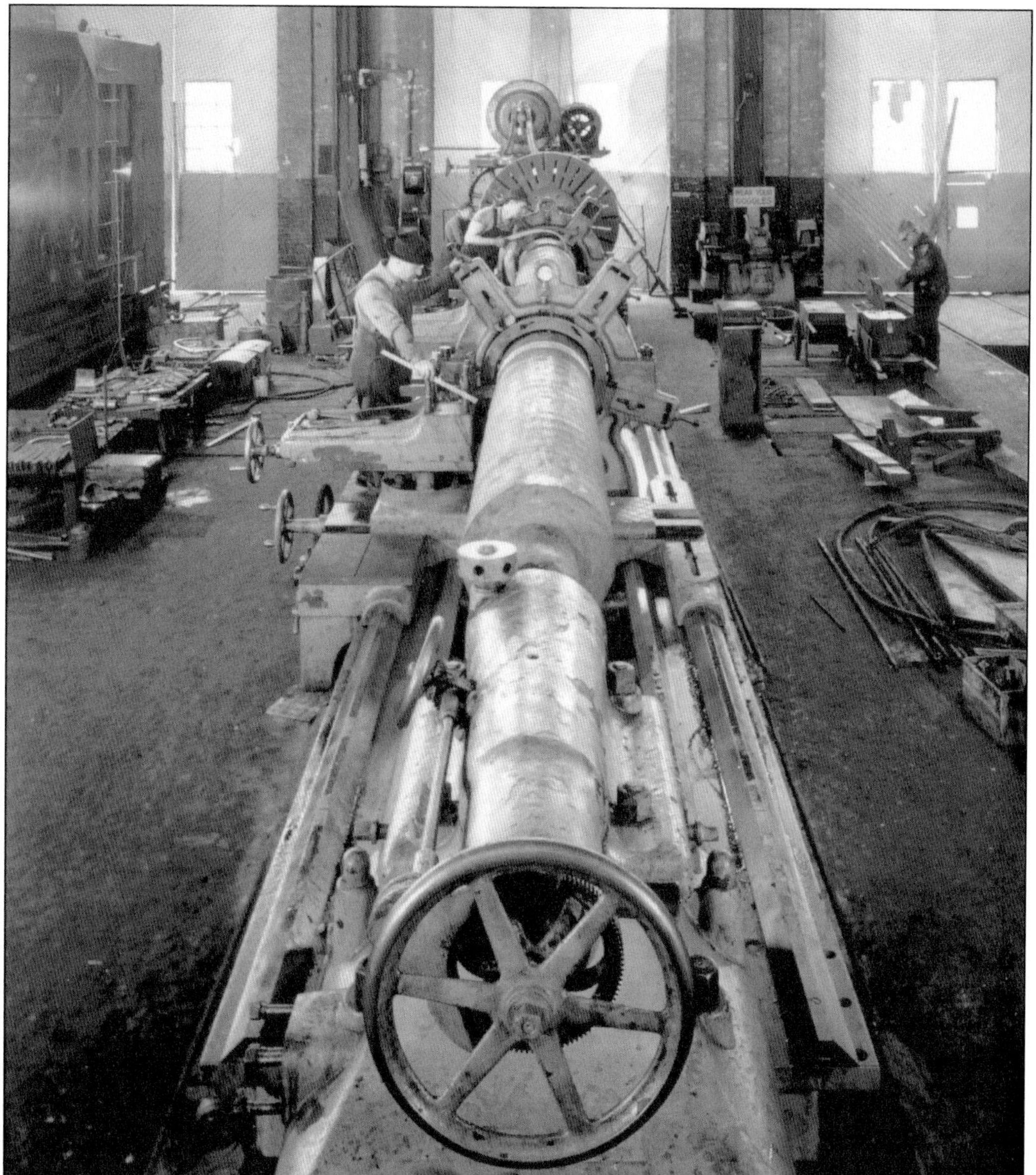

This machine is a lathe. The size of it compared to the man operating it at upper left gives some idea of the scale of the equipment needed to manufacture a railroad. (Courtesy of SAMCC.)

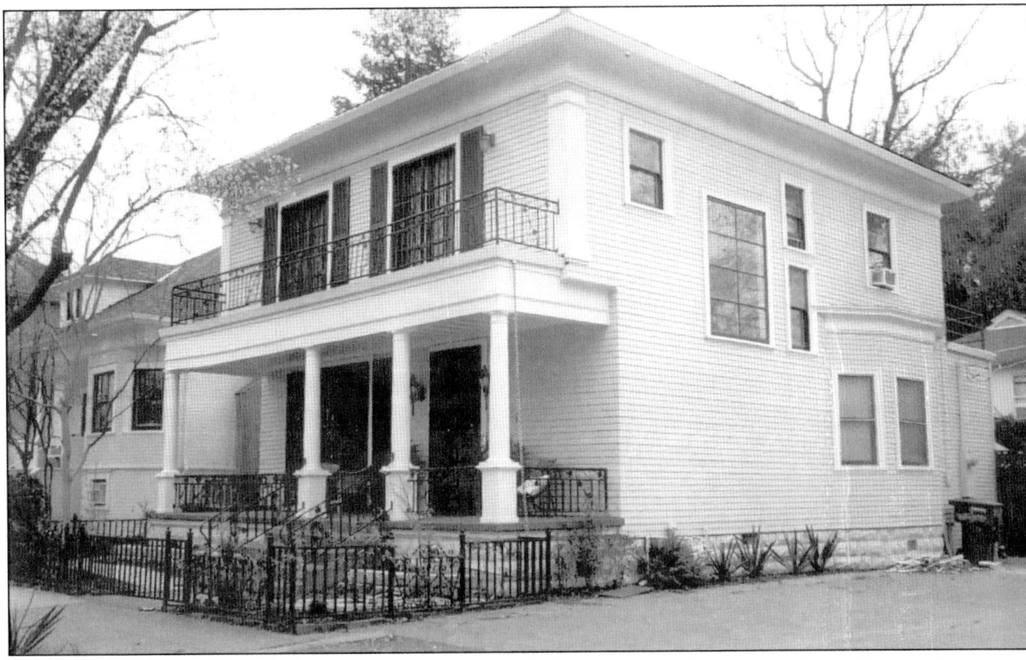

Josephine and Daniel McGee lived in this 1908 house at 816 Twenty-third Street. He was a foreman for the SP shops. (Photograph by Don Cox.)

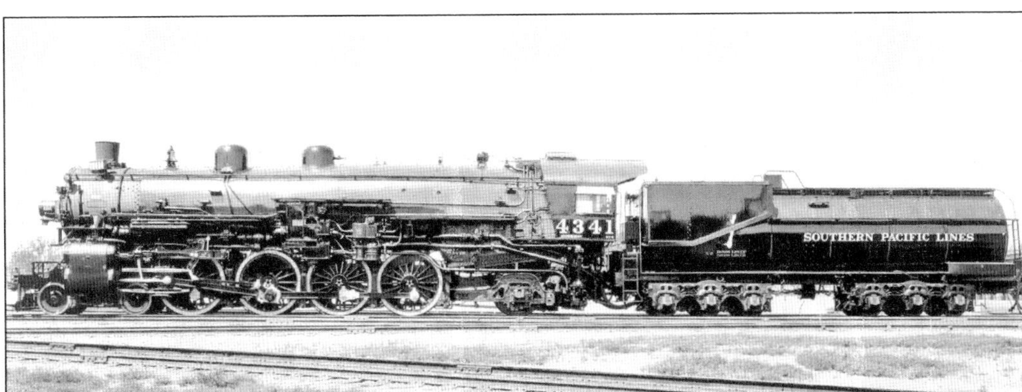

This locomotive is an example of one of the powerful mountain locomotives manufactured by SP in the 1920s. (Courtesy of SAMCC.)

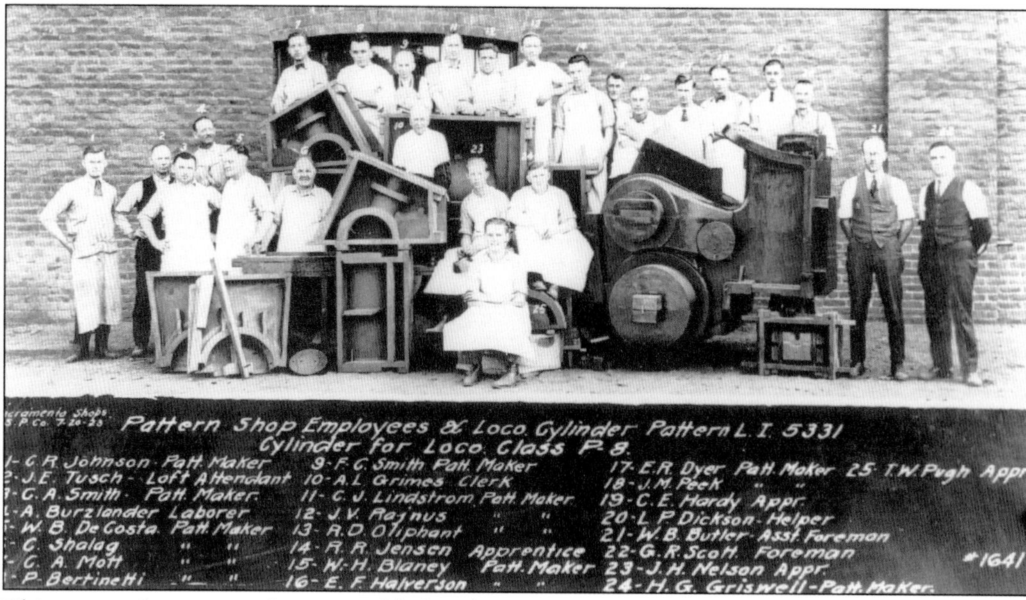

This group of pattern makers assembled in the 1920s with some of the patterns they have made, which will be used to make the molds that could accept the molten metal. While these men were highly skilled carpenters, many, when asked to list their occupation in a city directory, would simply put carpenter. (Courtesy of SAMCC.)

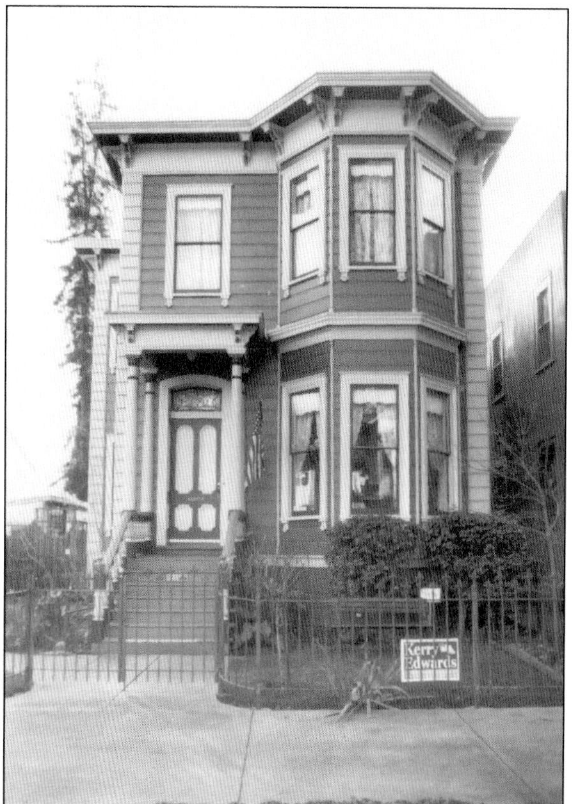

Peter Carlson was a cabinetmaker for SP. He lived in this Italianate house from 1905 until his death in 1935. In 1938, the house sold for $2,900. The house was built in 1878 for H. E. Parker, a salesman for W. R. Strong and Company, dealers in wholesale produce. (Photograph by Paula Boghosian.)

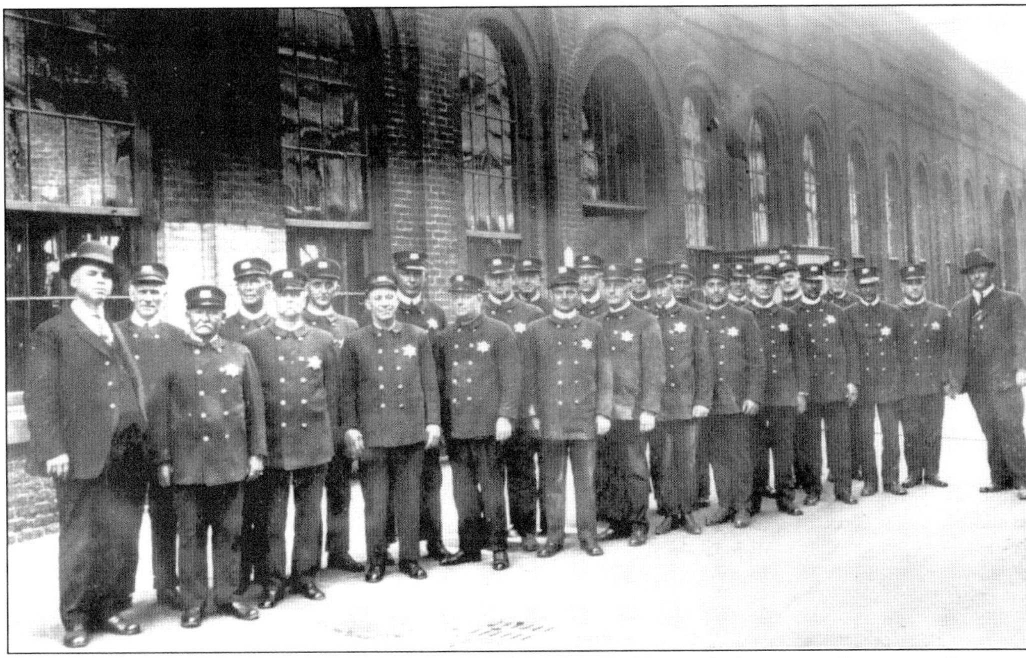

With a community of workers numbering 4,000 to 5,000, SP needed to provide many of its own services. The shops had their own police force and fire department. With a potentially dangerous working environment, SP could not have unknowledgeable outsiders wandering around the production plants. (Courtesy of SAMCC.)

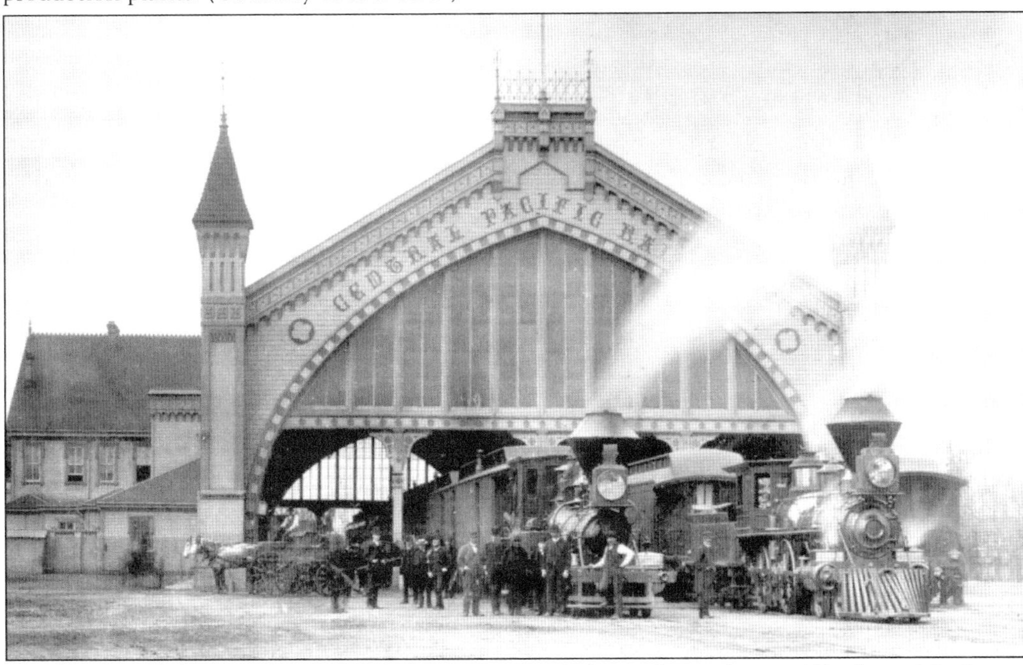

With its Victorian grandeur, this 1879 depot served the early residents of Boulevard Park, and because of its massive structure, the trains passed through the middle of the building. Note that the signage on the building indicates that it belonged to Central Pacific Railroad. It did not become the Southern Pacific Railroad until the 1890s. (Courtesy of Paula Boghosian)

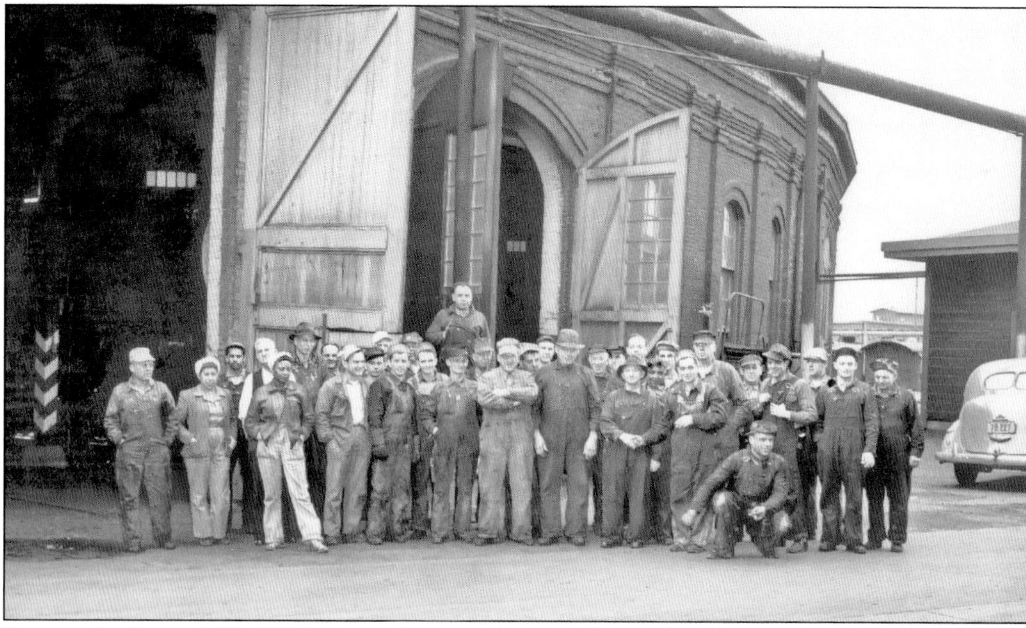

During the Second World War, this photograph was taken of the workers in the roundhouse. As one can see to the left in the photograph, women were starting to take spots in the SP workforce. (Courtesy of SAMCC.)

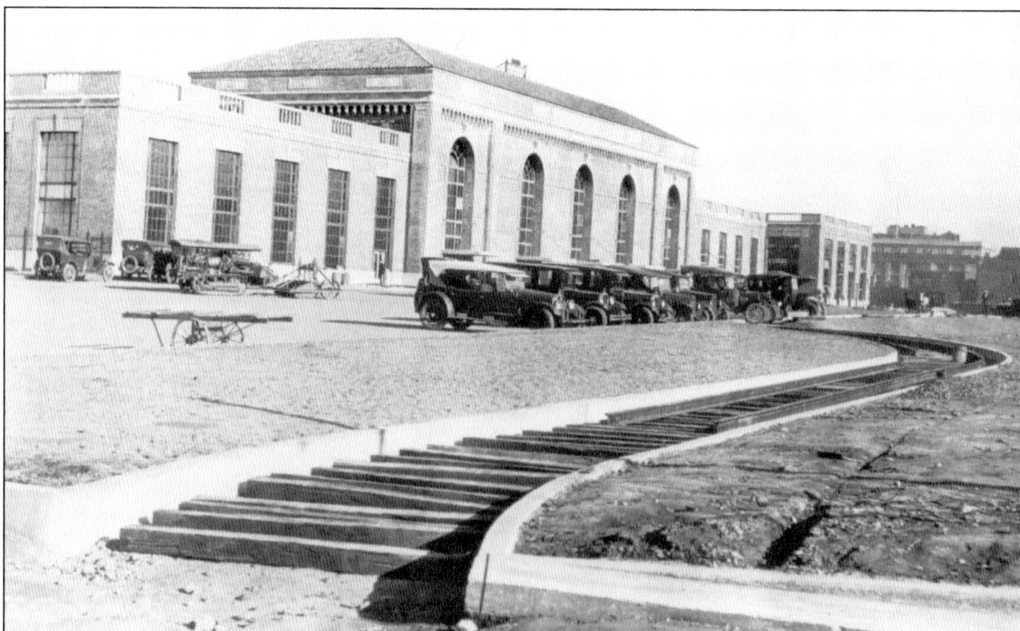

The new Southern Pacific Depot was completed in 1925. The building is still in use at the present time. (Courtesy of Paula Boghosian.)

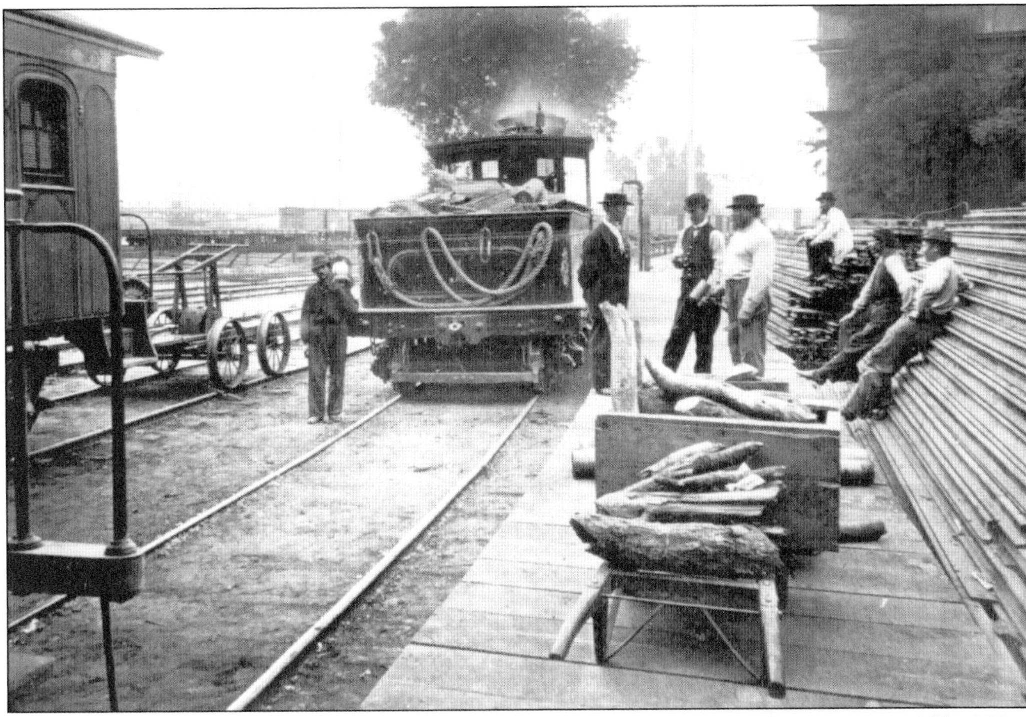

The first Central Pacific locomotive, the *Governor Stanford*, is seen in this rare 1864 Alfred Hart photograph of Front Street. The coach on the left was one of the railroad's first coaches. In the center, the conductor consults his watch. The men at the right are lounging on rails that will soon be sent to the railroad construction site, which was then near Newcastle.

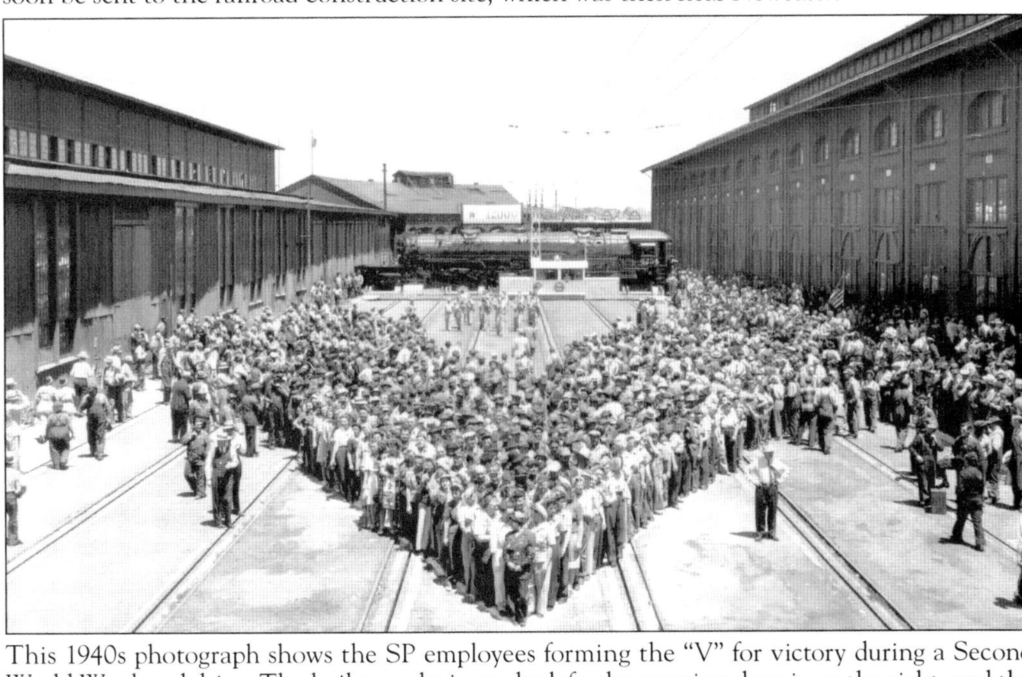

This 1940s photograph shows the SP employees forming the "V" for victory during a Second World War bond drive. The boiler works is on the left, the erecting shop is on the right, and the roundhouse is at the rear. (Courtesy of SAMCC.)

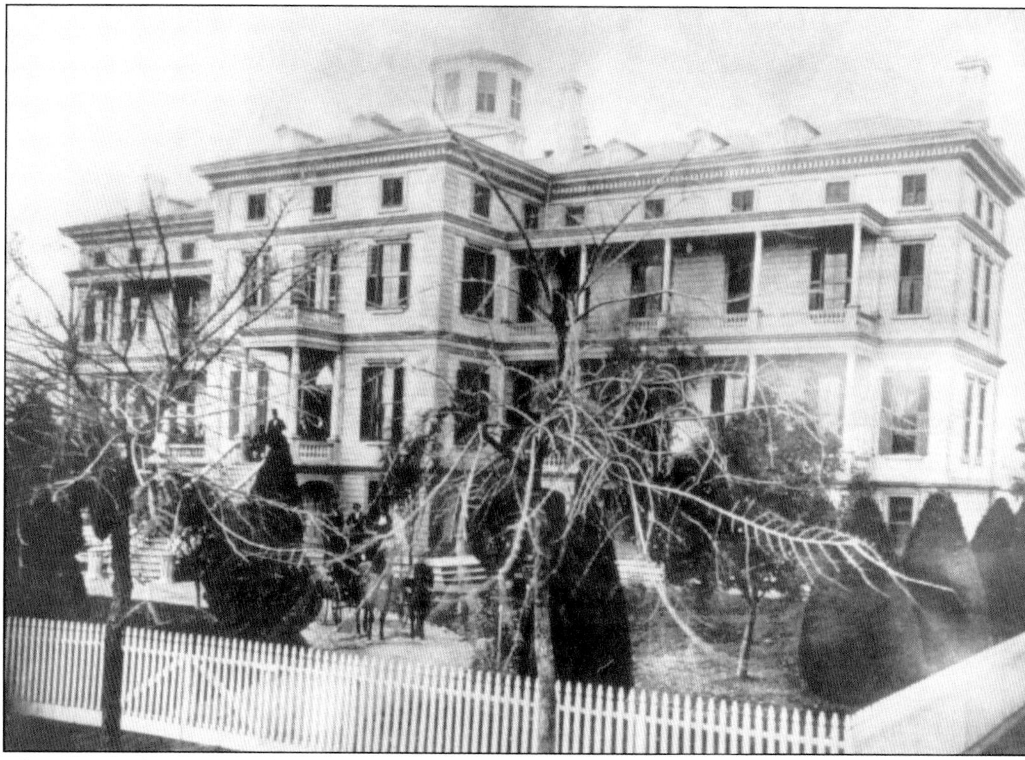

This 1890s photograph shows the SP hospital that the company built to care for its workers. It was located at Thirteenth and C Streets. (Courtesy of SAMCC.)

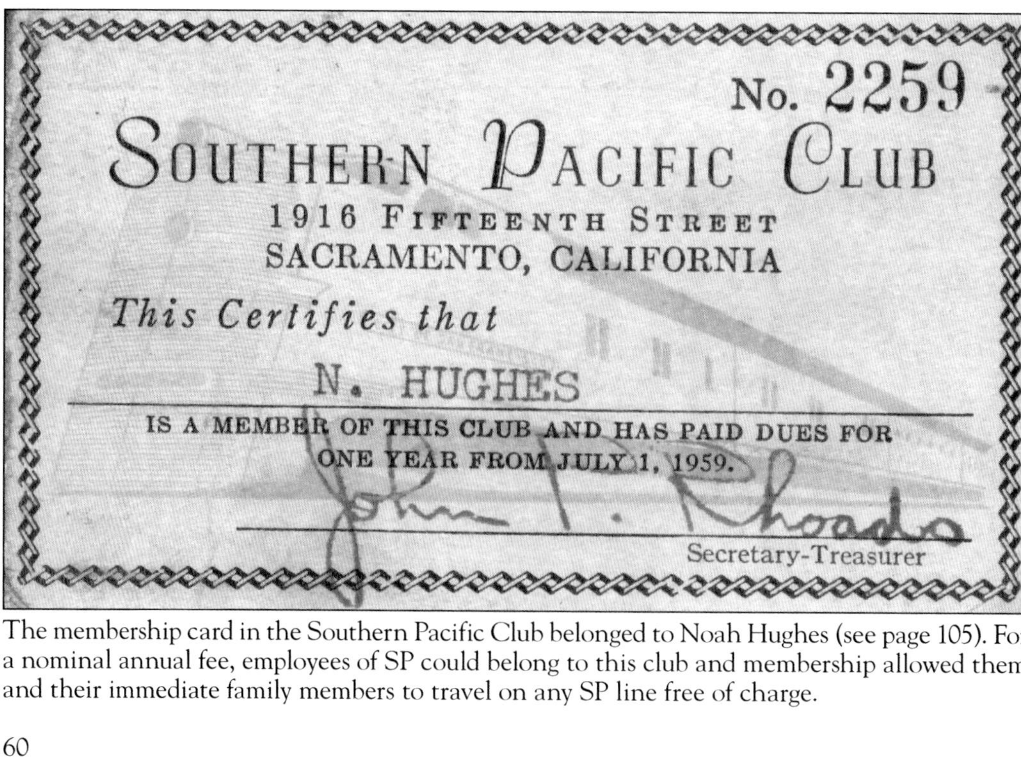

No. 2259

SOUTHERN PACIFIC CLUB

1916 FIFTEENTH STREET
SACRAMENTO, CALIFORNIA

This Certifies that

N. HUGHES

IS A MEMBER OF THIS CLUB AND HAS PAID DUES FOR ONE YEAR FROM JULY 1, 1959.

John P. Rhoads
Secretary-Treasurer

The membership card in the Southern Pacific Club belonged to Noah Hughes (see page 105). For a nominal annual fee, employees of SP could belong to this club and membership allowed them and their immediate family members to travel on any SP line free of charge.

Six

Money Matters

Money always matters in a new settlement but was a prime force in the gold rush town of Sacramento. The first stop for miners down from the mountains was Sacramento—a place to turn their gold into money and entertainment. Early pioneers performing banking services became wealthy just managing the money made from gold. Merchants also fared well since food and supplies were limited, and they were able to charge handsomely for their goods. Some individuals even traveled east to purchase goods at cost and bring them back for resale in California at high prices, often providing enough profit to begin a business or buy land to farm.

As the gold fields gave up the "easy" gold, people began to settle around Sacramento and farm the rich valley fields. Being vulnerable to crop transportation fees and existing banking practices, farmers formed their own associations, ultimately gathering enough power and money to establish their own banks with policies befitting their industry. They formed liaisons with steamboat companies to compete with railroads for lower fees. They adjusted bank requirements on repayment of agricultural loans so farmers could sell when the profits were best, and were more sensitive to climatic vagaries that affected crops. The Farmers and Mechanics Bank was such an institution. Cooperative associations were successful in marketing, lobbying, and coordinating crops for the good of the farmer. The California Fruit Exchange was an example.

The Bank of Italy, ultimately evolving into the massive Bank of America, was established in 1904 in San Francisco by A. P. Gianini. The purpose of its founding was to assist farmers, primarily of Italian descent, who were not serviced well by the large national banks dominating the banking scene at that time. Geared to local residents' social circumstances, financial needs, and plans, the Bank of Italy was a good fit for Sacramento. It occupied the former People's Bank building when it moved to Sacramento before the 1920s. In 1930, the name was changed to Bank of America, which became one of the largest banking institutions in the country. Agricultural-related pursuits and land and real estate development in and around Sacramento provided a good and growing market for banking, and Boulevard Park was home to many that were employed in the field.

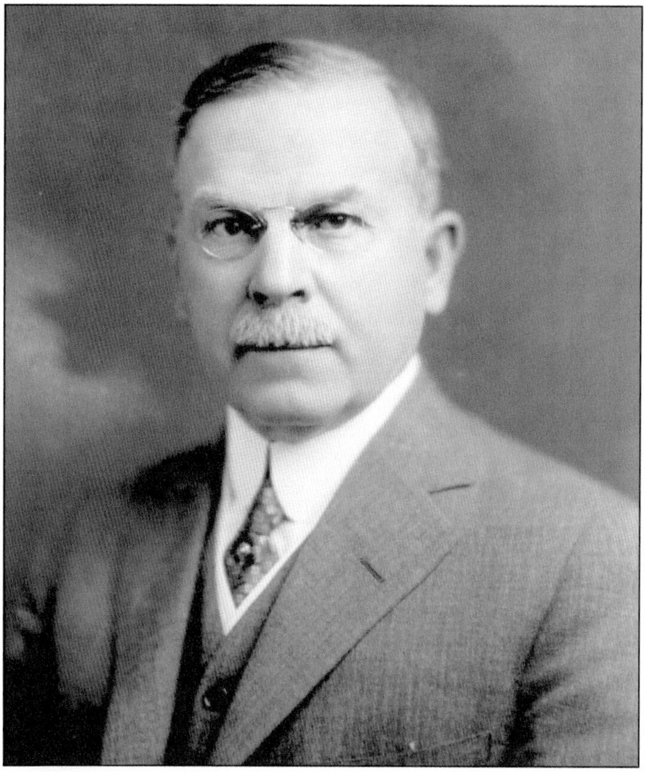

Alden Anderson was elected lieutenant governor of California, serving from 1903 to 1907. Before that, he served in the California State Assembly from 1897 to 1903, rising to the rank of speaker of the assembly from 1899 to 1901. In 1909–1910, Anderson was the state superintendent of banks. In the primary election of 1910, he was a nominee for governor of California. (Courtesy of CSL.)

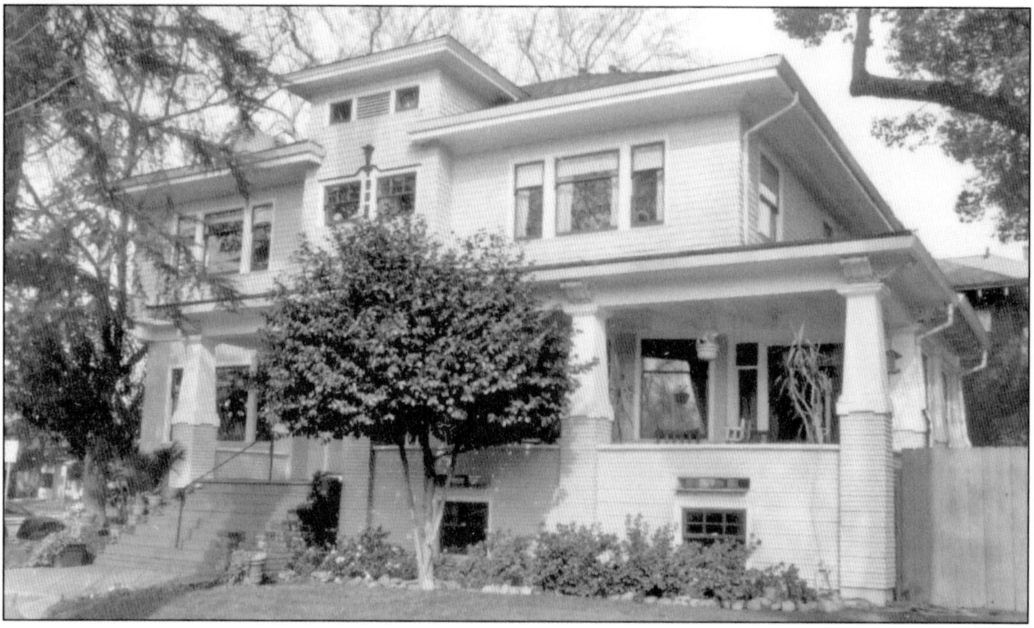

Alden Anderson lived in this beautiful house at 2101 H Street from 1916 to 1924. John Mayden, the manager of Baker and Hamilton Hardware had this house built in 1909. In 1913, Mayden was indicted for embezzling $20,000 from Baker and Hamilton. Mayden was able to settle out of court and went on to have some success as the founder of the Sutter Candy Company. (Photograph by Paula Boghosian.)

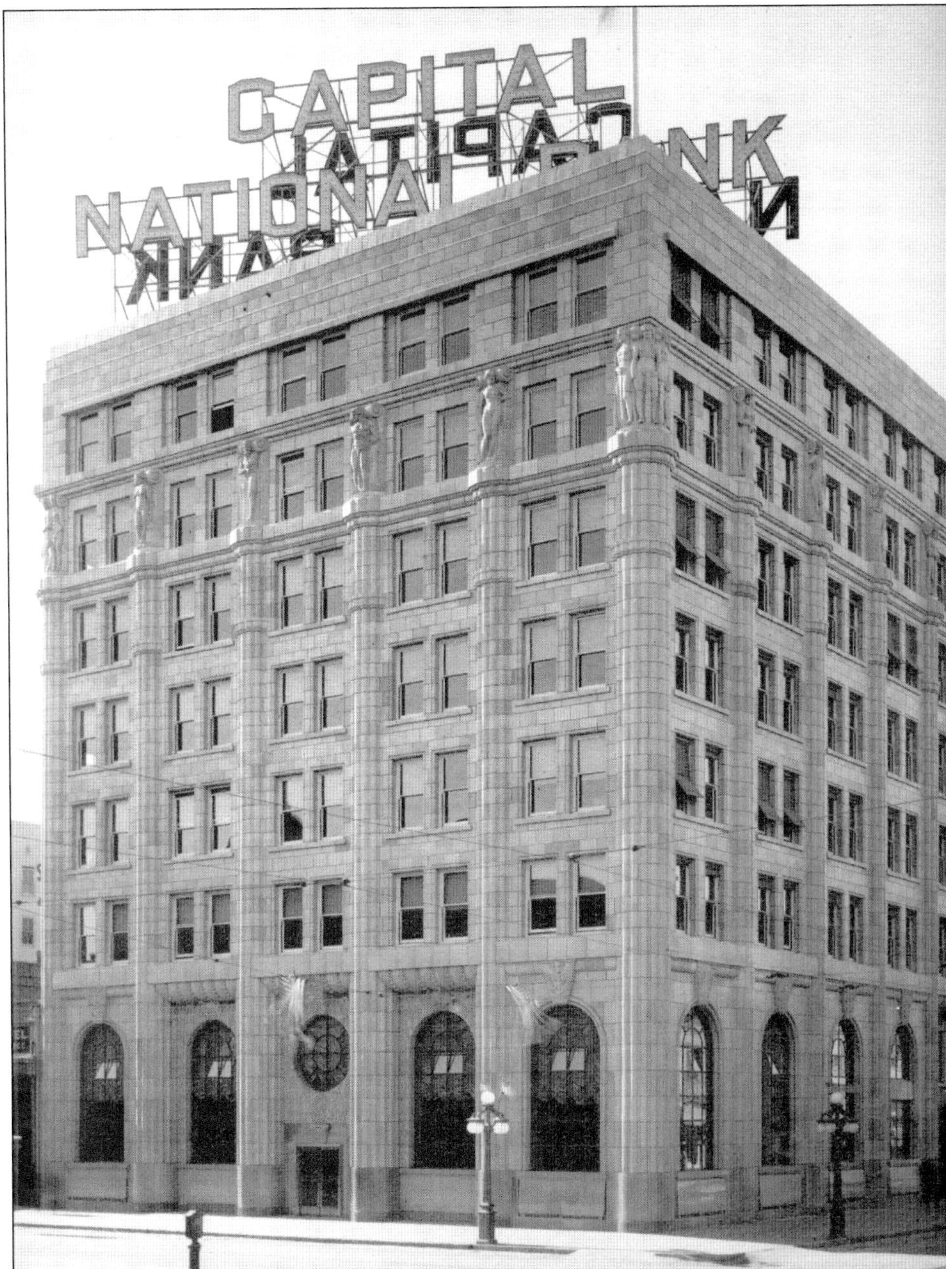

In addition to his political accomplishments, Alden Anderson was also a founder and president of the Capital National Bank, located on the southeast corner of Seventh and J Streets. He was chairman of the board for the California Western States Life Insurance Company and president of the Capital Federal Savings and Loan Association and the Hotel Sacramento Company. Anderson was the first state superintendent of banks in 1909–1910. He was the vice president of the Consumers Ice Company and director of the Bank of Rio Vista, the Natomas Water Company, the Rice Growers Association, the Capital Fire Insurance Company, and the Tide Water Associated Oil Company of New York. After Alden graduated from the University of Pacific, he went into business as an assistant in his father's fruit business. (Courtesy of SAMCC.)

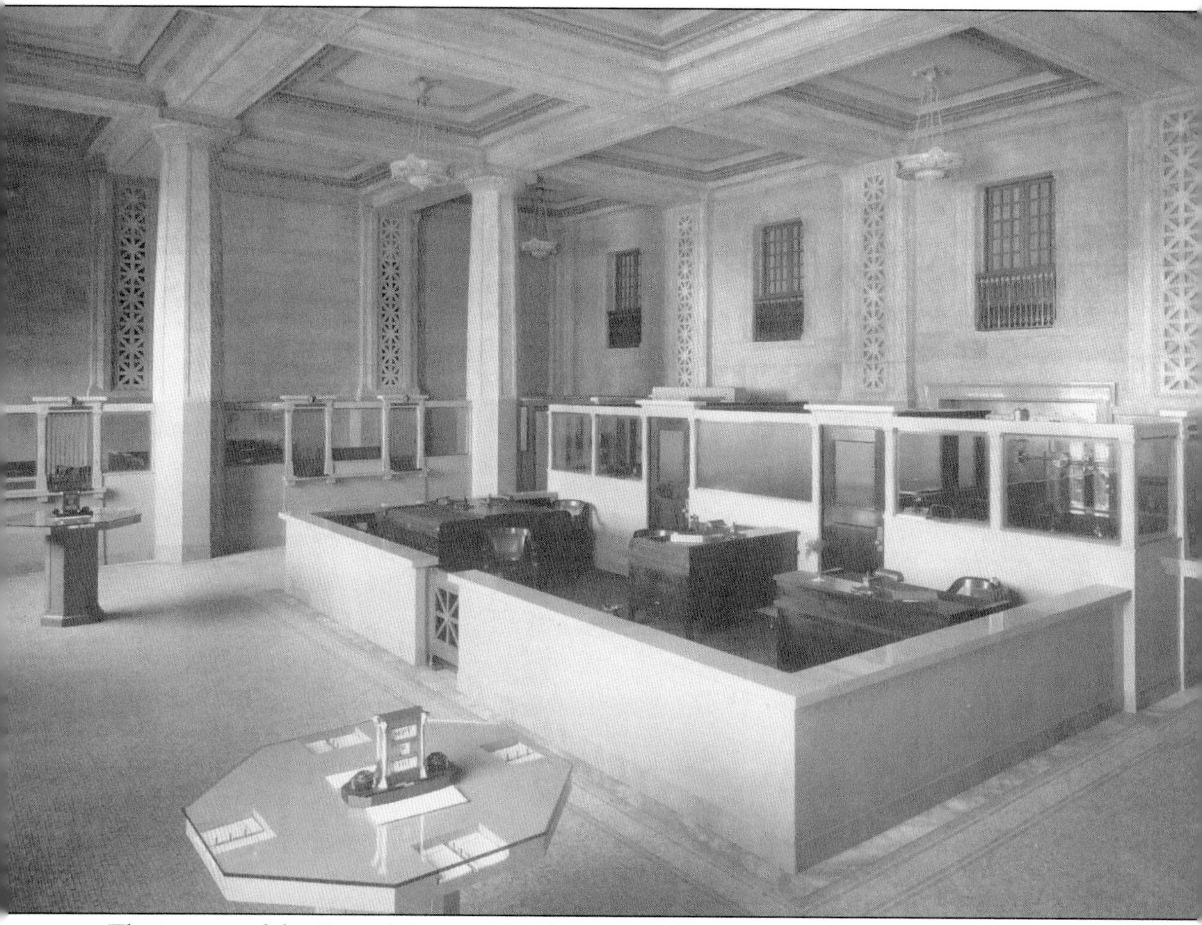

The interior of the Capital National Bank is pictured here at its opening in 1916. In those days, a bank wanted people to feel its grandeur, wealth, and financial strength when they walked in the door. The bank was designed by famous Sacramento architect Rudolph Herold, who also designed the Sacramento City Hall, Masonic temple, and a number of other Sacramento buildings. (Courtesy of SAMCC.)

The building in the center is The Peoples Bank. Alfred Folger (714 Twenty-first Street) was a vice president of this bank. Folger had an early background in agriculture. In 1890, he became a bookkeeper for the bank and rose through the ranks. Folger and Clinton E. White were directors of this bank. (Courtesy of SAMCC.)

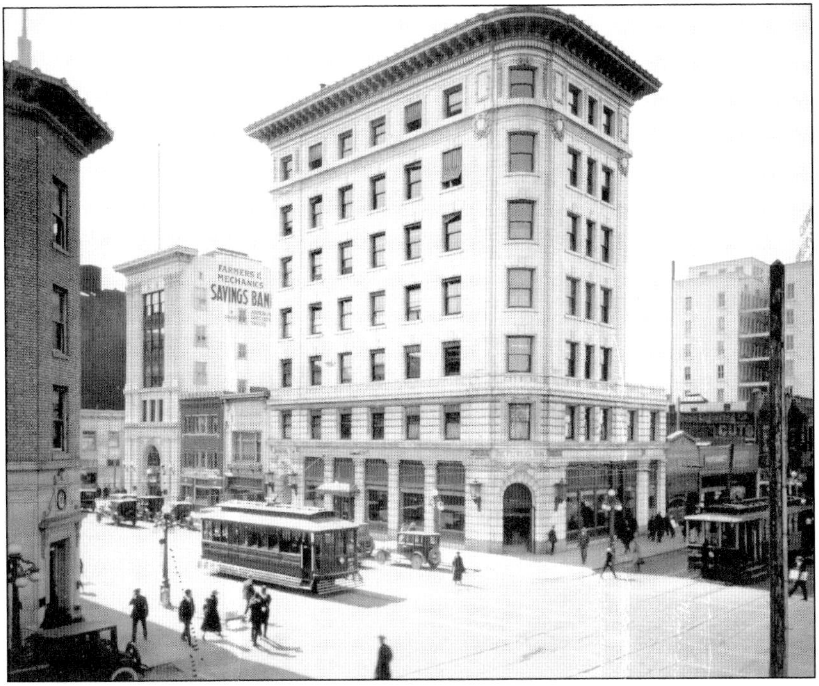

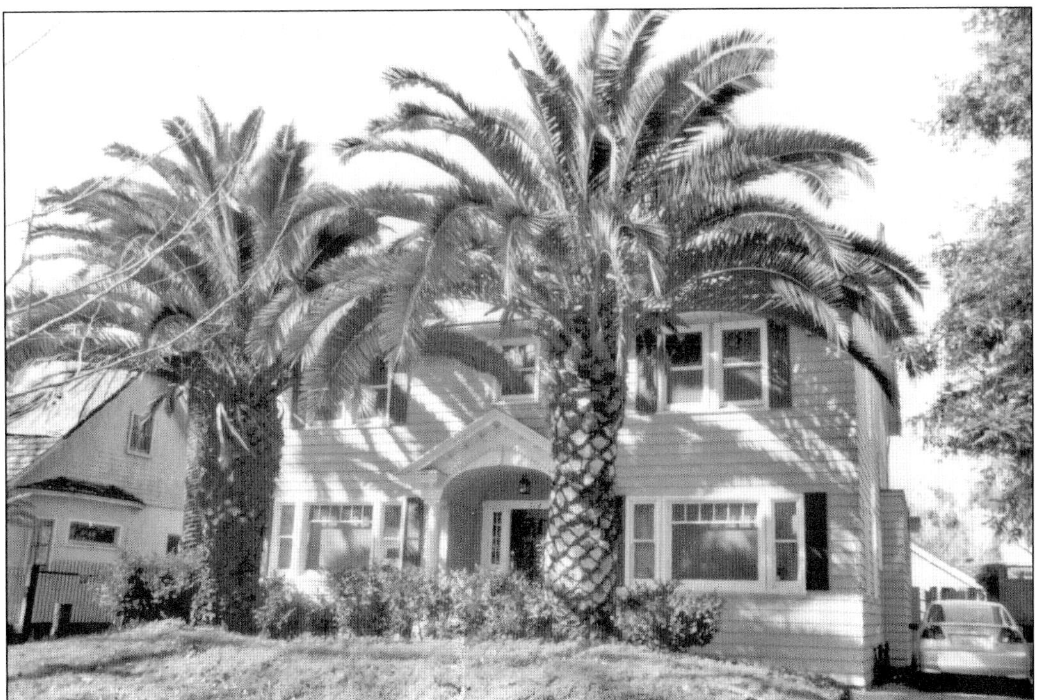

This is the home of Alfred and Ella Folger at 714 Twenty-first Street. Folger had the house built in 1920 and, after he died in 1925, Ella continued to live there into the late 1930s. When she passed away, she deeded it to her daughter Mrs. Ardell Armstrong. Ella Folger was well known for her charitable work, particularly with the Sacramento Orphanage and Children's Home. (Photograph by Paula Boghosian.)

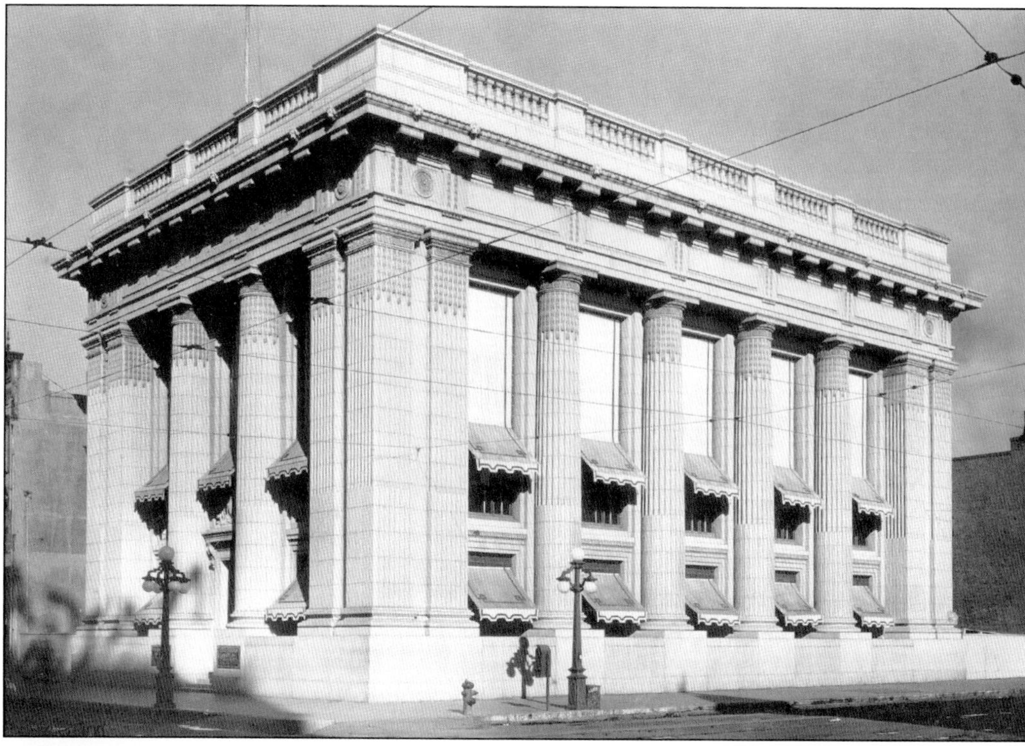

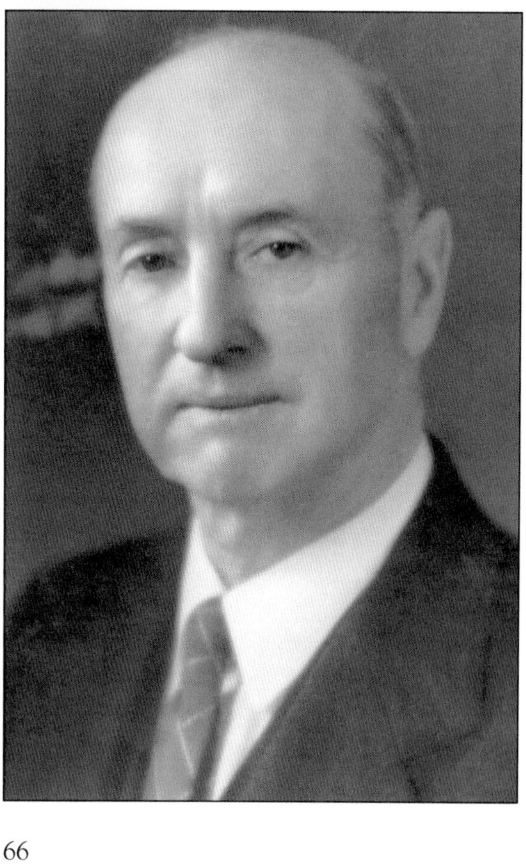

The Bank of D. O. Mills was organized in 1849 and was the second oldest bank in the West. This 1912 building, on the northwest corner of Seventh and J Street, was attributed to the famous Bay Area architect Willis Polk. Joseph F. Didion (2019 D Street) and Claude M. Adams (2118 E Street) were tellers for this bank. In 1925, it merged with the Capital National Bank and the California National Bank. (Courtesy of SAMCC.)

Here is local attorney Arthur Miller (725 Twenty-first Street, page 29) as he appeared in his latter years. He was a director for the Bank of D. O. Mills pictured above. (Courtesy of Joseph Wolfenden.)

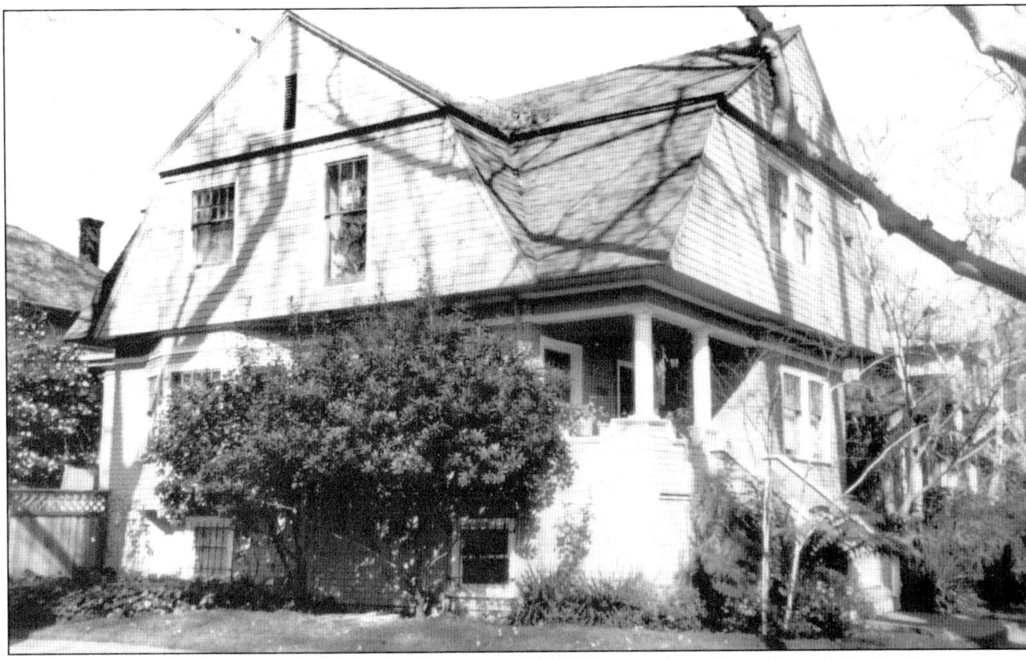

This 1913 house was built for Harrison Bennett (530 Twenty-first Street), a teller for Sacramento Bank for 35 years. Bennett was a lieutenant in the Civil War with the 1st Michigan and fought at Bull Run, Fredericksberg, and The Wilderness. (Photograph by Paula Boghosian.)

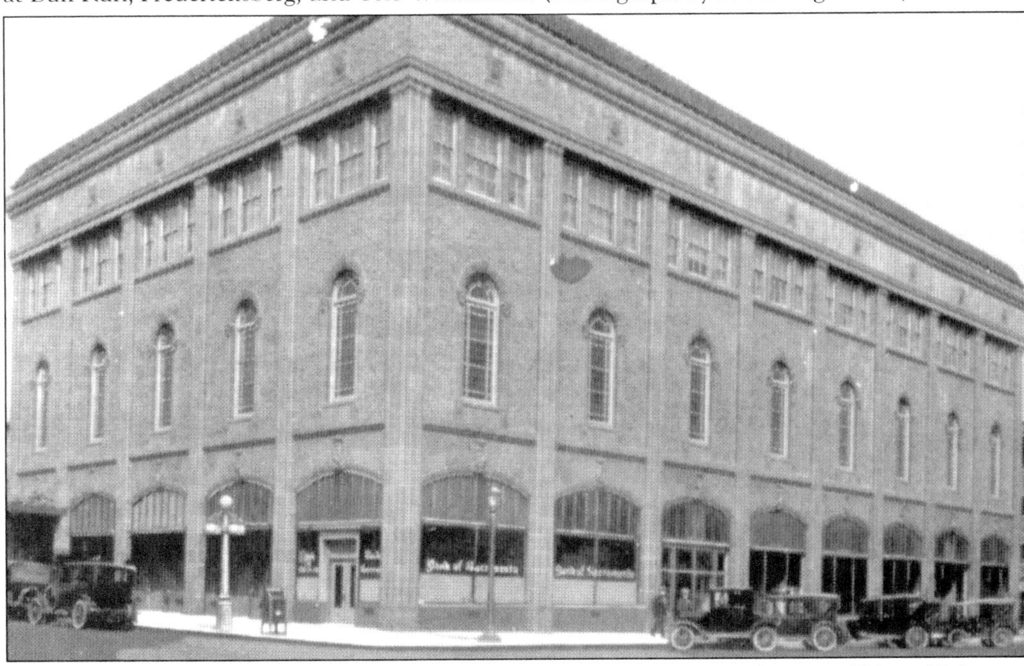

Sacramento Bank was housed in the ground floor of the Masonic temple at Twelfth and J Streets. James M. Henderson (618 Twenty-second Street) was its president, as well as president at the Fort Sutter National Bank and Hickman and Coleman Real Estate. Due to various bank mergers in the 1920s and 1930s, Henderson was one of the most powerful financial men in Northern California. (Courtesy of SAMCC.)

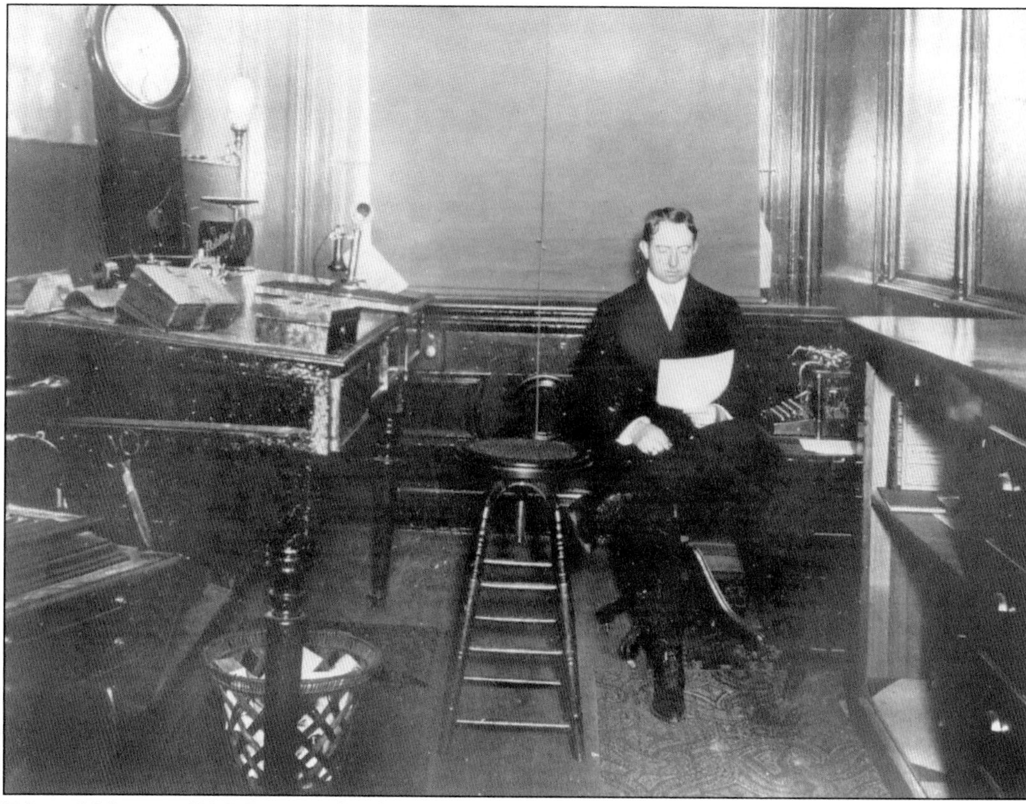

Edward Huston (726 Twenty-third Street) was the local manager of the Pacific Mutual Life Insurance Company. This interior photograph of the office was taken around 1905. Note the typewriter to the right and the telephone on the table. Huston later worked for the Carly Real Estate Company. He retired from Carly in 1920 and bought into Elliot and Huston Real Estate and Insurance. (Courtesy of SAMCC.)

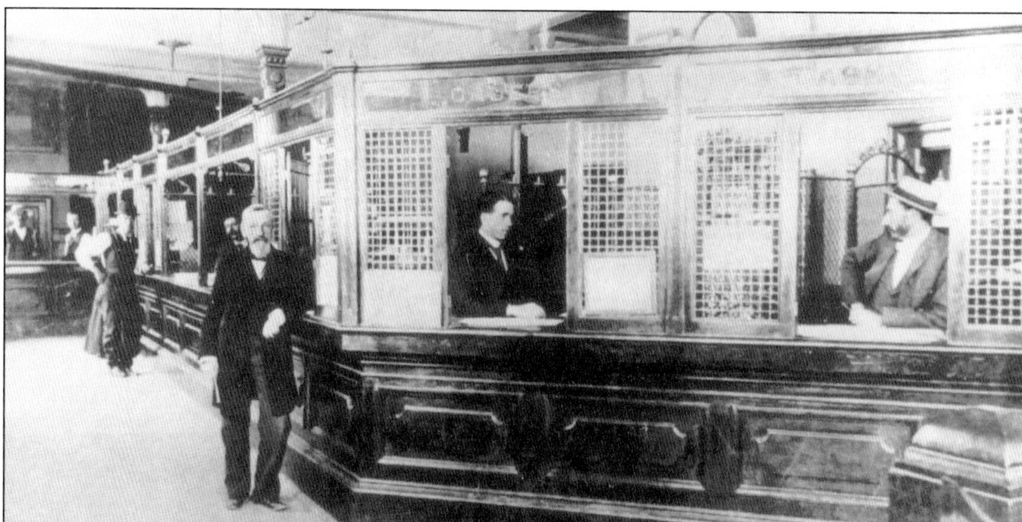

Here is a typical interior of a small bank and its employees, *c.* 1905.

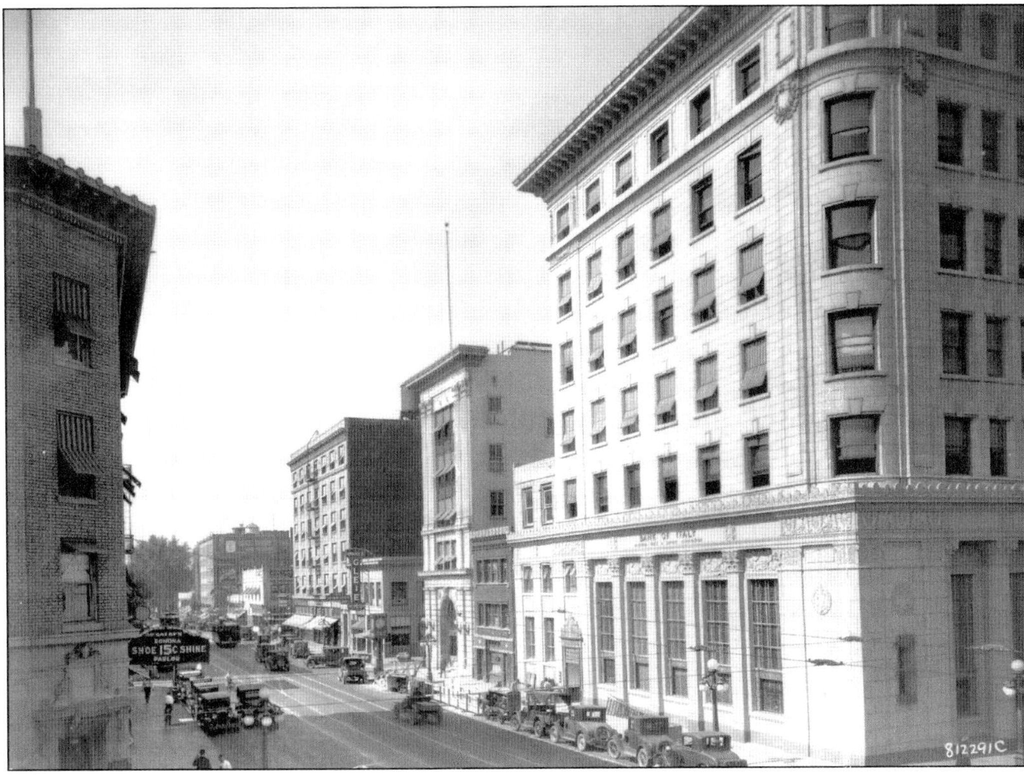

On the right is the old People's Bank building, which was acquired, remodeled, and expanded by the Bank of Italy (later Bank of America). Robert Lorenz (2100 F Street) was a vice president at this bank. Just beyond is the office of Elliot and Huston. Next is the Farmers and Mechanics Bank. Peter Huth (2001 H Street) was a vice president of that bank. (Courtesy of SAMCC.)

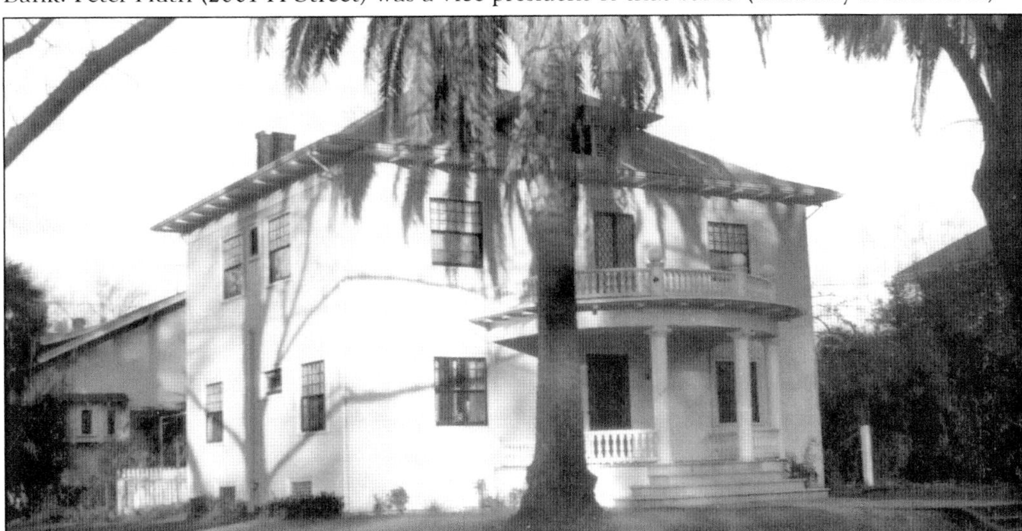
This 1910 house was built for John Hoesch, an auditor for the California Secretary of State. Clark E. Bell (New York Life) lived here in the late 1910s. He moved to Los Angeles to become director of their chamber of commerce and president of California Life Underwriters. Peter and Susie Huth (Farmers and Mechanics Bank) lived here for many years. (Courtesy of SAMCC.)

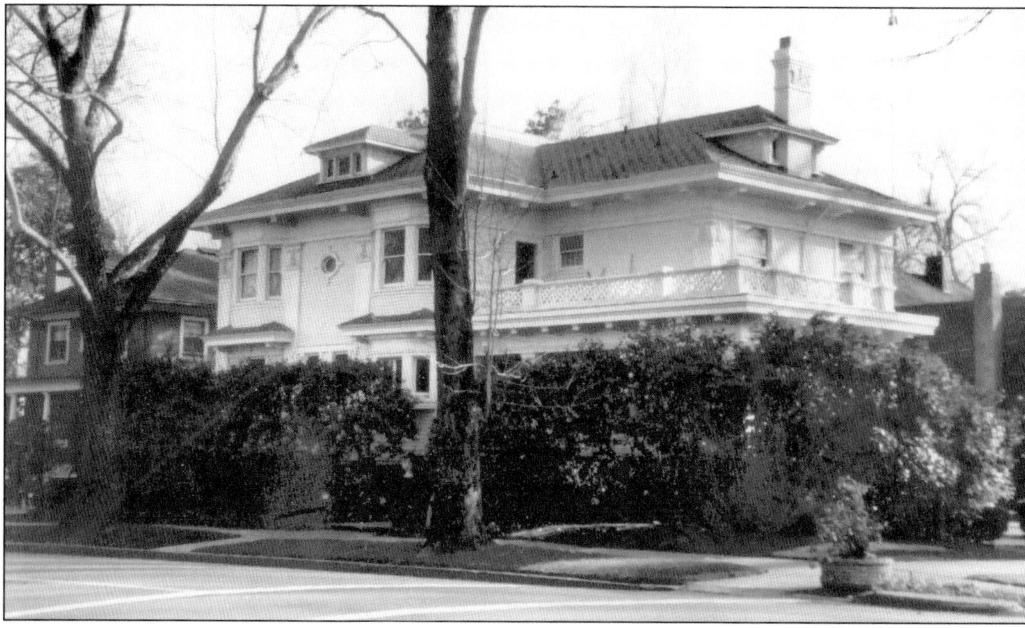

Catherine and Joseph Marzen, a forty-niner and successful Nevada cattlemen, retired to Sacramento in 1910 and had architects Seadler and Hoen design this house at 2100 F Street. He died in 1918, and Catherine passed away in 1928. After that, Robert W. (assistant vice president, Bank of Italy) and Eleanor Lorenz lived here for about 10 years. Lorenz was president of the local American Bankers Association. (Photograph by Paula Boghosian.)

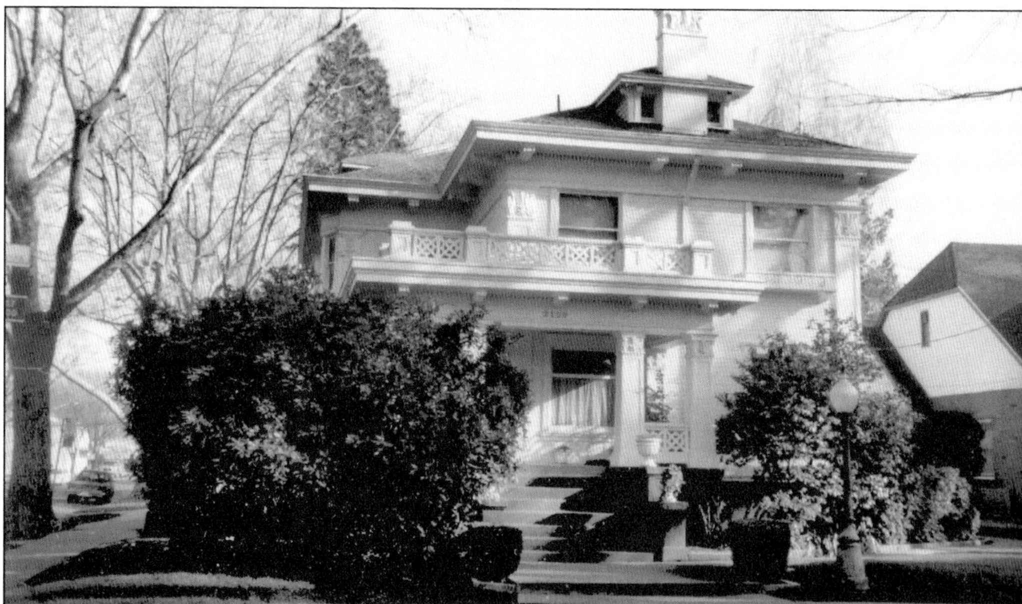

In 1979, local realtor Bonnie Fitzpatrick bought 2100 F Street and began restoration. One night, policemen appeared. They had been digging up bodies planted by Dorthea Puente in her yard when they learned she had once operated a boardinghouse at this house. The police wanted to dig up the recently replanted backyard. Hostilities ensued, but the police finally agreed to use probes. (Photograph by Paula Boghosian.)

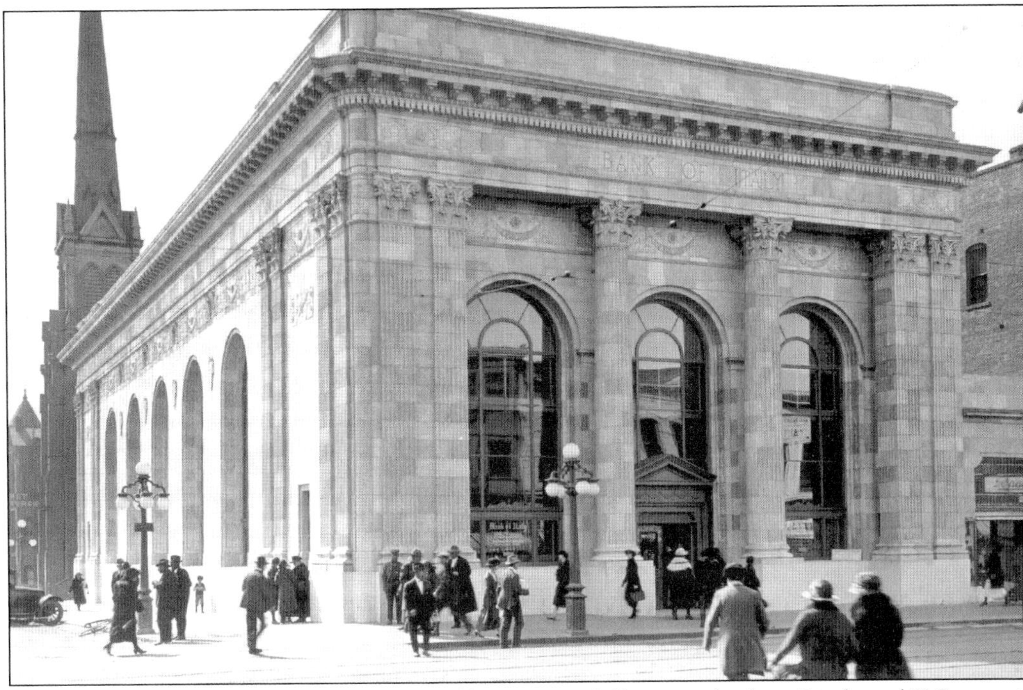

This branch of the Bank of Italy, designed by George Sellon, was built at Sixth and K Streets in 1923. In 1930, the bank became the Bank of America, and it began an aggressive expansion via a network of local branches, with a focus of developing local agriculture and commerce. Even for a small bank, it has intricate architectural detail and exudes solidity and elegance. (Courtesy of SAMCC.)

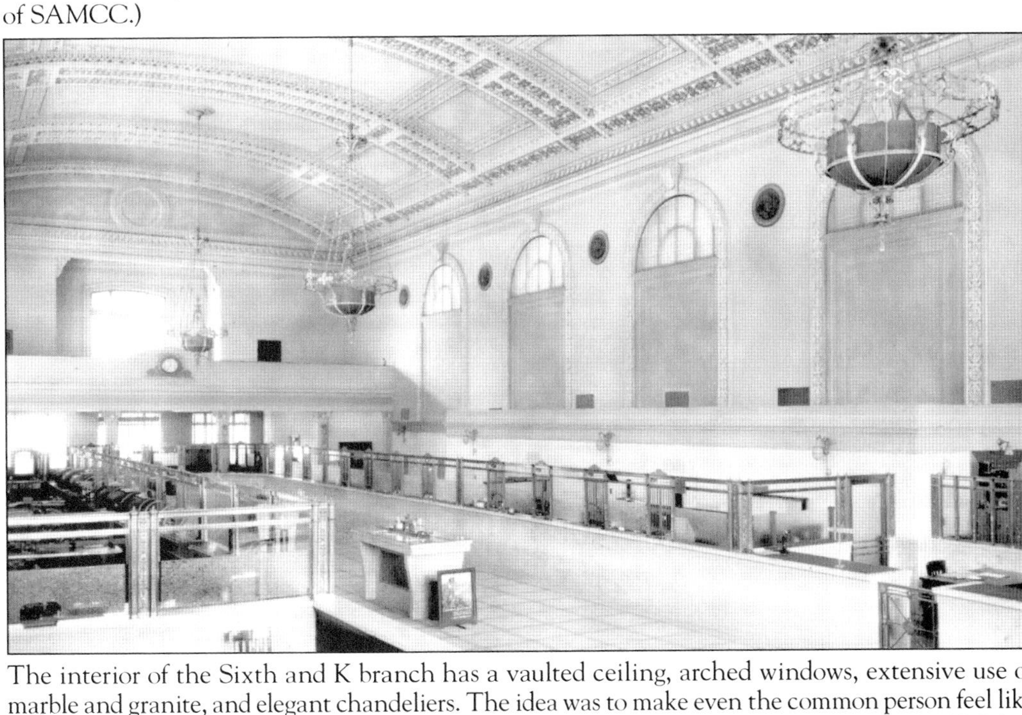

The interior of the Sixth and K branch has a vaulted ceiling, arched windows, extensive use of marble and granite, and elegant chandeliers. The idea was to make even the common person feel like this great institution was going to take care of them and their needs. (Courtesy of SAMCC.)

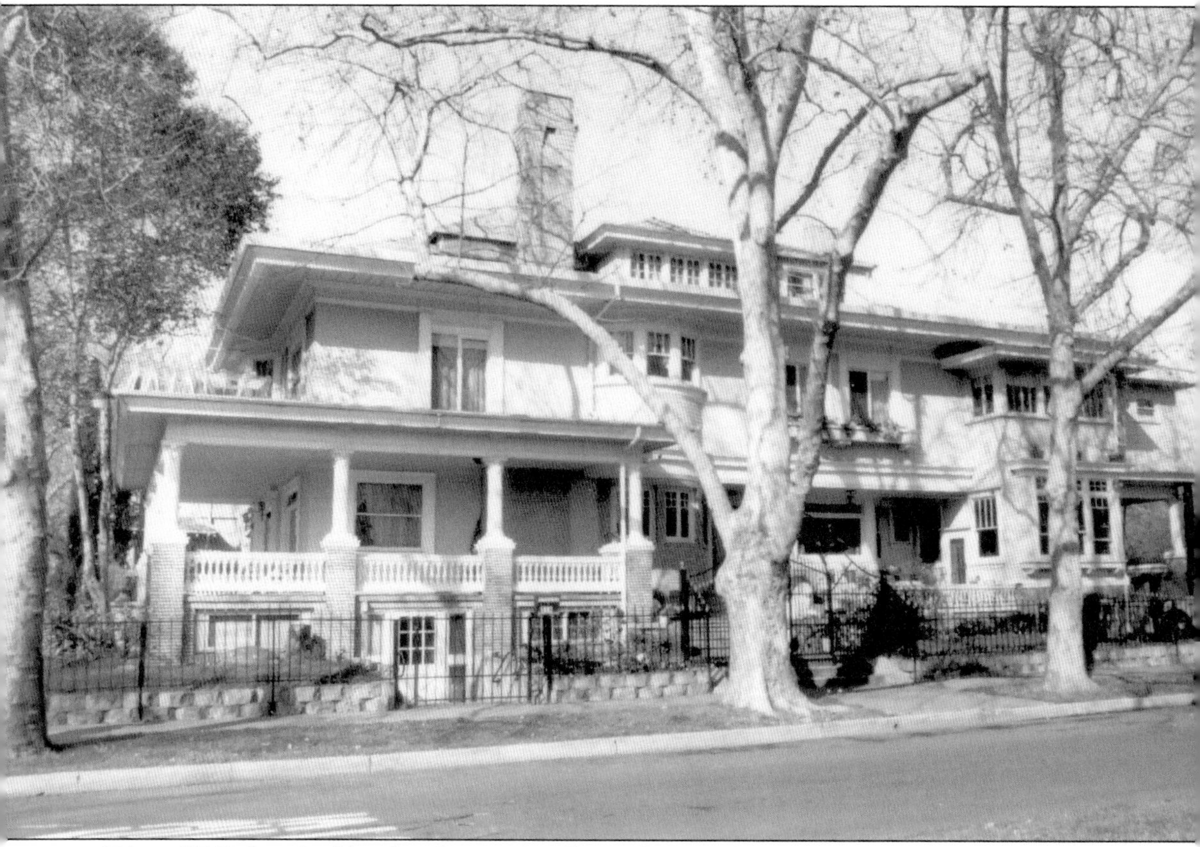

Edward F. Dalton had local architects Seadler and Hoen design this house for him. Completed in 1913, Dalton lived here into the mid-1920s. His wife was not mentioned in his obituary in 1934, so she probably predeceased him in the mid-1920s. They had five children. (Photograph by Paula Boghosian.)

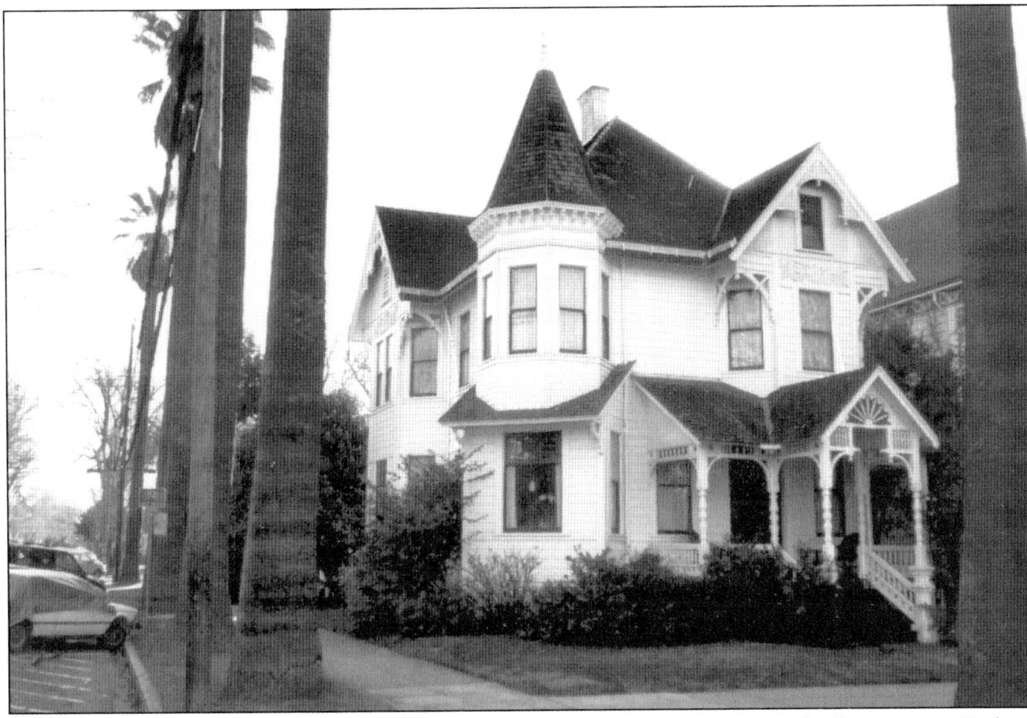

Edward F. Dalton lived at 2330 F Street from around 1905 to 1913. In the beginning, Dalton was a rancher and had extensive land holdings throughout Sacramento County. He served for nearly two decades as a director of the California Western States Life Insurance Company. He also served as vice president and treasurer. His mother came to California with her family in 1846. (Photograph by Paula Boghosian.)

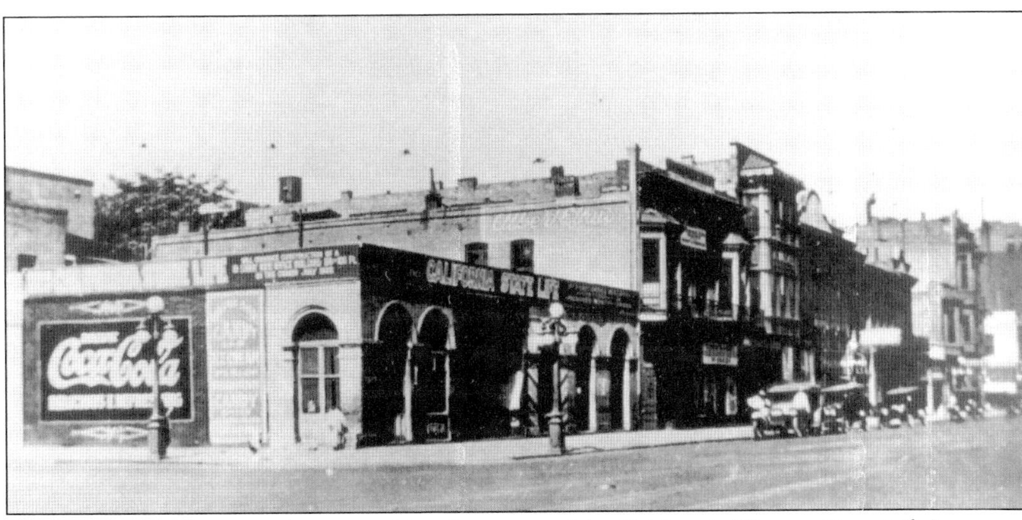

This modest building was the original headquarters of the California Western State Life Insurance Company. The company and the building to the west of it were torn down to make way for its successor in 1925. (Courtesy of SAMCC.)

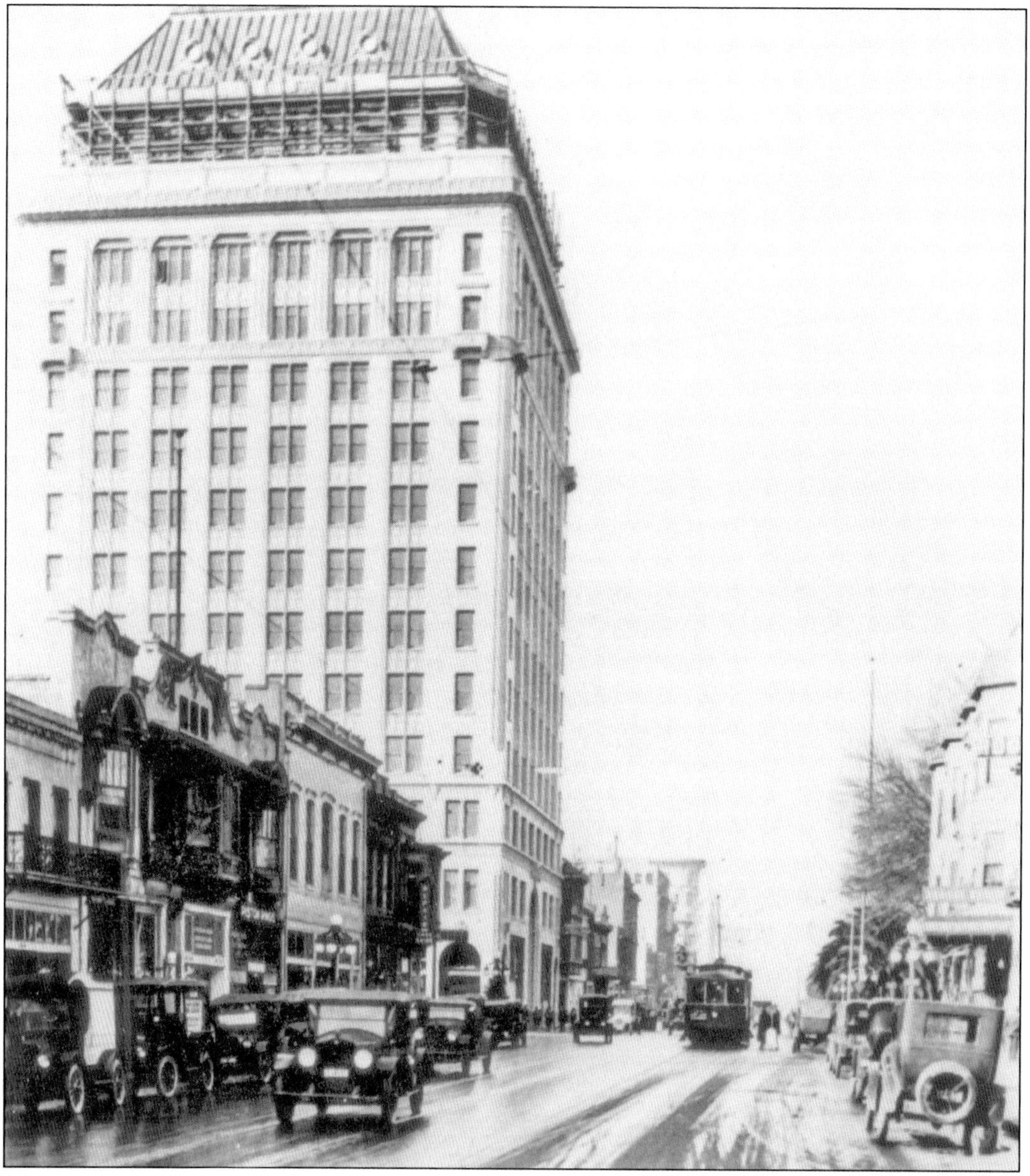

The 14-story building at 926 J Street was the headquarters of the California Western States Life Insurance Company. It was Sacramento's first skyscraper and was designed by Sacramento architect George Sellon, the first California state architect in 1908–1909. The building was completed in 1925, and one can see the wood scaffolding at the upper level. A recent proposal suggests this office building be turned into a boutique hotel. (Courtesy of SAMCC.)

Seven

Law and Order

This chapter is about the people who make law and those that enforce it. Residents of Boulevard Park were well represented in the bodies that make law, such as the city, county, and state governments, as well as the bodies that enforce law and create order, such as the state agencies, courts, and police.

Since the gold rush, Sacramento had a freewheeling, old-west reputation for rough politics, gambling, prostitution, pool halls, and saloons. However, by the end of the 1800s, change was in the wind. One political trend that marked the early years of Boulevard Park was the growth of the Progressive movement. It began in the early 1890s, but gathered political mass through the first 25 years of the 20th century. The Progressives saw the opportunity for real civic improvement, including municipal services for water filtration, sewers, garbage removal, and street improvements. However, their first task was to put an end to ward-style politics and the corruption that went with it. The ward boss was not always a politician, but he was the one who doled out the political power and votes to get people elected to the city council. A successful ward boss could count on being able to supply the people who worked for him, or supported him, with city jobs and contracts.

One of the acknowledged leaders of the Progressive movement in Sacramento was a Boulevard Park resident, attorney Clinton L. White. He was elected as one of the 15 freeholders that redrafted the city's charter in 1893, thus creating a more effective government to deal with Sacramento's problems. As a succession of reform-minded Progressives were elected to the city council and the office of mayor, they turned to another Boulevard Park resident and appointed honest John Sullivan as chief of police, giving him the job of tackling vice and corruption. The victories came slowly, but eventually prostitution and illegal gambling were more tightly controlled. The pool halls and saloons were licensed and watched more closely. The streets were paved and the sewer system built, as well as the water filtration plant and the city incinerator.

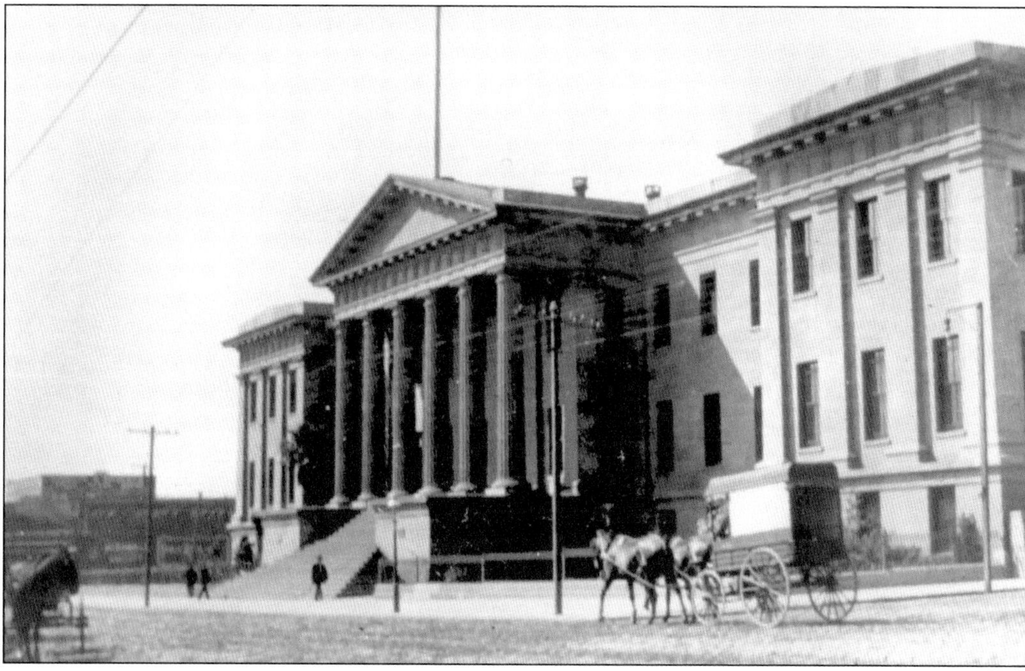

When Boulevard Park first began to develop in 1906, this was the county courthouse that existed. Note the horse-drawn delivery wagon and the unpaved street. Just a few years later, in 1913, it was replaced by the building pictured below. (Courtesy of SAMCC.)

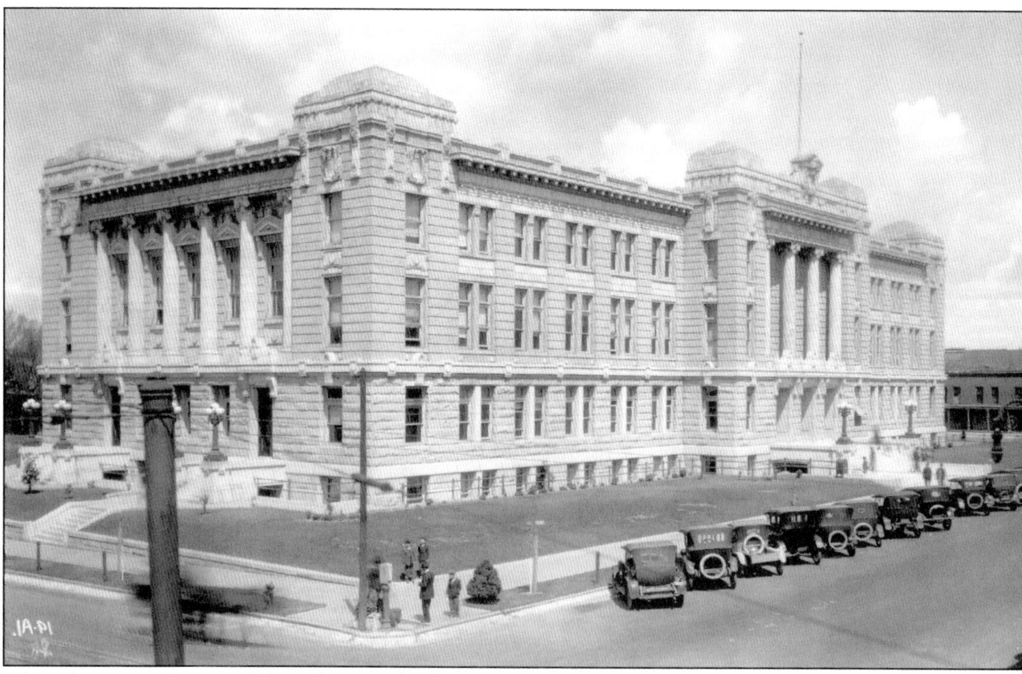

This photograph, probably taken in the late 1910s to early 1920s, shows the county courthouse that was completed in 1913. It was designed by Rudolph Herold. Automobiles line the front of the building, and the streets are paved. (Courtesy of SAMCC.)

Pictured are Superior Court judge Malcolm Glenn and his wife, Olive, on their 58th wedding anniversary. When he retired from the bench in 1956, Glenn had served for almost 43 years, the second longest term in the history of the Superior Court at that time. Before his appointment to the bench in 1914, he had served as a deputy attorney general for the state. (Courtesy of SAMCC.)

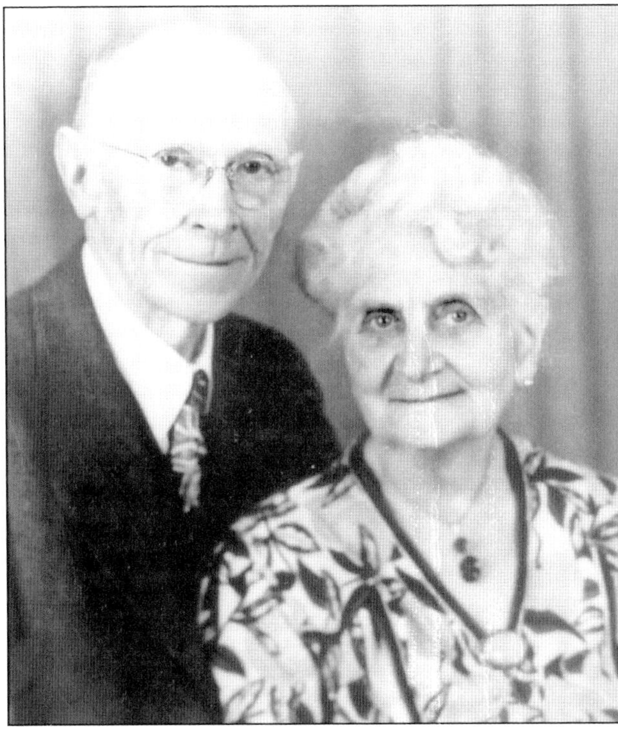

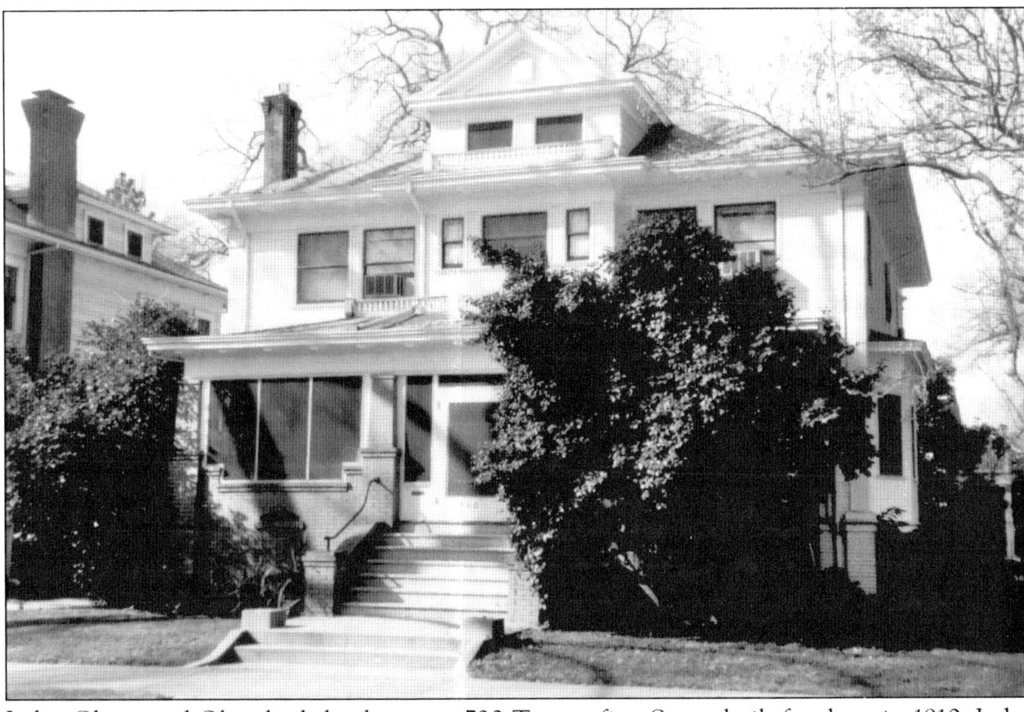

Judge Glenn and Olive had this house at 700 Twenty-first Street built for them in 1910. Judge Glenn died in 1960, just a few weeks after celebrating his 60th wedding anniversary with Olive. Olive died just two years later, ending more than half a century of occupancy by the Glenn family. (Photograph by Paula Boghosian.)

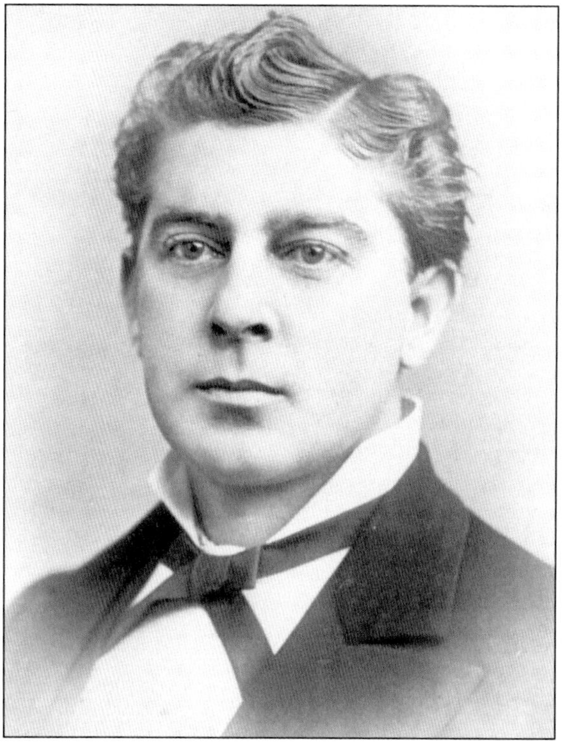

During the late 1910s, attorney Charles T. Jones lived in Boulevard Park at 2106 H Street. At the time, he was a deputy district attorney. He also served as district attorney and had a reputation as one of the best prosecutors in California. (Courtesy of CSL.)

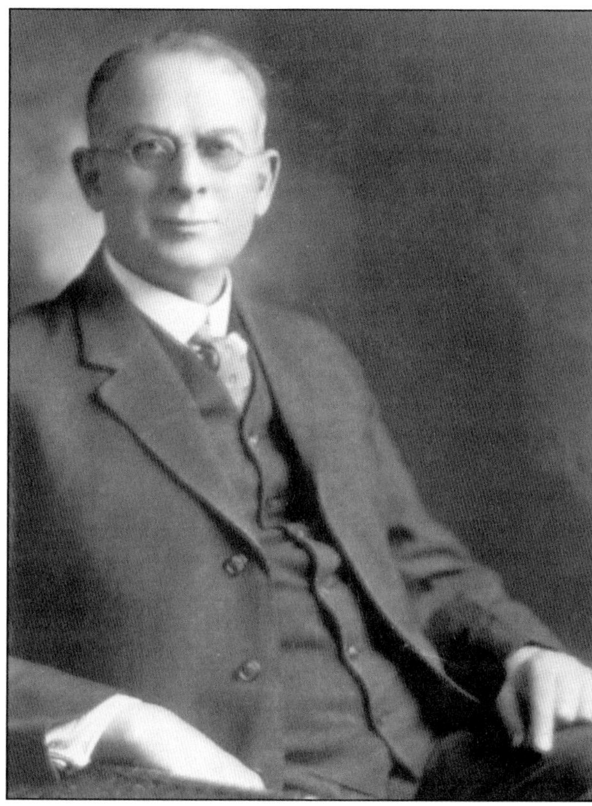

Ashley R. Tabor practiced law with his brother Benjamin in the firm Tabor and Tabor. He specialized in mining law, and Benjamin served for a time as a deputy district attorney. Ashley and his wife, Anna, lived in a flat at 715 Twenty-fourth Street, and they owned the building. Ashley died in 1927, but Anna continued to live there until 1939, when she sold the building. (Courtesy of CSL.)

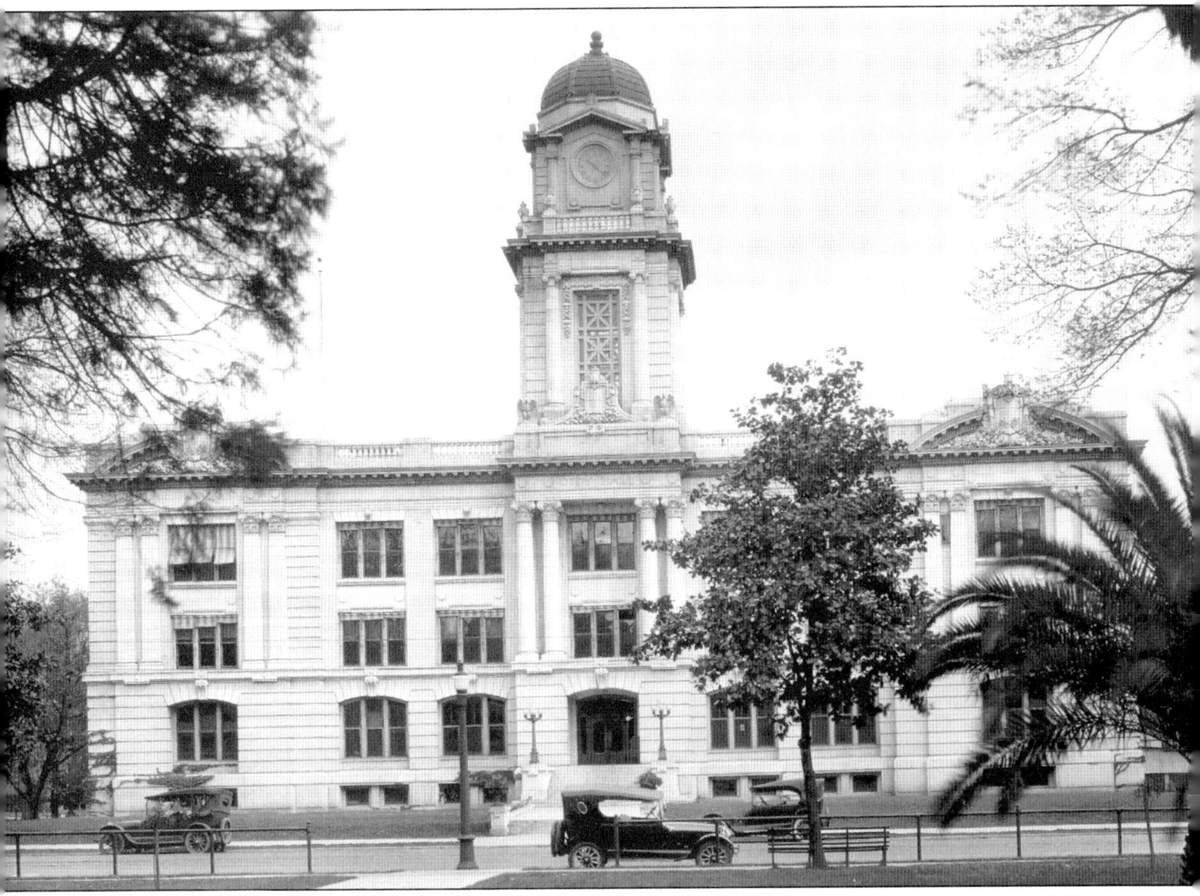

Sacramento's city hall building was designed by Rudolph Herold and was completed in 1911. A number of early Boulevard Park residents served the city with distinction. The building was recently rehabilitated as part of the project that constructed a new city administration building located behind it. (Courtesy of SAMCC.)

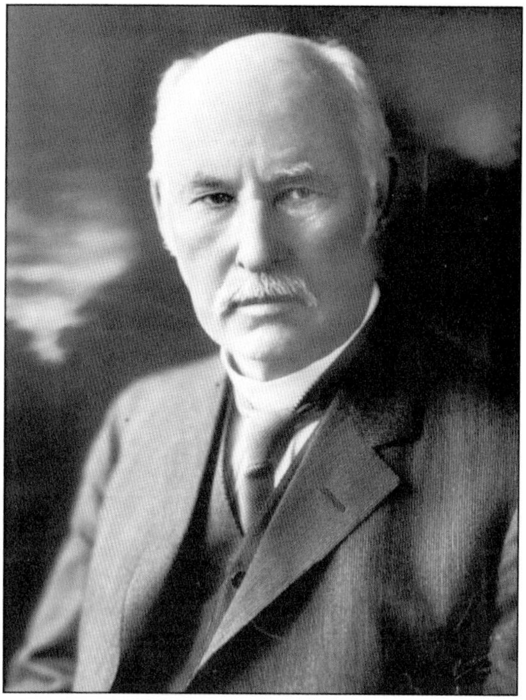

Clinton L. White was the kind of attorney that other attorneys look up to. One of his partners was Arthur Miller (see pages 28–29). In 1880–1881, he was secretary of the Judiciary Committee of the State Senate and was a deputy attorney general in 1881–1882. White was mayor of Sacramento in 1908–1909. He was president of the Park Realty Company that purchased the old Union Park track. (Courtesy of CSL.)

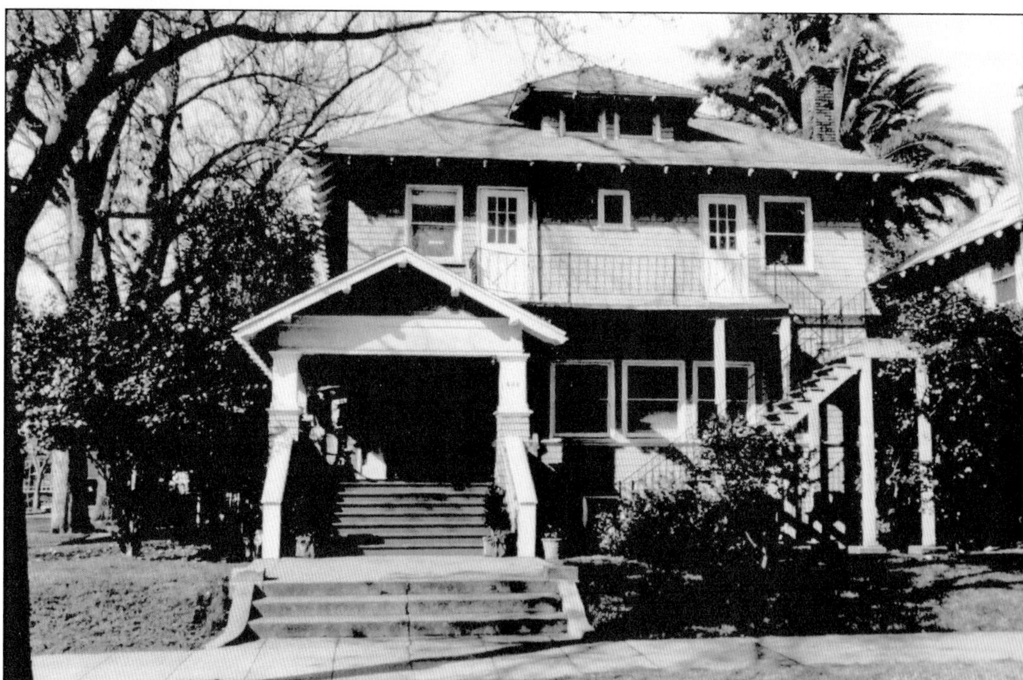

The house at 630 Twenty-first Street was built in 1909 for Clinton White. When White died in 1925, he deeded the house to his daughter Edith and her husband, Samuel H. Cohn. Edith was on the city's board of education, and Samuel was superintendent of the Washington School District. Edith died in 1959. The house was vacant by 1960, ending a half-century of White-Cohn occupancy. (Photograph by Paula Boghosian.)

In addition to his law practice, Raphael Platnauer was the corporate counsel for the city for a four-year term. Later in his career, he was the administrator for the County Law Library. (Courtesy of CSL.)

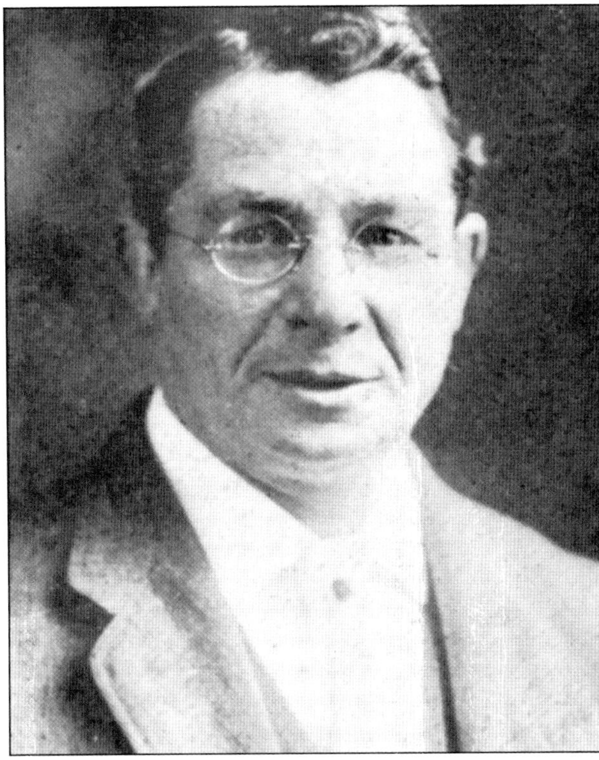

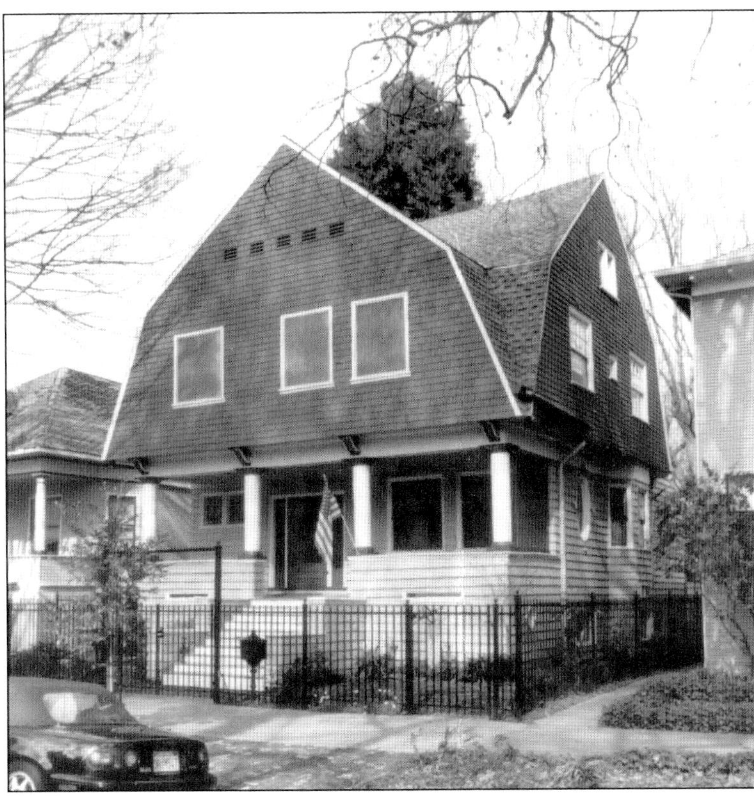

The Platnauers lived in this Colonial Revival house, completed in 1908. His sister Florence became the second wife of David Lubin of Weinstock-Lubin and Company. Raphael died in 1943, thus ending 35 years of occupancy in the house by that family.

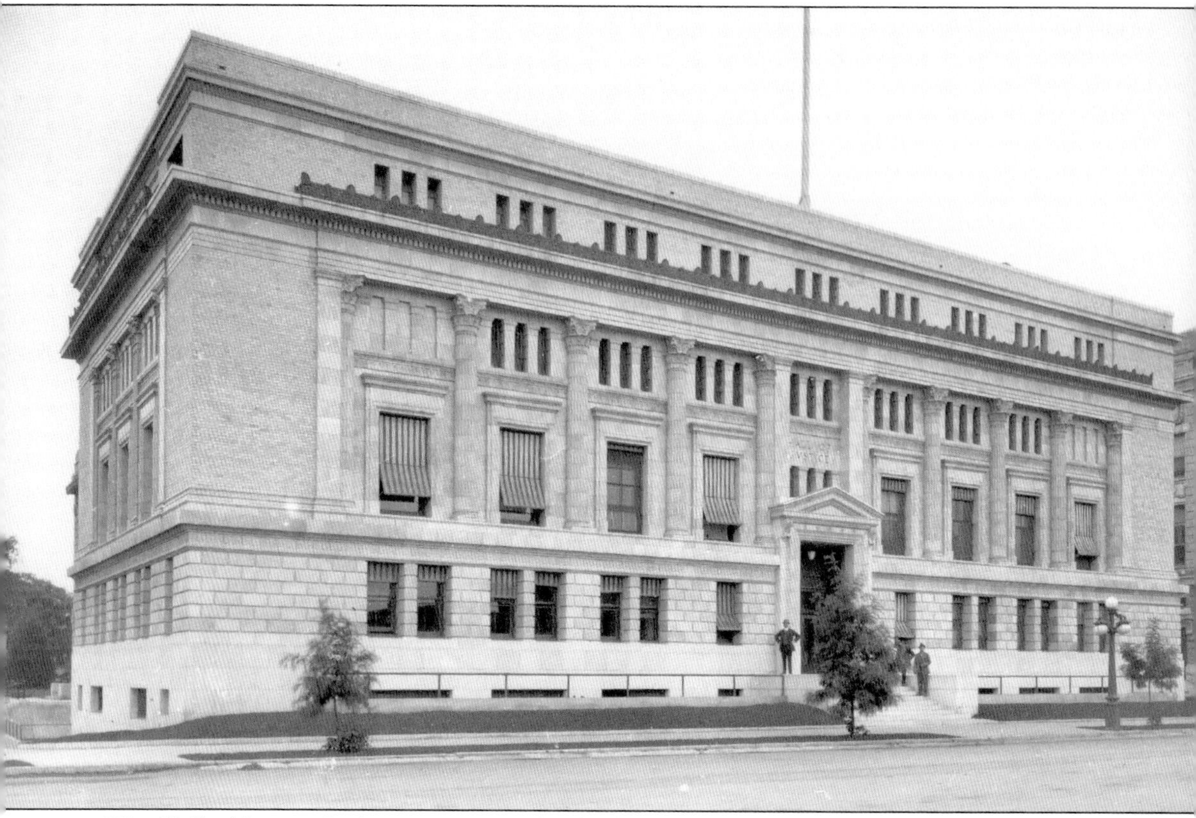

The Hall of Justice, built in 1916, served as both police station and jail. Recently rehabilitated, it now houses the County Law Library. Two police chiefs and several law officers lived in early Boulevard Park. (Courtesy of SAMCC.)

John Sullivan was chief of police from 1900 to 1904 and was appointed chief again by Clinton White (see page 80) in 1908–1909. Before his stint with the police, Sullivan was fireman and deputy county assessor. He ran unsuccessfully for mayor in 1910 and turned to real estate with Sullivan and Woodard. (Courtesy of CSL.)

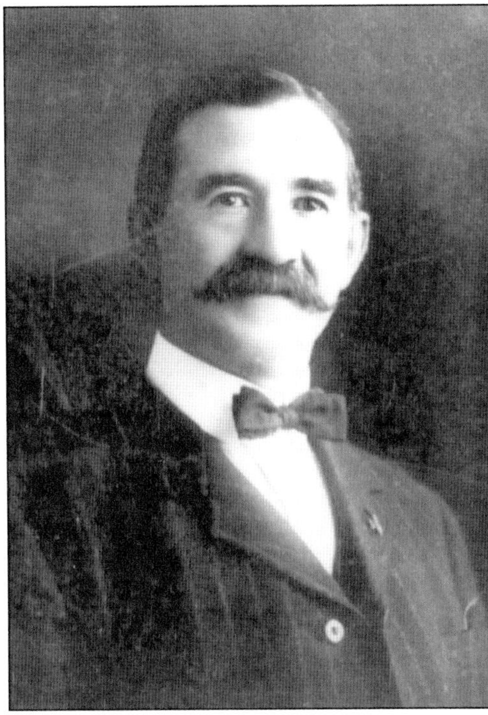

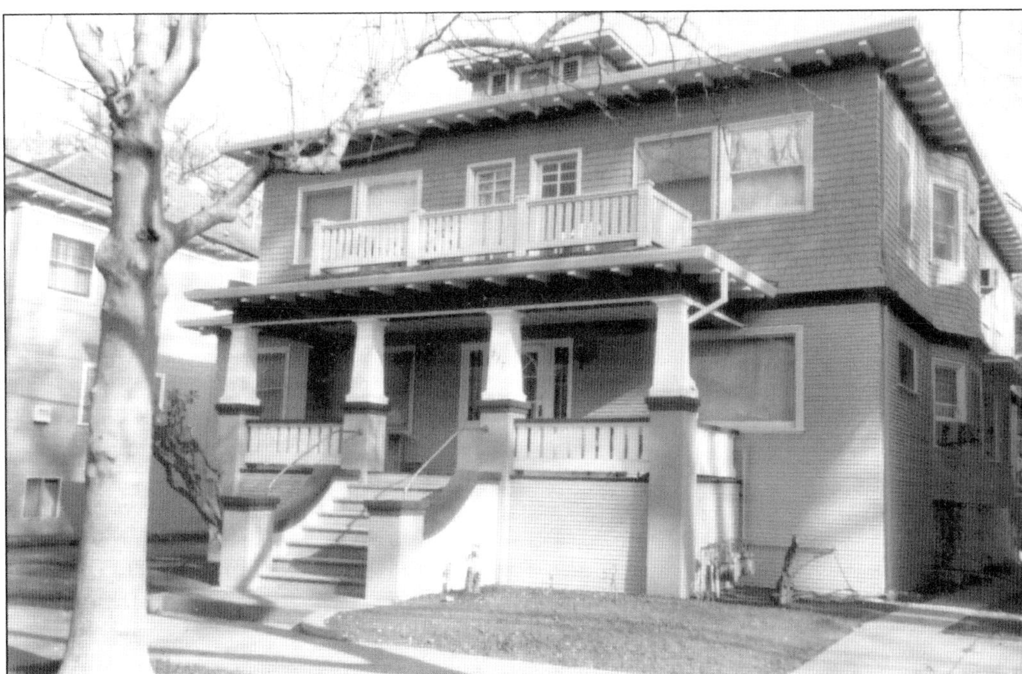

This two-story Craftsman duplex was built for Ralph Head, the chief pharmacist at Owl Drugs in 1913. By 1921, Annie and John Sullivan were living in 717 Twenty-second Street and owned the building. They also owned the flats next door at 721. John died in 1934, but Annie continued to live there until her death in 1951, some 30 years of possession by the Sullivans. (Photograph by Paula Boghosian.)

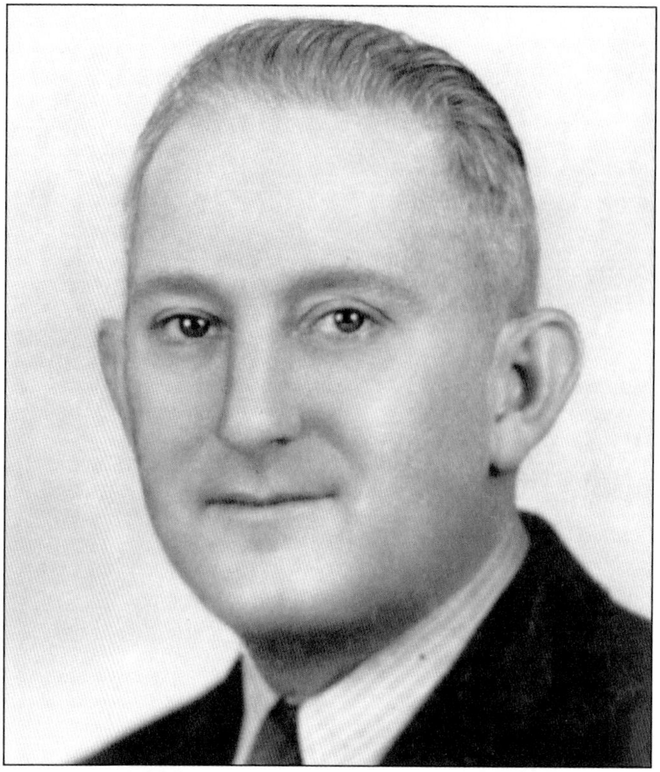

Fritz Kaminsky had a 30-year career in the Sacramento Police Department, finally becoming chief of police in 1951. Kaminsky graduated from the FBI National Academy in 1936 and set up the Sacramento department's first regular training school. His many years of service involved him in all kinds of police and investigative activity, including the killing of a man who shot a Yolo County constable. (Courtesy of SAMCC.)

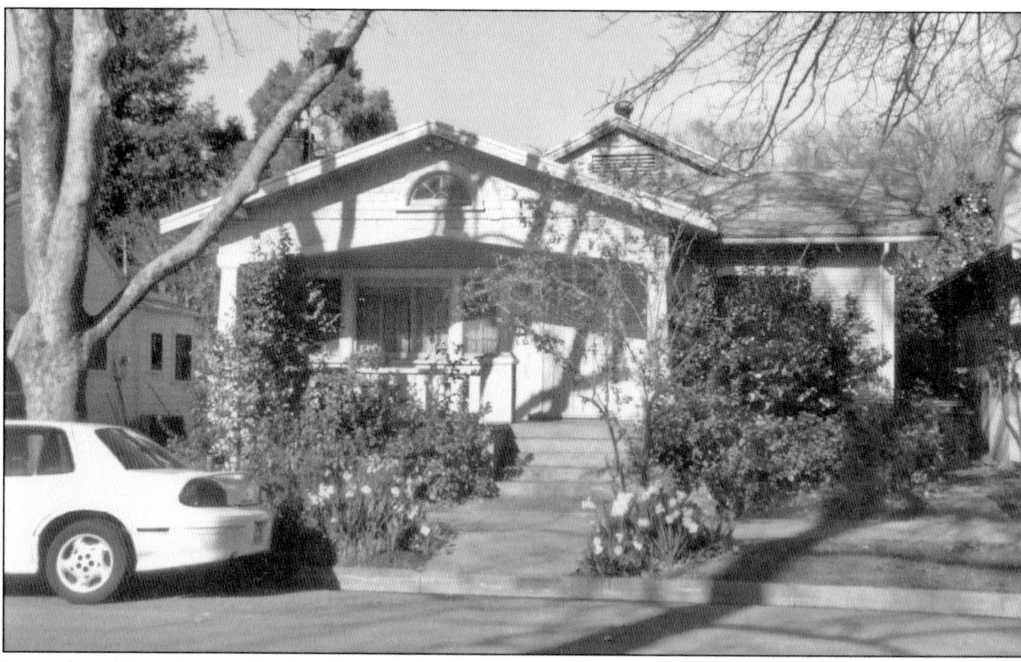

Muriel and Fritz Kaminsky lived in this house at 2215 D Street. Kaminsky was serving as assistant chief in 1951 when Chief James Hicks was called to duty in the Korean War. Kaminsky was elevated to chief, but when Hicks returned, Kaminsky decided to step aside and retire. He announced to the press that he had some fishing he wanted to catch up on. (Photograph by Paula Boghosian.)

Known as "the man who never forgot a face," police captain Max Fisher was nationally known for his fingerprint and visual identification programs, which he started in 1899. Fisher was offered the chief of police position in Sacramento, and in several other cities, but he turned them down to continue his fingerprinting work. Fisher retired from the force in 1932. (Courtesy of SAMCC.)

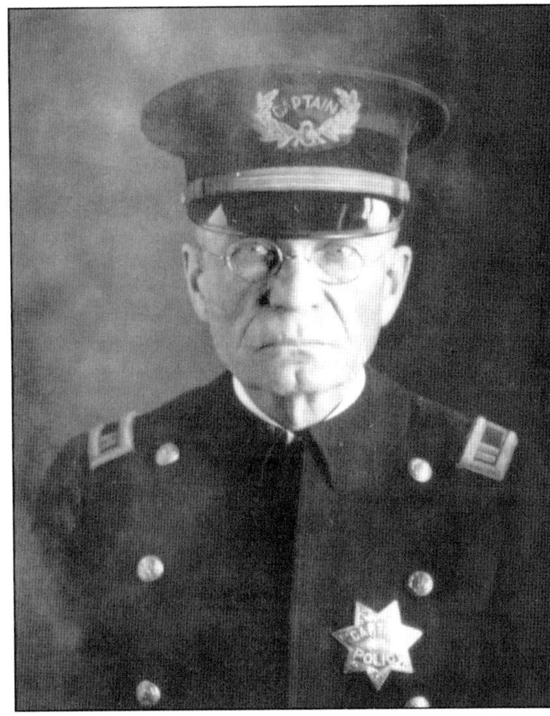

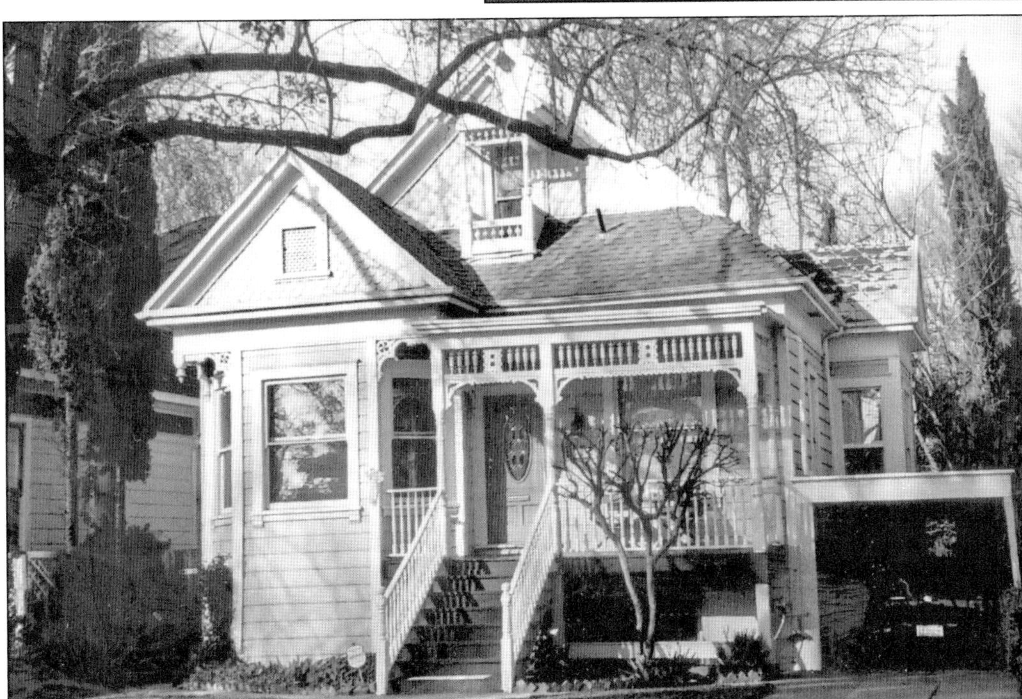

Max Fisher lived in this house at 2405 I Street from 1905 to 1932. After his retirement from the police force in 1932, he went to live with his daughter Alice and her husband, William Simpson. In September 1940, Fisher deeded the house to Alice. He died in August of the next year after a long illness. (Photograph by Paula Boghosian.)

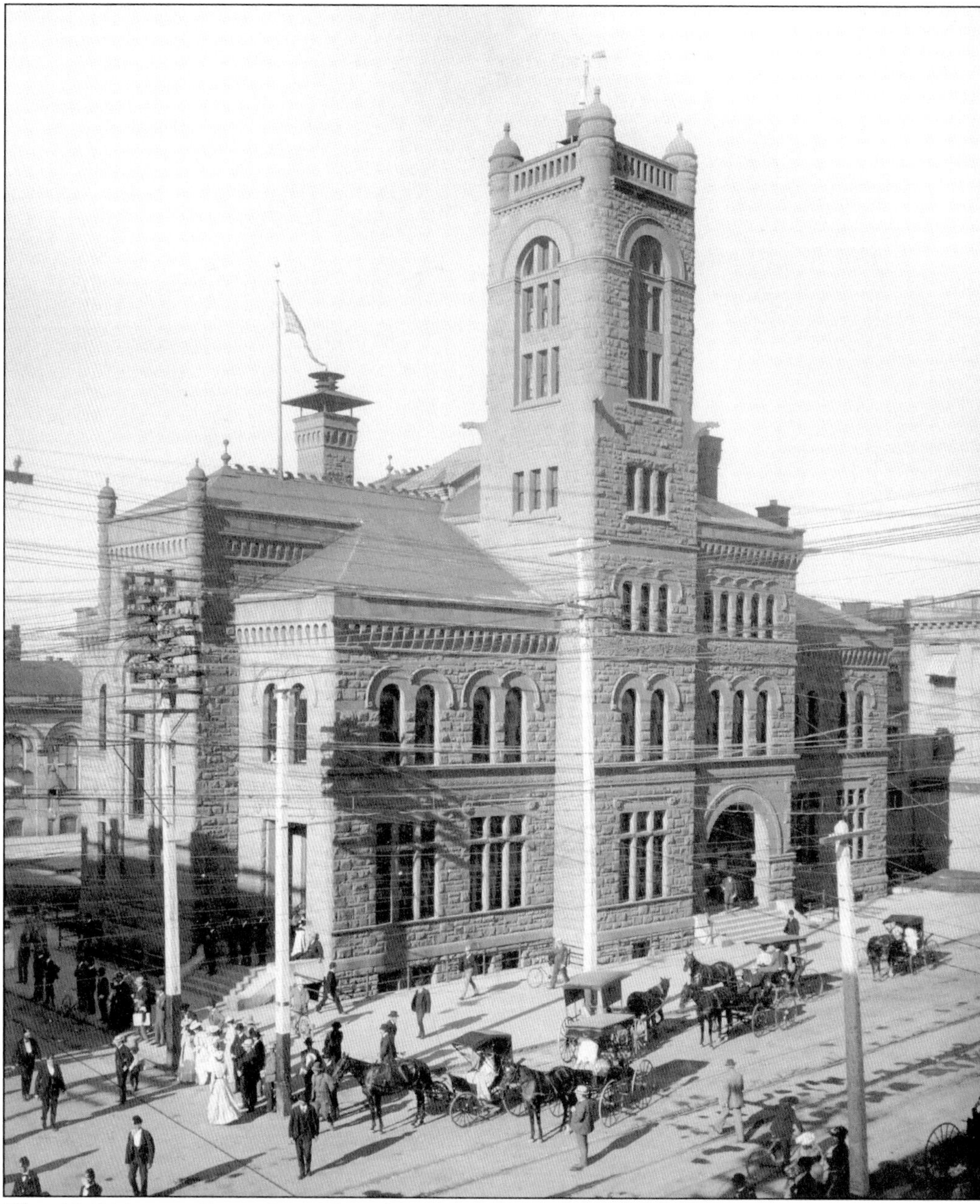

The old 1894 post office at Seventh and K Streets, which existed during the early years of Boulevard Park, was originally the site of the St. Rose of Lima Catholic Church. This building was replaced by the current post office at 801 I Street in 1933 and was demolished in 1967. A number of postal workers have made Boulevard Park their home probably worked here. (Courtesy of SAMCC.)

Eight

Is the Doctor In?

As Sacramento grew, so did its need for larger, more modern hospitals. The explosive growth period for Sacramento was from 1905 to 1915. However, by 1915, war clouds hung over Europe and the economic picture turned somewhat gloomy. Despite the fact that the United States did not enter World War I until 1917, concerns over the future created a softening economy and, starting in 1916, economic growth and home building in Sacramento dropped noticeably.

By the end of the war, it was time to build new hospitals. The return of so many soldiers from overseas brought the great influenza epidemic, and thousands of people in Sacramento were stricken by this particularly virulent strain of the disease. The hospitals filled, and they soon ran out of beds; people were lying in the hallways and hundreds died. It became so bad that at one point the city council passed an ordinance that allowed no person outdoors or into public places without a mask on. By the time the ordinance passed, the disease had begun to decline. However, Sacramento's need for more hospital beds and modern hospitals had been exposed.

Sacramento's medical community responded to the chaos of the epidemic. Committees were organized to publicize the problem and to engage in fund-raising. The medical community, Sacramento's businesses, and the general public contributed generously and, by the early to mid-1920s, two brand new state-of-the-art hospitals were built—Mercy and Sutter General. It is no coincidence that some of the physicians who organized this effort were residents of Boulevard Park.

Paralleling the need for better medicine in Sacramento was the formation and growth of the Kirk-Geary wholesale pharmaceutical house on Front Street. It kept the community and its pharmacies supplied with the best medicine available. Eventually that company became part of the nationwide giant McKesson and Robbins. Boulevard Park residents played an integral role in the whole chain that brought good health and prompt care to Sacramento residents.

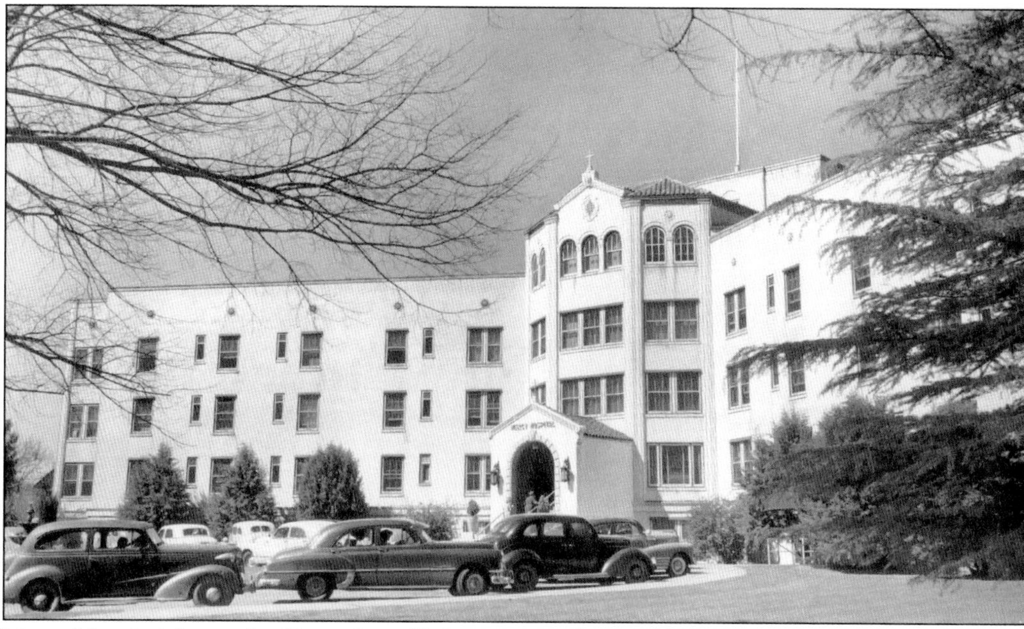

Mercy Hospital, located at Fortieth and J Streets, was designed by Rudolph Herold and completed in 1925. Dr. George Dufficy (see below) was associated with the hospital for 35 years. He was on the board of directors for many years and he aided the Sisters of Mercy in the planning and construction of this building. He was also a chief instructor in the School of Nursing. (Courtesy of SAMCC.)

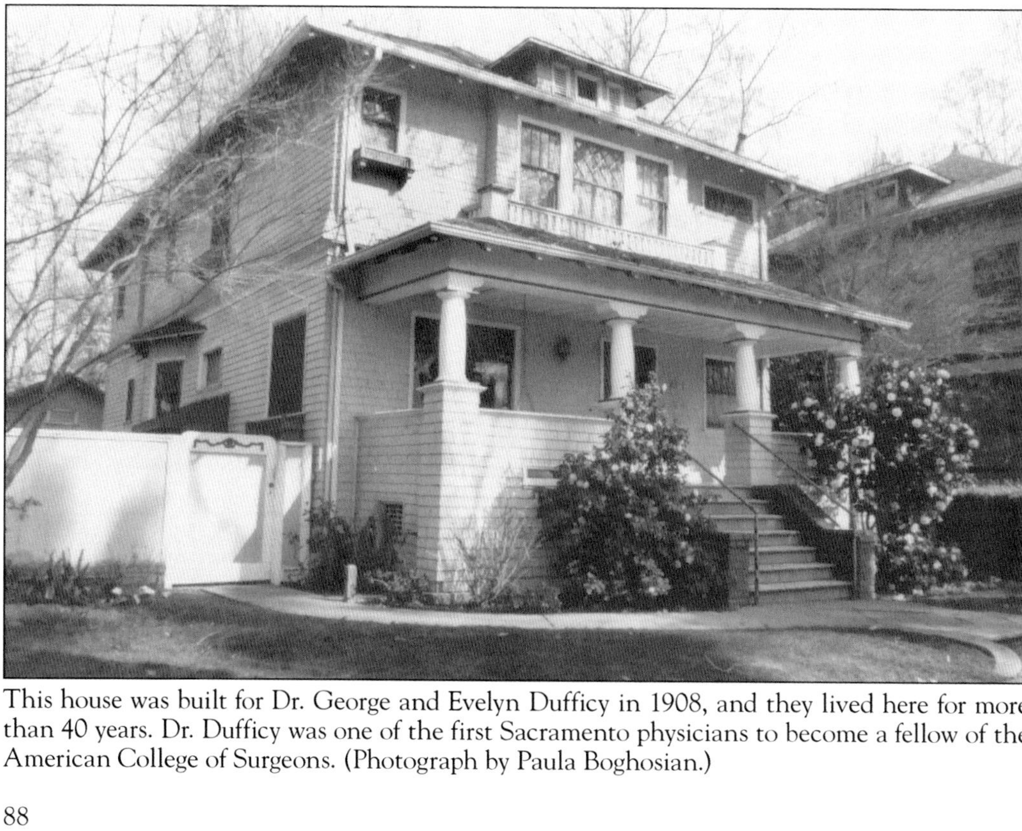

This house was built for Dr. George and Evelyn Dufficy in 1908, and they lived here for more than 40 years. Dr. Dufficy was one of the first Sacramento physicians to become a fellow of the American College of Surgeons. (Photograph by Paula Boghosian.)

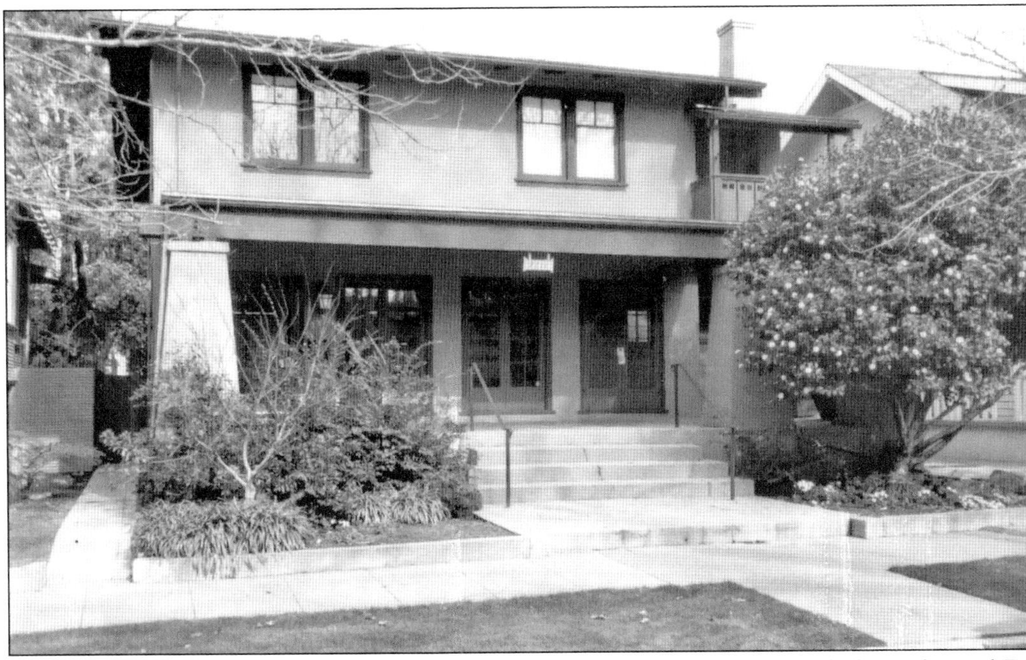

This 1911 Craftsman house has some Prairie School influences; it was built for Sadie and Dr. Asahel E. Briggs. He was a physician and surgeon and was the patriarch of an extended family that produced at least three generations of Sacramento doctors. (Photograph by Paula Boghosian.)

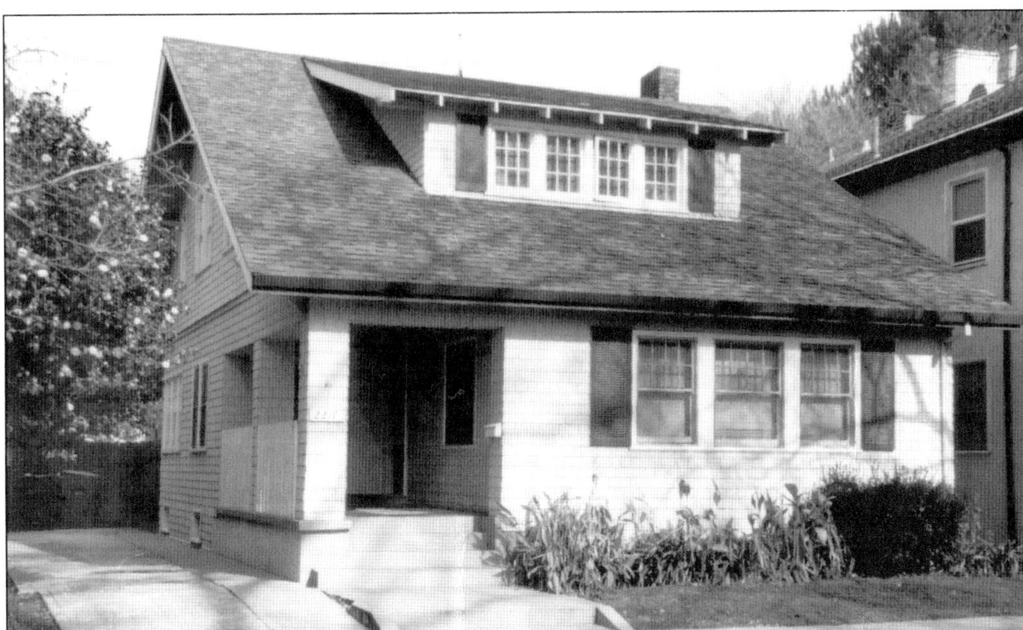

In 1918, Dr. George Briggs moved to this house at 2217 H Street to be near to his father, Asahel (2211 H Street), during the last years of his life. He was an eye, ear, and throat specialist who received nationwide recognition for his work. He was one of the organizing trustees that founded Sutter Hospital and was secretary-treasurer of the board of directors for about 30 years. (Photograph by Paula Boghosian.)

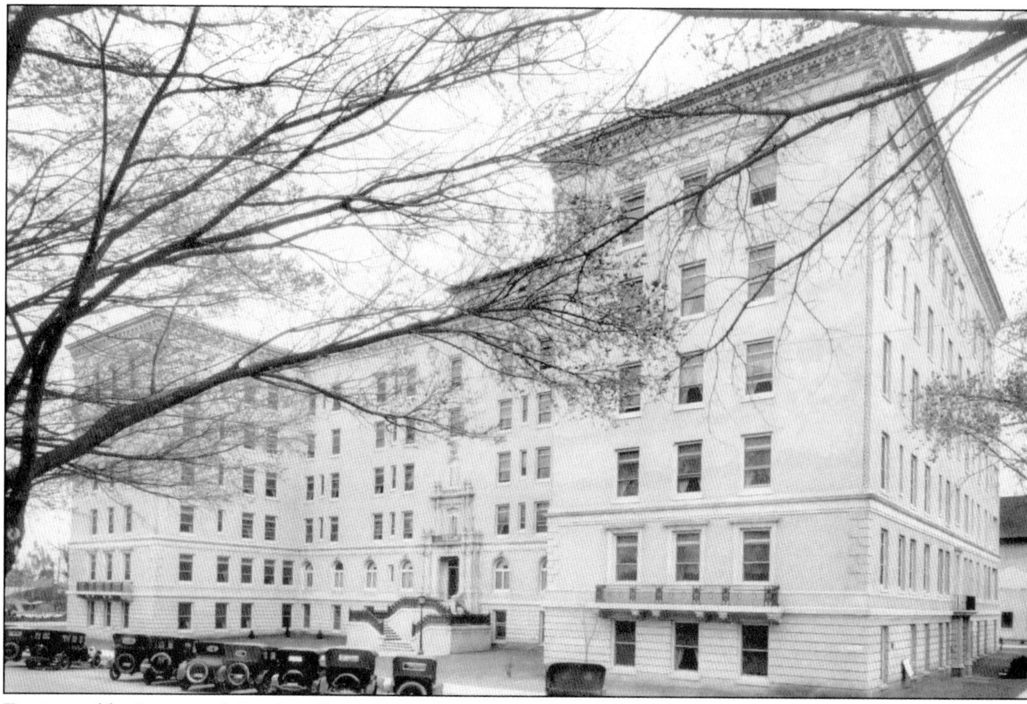

Designed by Leonard Starks, this 1920s photograph shows Sutter Hospital, which was completed in 1923. Both Dr. George Briggs (2217 H Street, page 89) and Dr. Aden C. Hart (2131 H Street, below) were founders of Sutter Hospital. (Courtesy of SAMCC.)

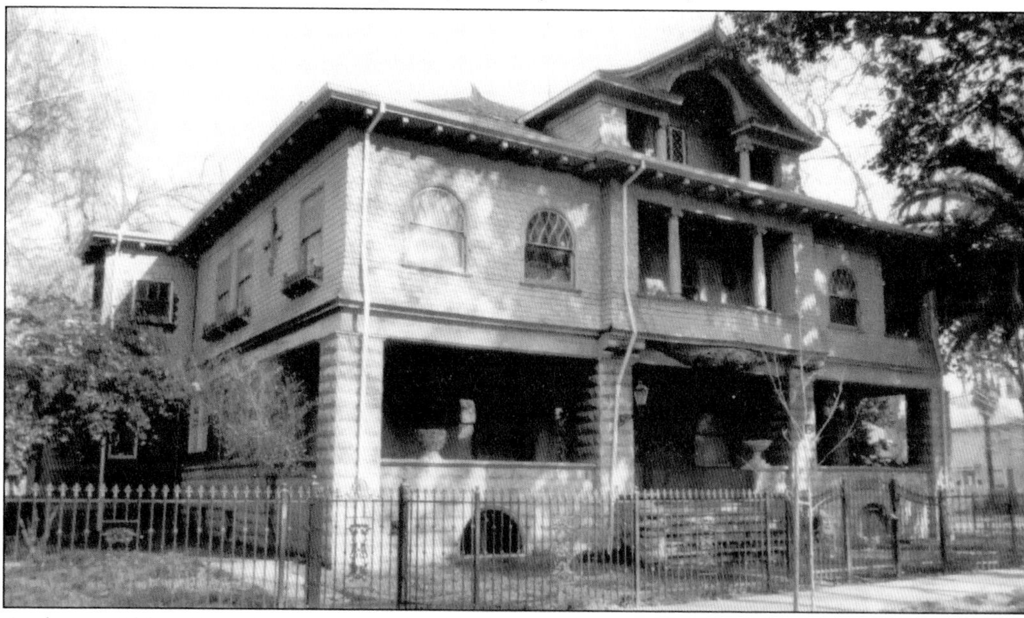

Architect Alden Campbell designed this 1907 house for Dr. Aden C. and Alice Hart. Hart was a founder of Sutter Hospital and the Sacramento Society for Medical Improvement. He was widely recognized as an outstanding surgeon and was elected as an honorary member of the American College of Surgeons. He traveled to John Hopkins Hospital and the Mayo Clinic to study advanced medicine. (Photograph by Paula Boghosian.)

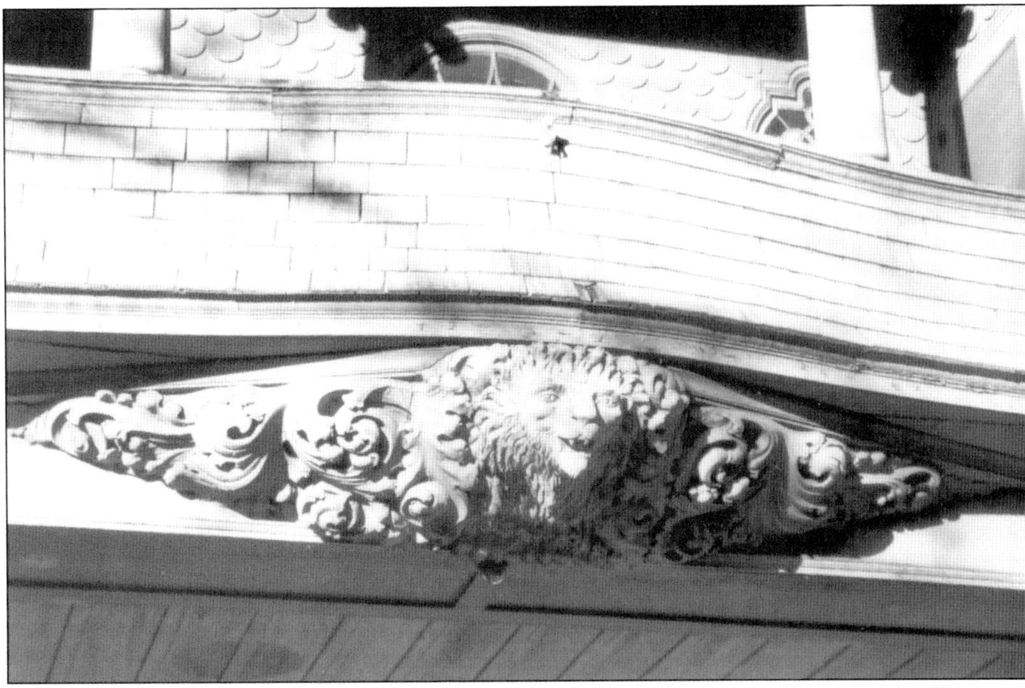

Alden Campbell designed mostly residences and Dr. Hart's house is the finest example of his work. Another good example of Campbell's work is the Cecil home near Grimes, California, which has been placed on the National Register of Historic Places. (Photograph by Paula Boghosian.)

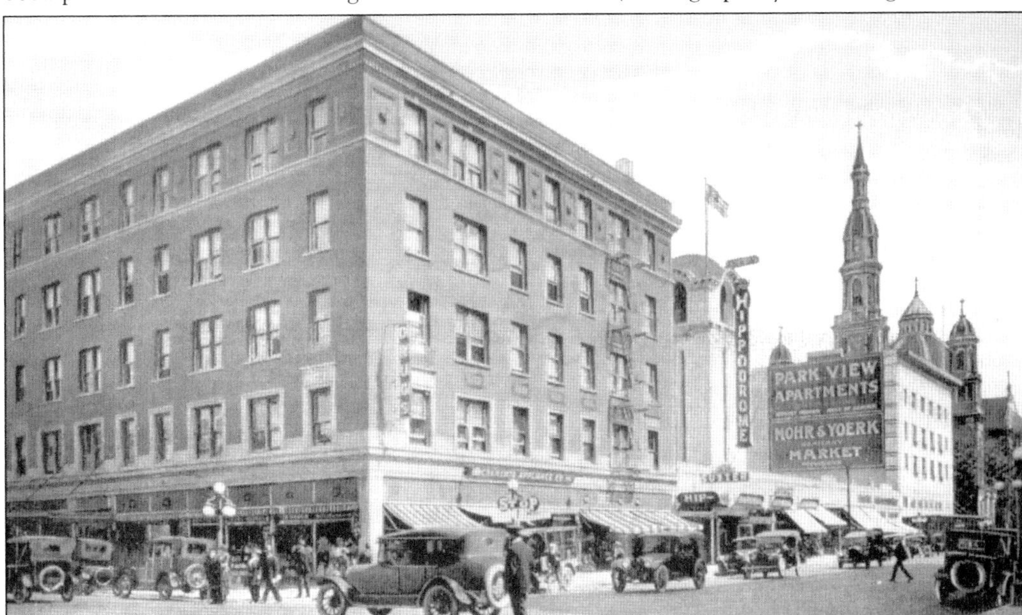

From its location on the northeast corner of Tenth and K Streets, the Physicians Building, pictured here c. 1919, housed many Sacramento doctors, dentists, and medical practitioners. Other doctors who lived in early Boulevard Park were Charles Murray, Charles Jones, Jacob Abrogast, James O'Brien, Theodore Rulison, and Philip Young. The dentists were represented by Edward Dreimeyer, Edward Kendall, Charles J. Tolton, and Cyrus Frantz. (Courtesy of SAMCC.)

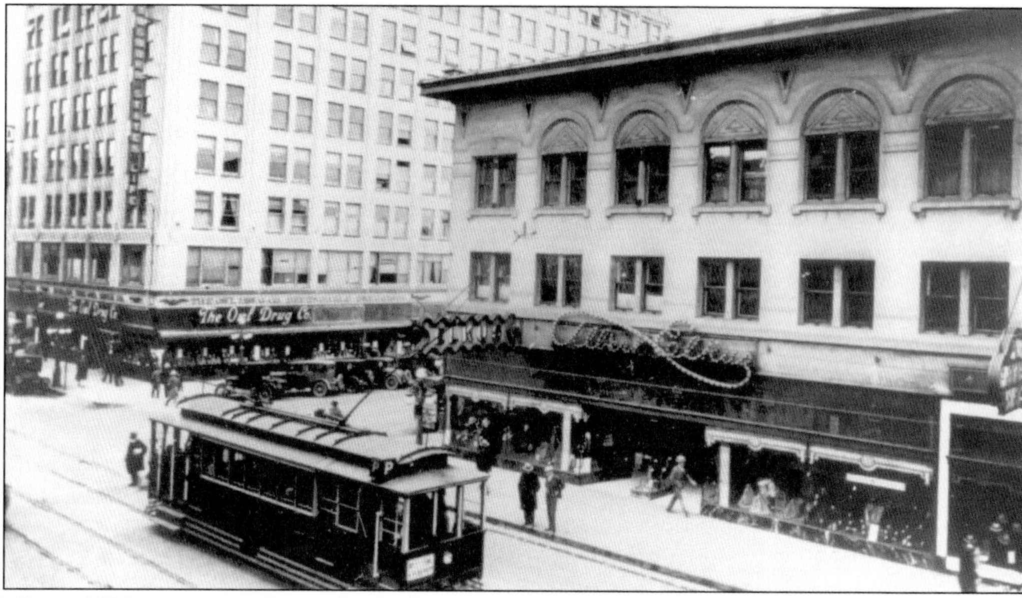

This *c.* 1920 streetscape shows the Owl Drug Store in its prominent location on the ground floor of the Forum Building (left of center). Ralph Head, the chief pharmacist of the store, had a duplex built at 717 Twenty-second Street. It later housed chief of police John Sullivan and Dr. Charles B. Jones. The Owl Drug Store went out of business during the Great Depression. (Courtesy of SAMCC.)

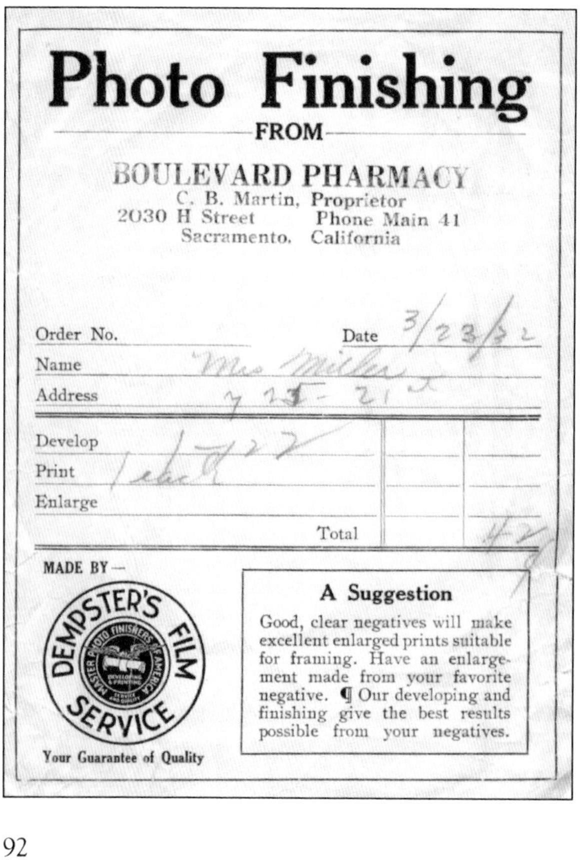

Photo Finishing

FROM

BOULEVARD PHARMACY
C. B. Martin, Proprietor
2030 H Street Phone Main 41
Sacramento, California

Order No. Date
Name
Address

Develop
Print
Enlarge
Total

MADE BY—
DEMPSTER'S FILM SERVICE
Your Guarantee of Quality

A Suggestion
Good, clear negatives will make excellent enlarged prints suitable for framing. Have an enlargement made from your favorite negative. ¶ Our developing and finishing give the best results possible from your negatives.

This bag held photograph prints that were purchased by Emma Groth Miller (see pages 26–31) from Cyrus B. Martin's Boulevard Pharmacy. In 1913, Martin had a house built at 510 Twenty-first Street. He lived there until his death in 1949. At one time, Martin had two other pharmacies at 212 and 1001 J Street. (Courtesy of Joe Wolfenden.)

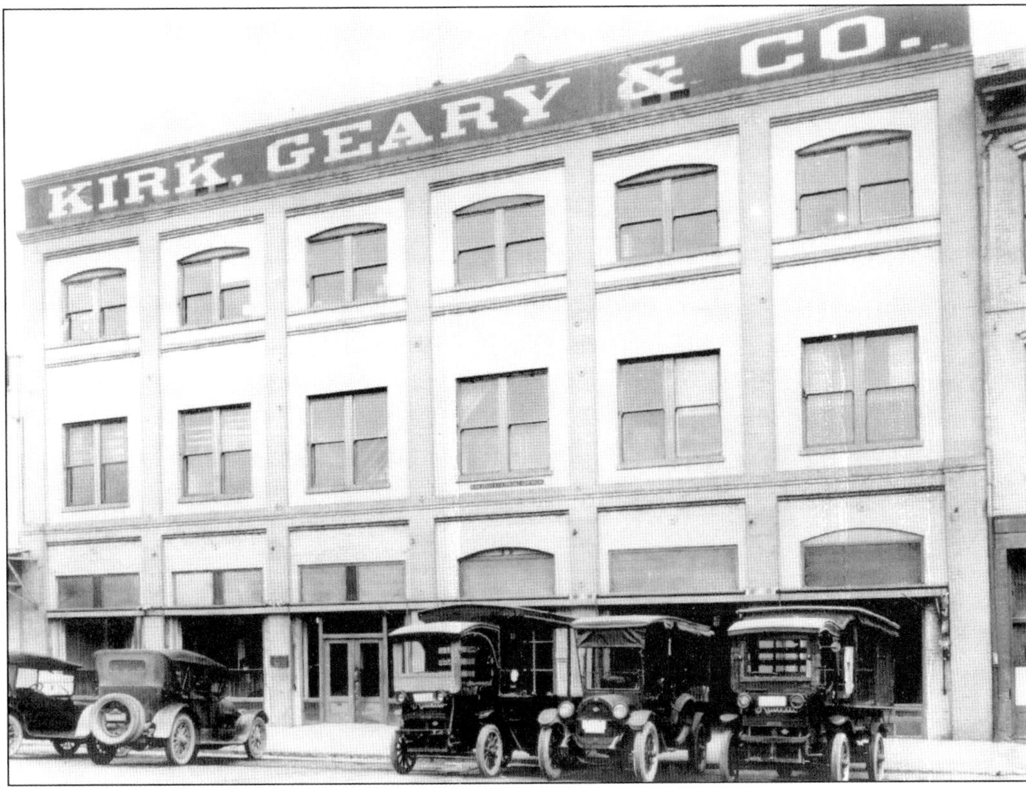

William and Isabella Geary formed a wholesale drug company in San Francisco in the 1860s. In 1882, William Geary brought his son William F. to Sacramento to establish a partnership in a wholesale retail drug firm, operated by the widow of H. C. Kirk. In 1906, the firm was incorporated with William Geary as president, William F. as vice president, and H. S. Kirk as secretary-treasurer. (Courtesy of Peter Bramson.)

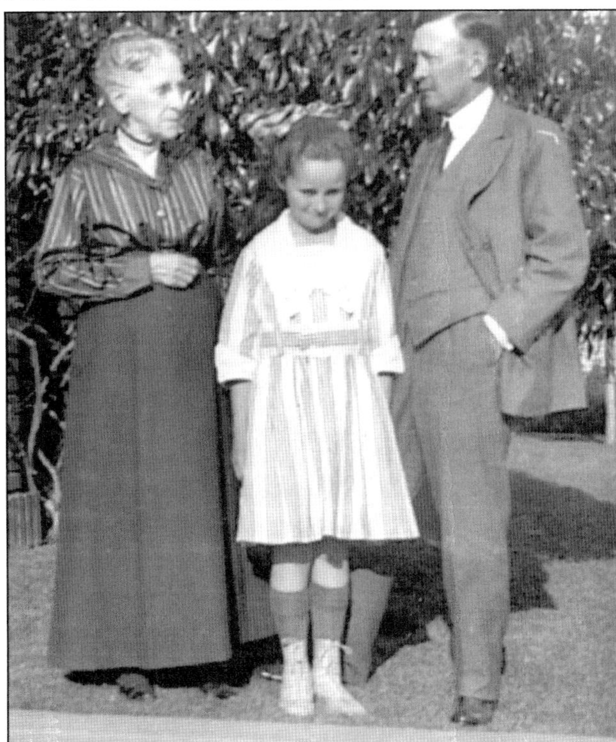

When Geary's father died in 1913, H. S. Kirk became president of the company and William F. Geary was vice president. A few years later, Isabella came to Sacramento for visit. Pictured, from left to right, are Isabella Geary, Katherine Geary, and William F. Geary. They are standing in the front yard of their home at 2101 G Street. (Courtesy of SAMCC.)

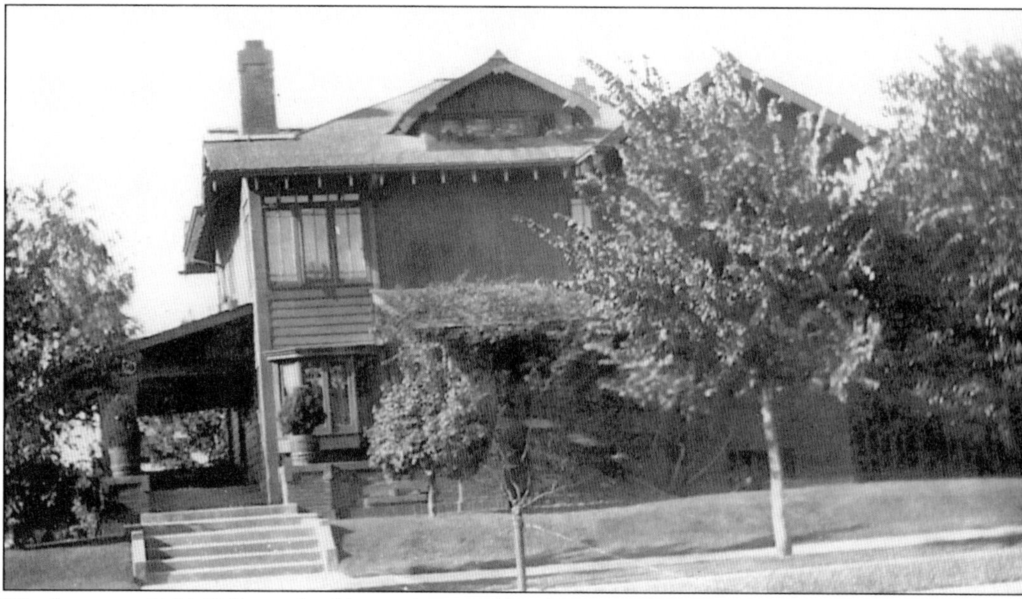

The house at 2101 G Street had been designed by George Sellon and built in 1909 for Mary and Robert E. Cranston, a mining engineer. The Geary's purchased the house in 1913. The house is an outstanding example of Sellon's residential work and has been placed on the National Register of Historic Places. (Courtesy of Peter Bramson.)

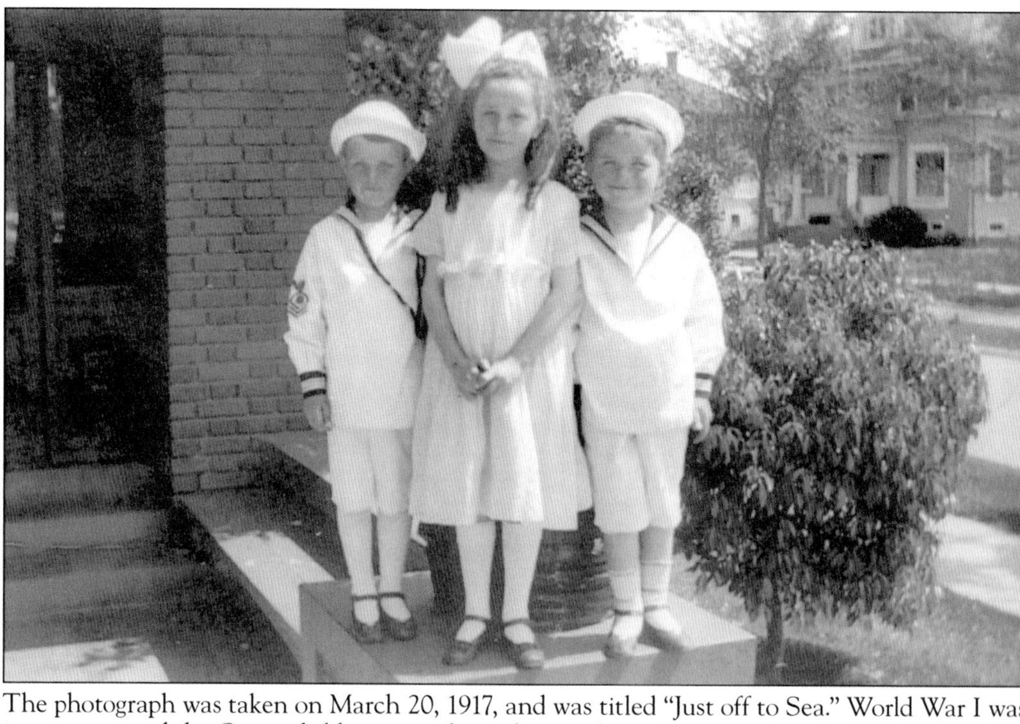

The photograph was taken on March 20, 1917, and was titled "Just off to Sea." World War I was in progress, and the Geary children were dressed up to show their patriotism. Pictured, from left to right, are John, Katherine, and William. (Courtesy of Peter Bramson.)

This photograph was taken in the spring of 1919, and the headline on the paper in Julia's hands reads, "Germany Disarmed By Armstice Terms." (Courtesy of Peter Bramson.)

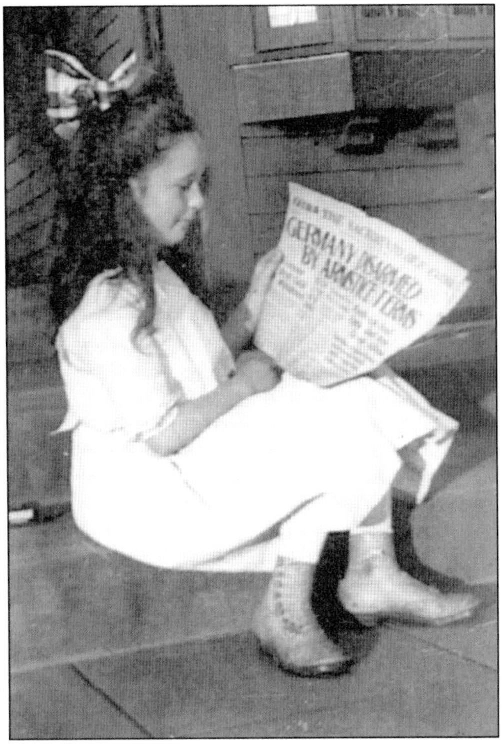

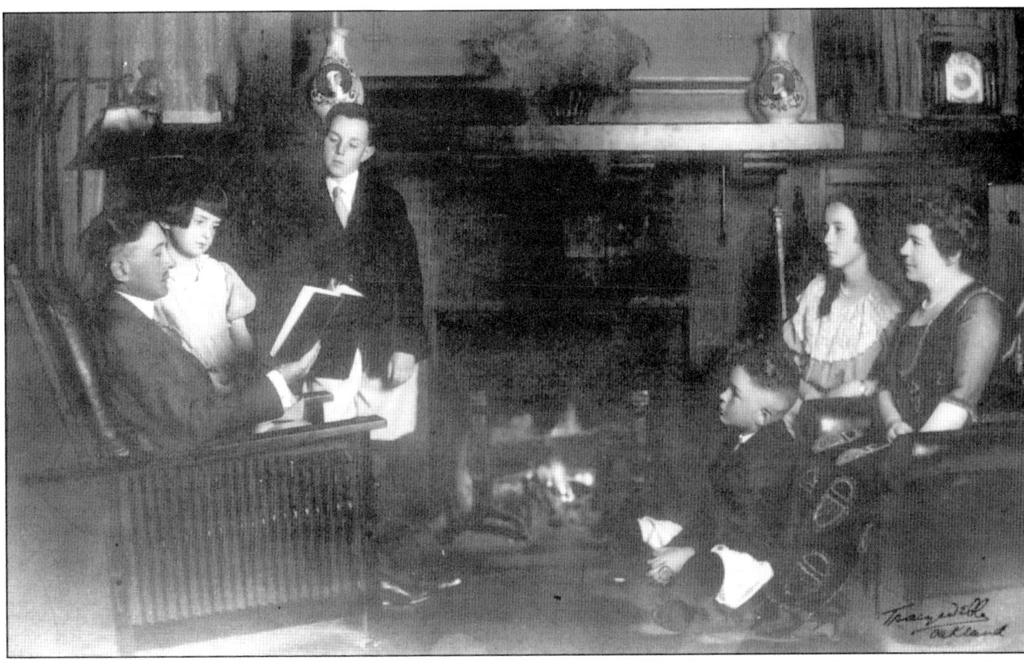

In the early 1920s, the Geary family gathers around the fireplace in the parlor to hear father read from a book. Pictured about the time H. S. Kirk passed away and William F. became president of the company, from left to right, are William F., Mary, John, William G. (seated on floor), Katherine, and Julia. Geary was also a director of the Farmer's and Merchants Bank. (Courtesy of Peter Bramson.)

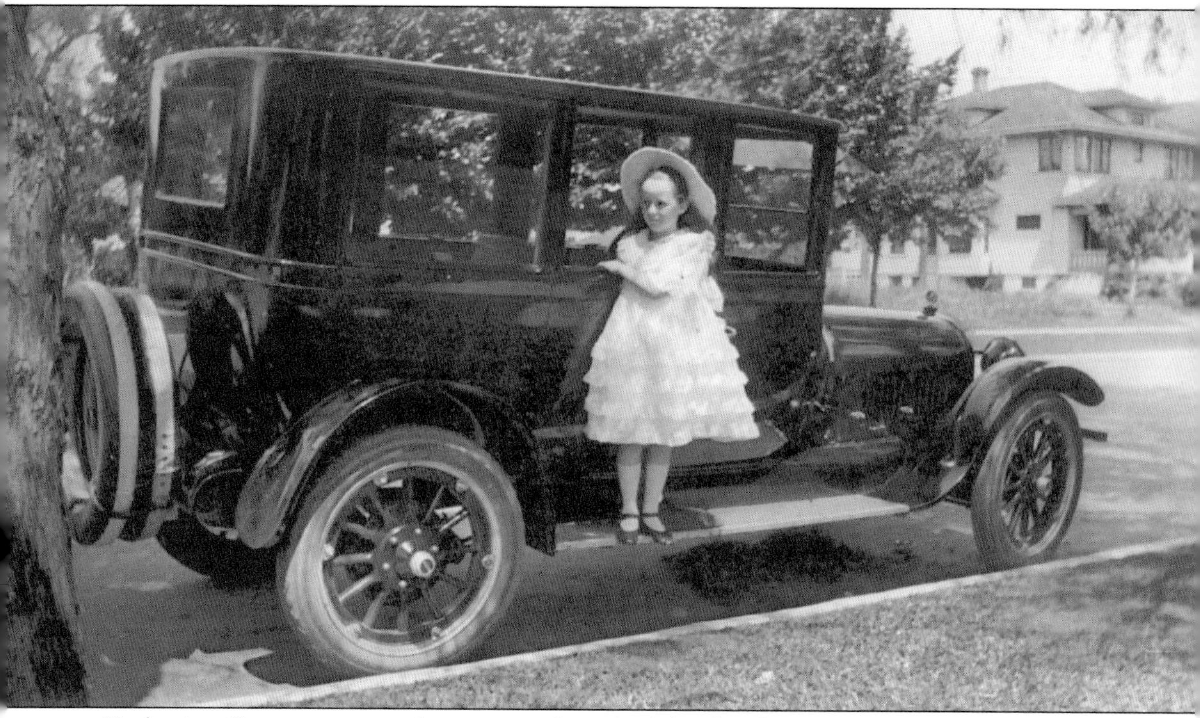

Katherine Geary poses on the running board of the family car in June 1919. (Courtesy of Peter Bramson.)

William G. Geary mugs for the camera in this c. 1913 photograph. He looks to be about three years old. Before they moved to the G Street house, they lived at 2431 H Street from 1907 to 1913. Note the hitching post in the background. (Courtesy of Peter Bramson.)

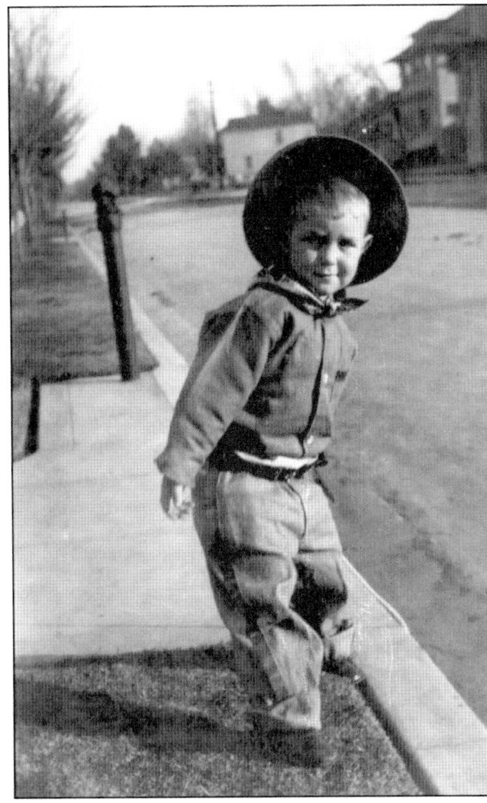

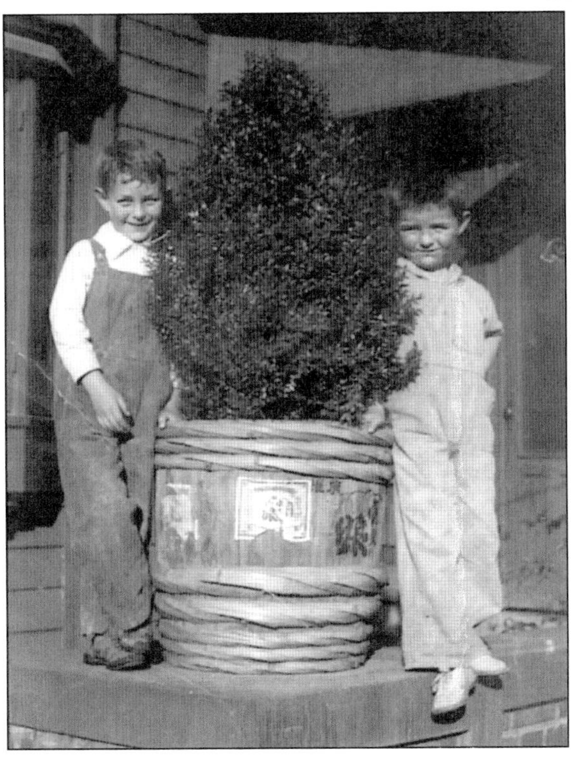

In this photograph, from left to right, are John and William. They look to be seven to eight years old so this photograph taken on the front porch of their house would have been taken around 1921. By 1941, John was a salesman for the Sacramento office and William was an assistant to the divisional vice president of the San Francisco office of Kirk-Geary, McKesson and Robbins. (Courtesy of Peter Bramson.)

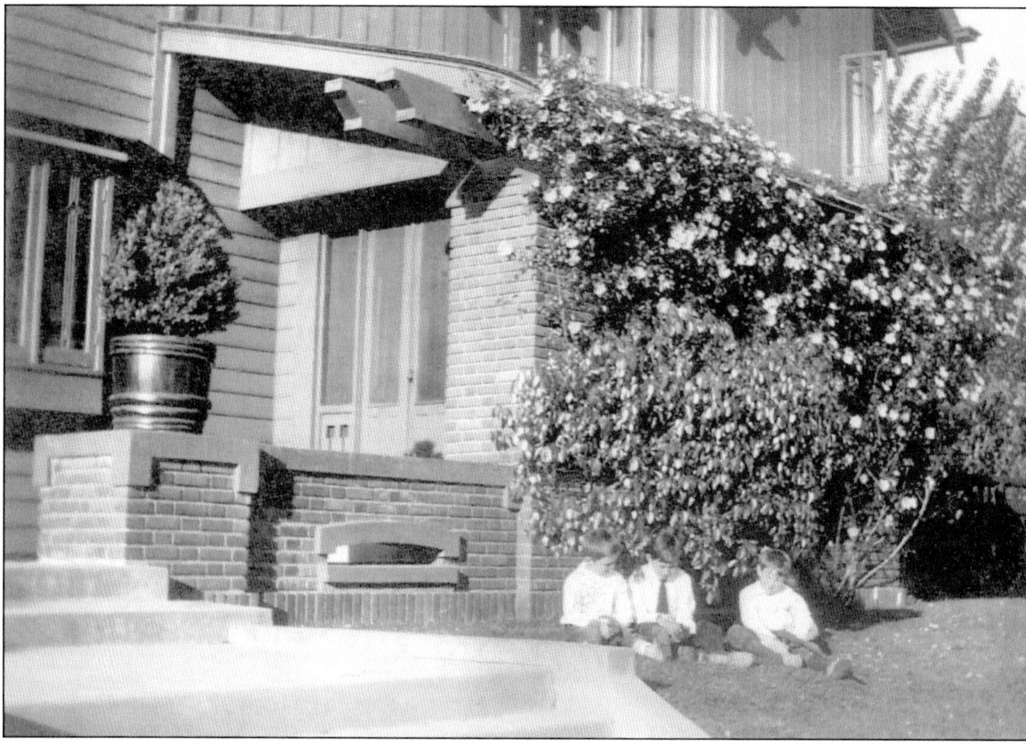

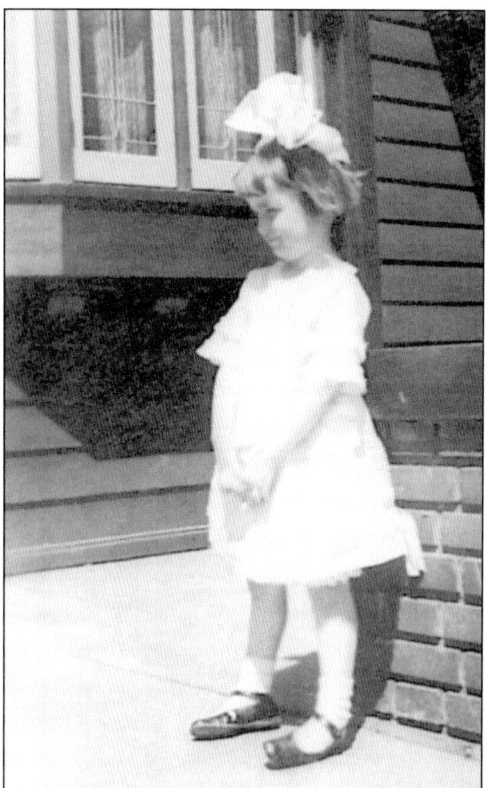

The boys enjoy a warm day in the front yard of their home around 1918. Pictured, from left to right, are William, John, and unidentified. In 1928, the Kirk-Geary Company became the Sacramento branch of the nationwide pharmaceutical company McKesson and Robbins. William F. Geary became a vice president at McKesson and Robbins. (Courtesy of Peter Bramson.)

In 1922, Mary Geary, the youngest of the family, poses for the camera, but she does not appear to be enjoying the event. When William F. Geary passed away in 1941 at the age of 72, all the children had left the nest. Julia Geary sold the house soon after.

Nine

Build It and They Will Come

Real estate in Sacramento has been an important issue since its founding by John Sutter, who ultimately lost full ownership of his land grant to the overwhelming hoard of gold seekers after 1849. There were many tangled land titles and quit claims as a result, and squatters who simply refused to leave. The first shelters were canvas and wood, then brick—for a number of years, brickyard excavations checkered the old city area. Real estate businesses established themselves early in the city's history and, combined with developers, continue to play a major economic role.

Sales fluctuated somewhat in the 19th century, with a few booms, such as that from 1887 to 1893, and downturns accompanying a national depression in the 1890s. However, between 1900 and 1920, Sacramento's population grew by 60 percent. An influx of easterners during the early years of the 20th century and the prosperity of Sacramento created an enormous building boom during the 1910s to about 1925. A number of land tracts became available for subdivision and construction, such as the Boulevard Park area and the 44,000-acre Haggin Ranch, north of the American River.

The building boom proved profitable for many in the building trades, allowing them to become homeowners in suburbs such as Oak Park, Boulevard Park, and New Era Park. A number of people in the building trades settled there, such as carpenters, plasterers, plumbers, concrete workers, electricians, and mechanics, as well as policemen, firemen, and railroad personnel. The Boulevard Park developers even had their own design and construction department, hiring a number of workers that became homeowners in the development themselves.

The opening up of new real estate lands and the building boom spawned the creation of many realty companies, including those marketing various areas some distance outside of the city, such as the Carmichael Land Company and North Sacramento Land Company. Wright and Kimbrough moved on to suburbs as well, completing 40 subdivisions by 1939. In all, their major work included areas such as Oak Park, Florin, Arden Park and Arden Fair, East Sacramento, Arden Bluff, Madison Oaks in Fair Oaks, and Lakeridge at Folsom Lake.

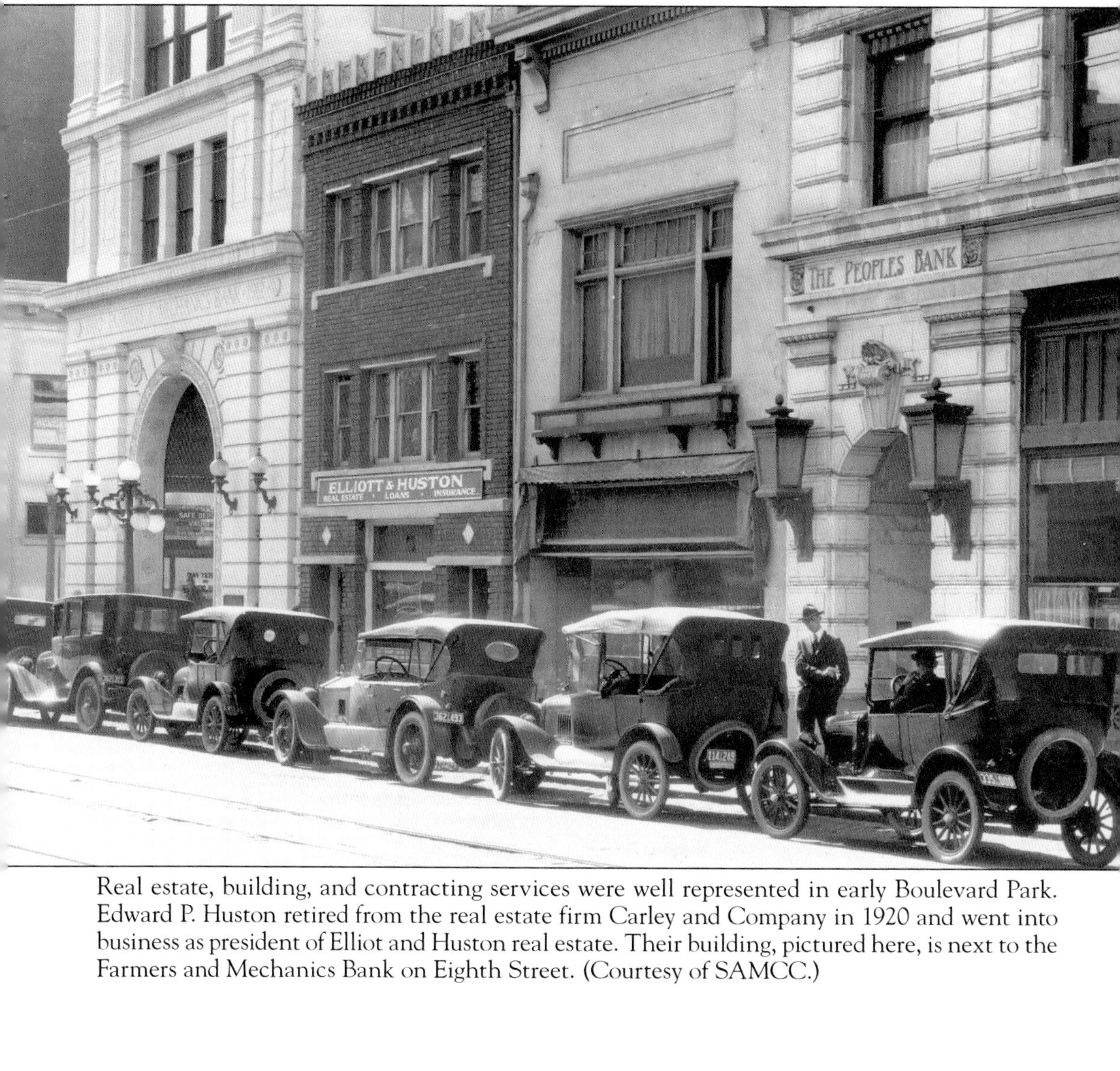

Real estate, building, and contracting services were well represented in early Boulevard Park. Edward P. Huston retired from the real estate firm Carley and Company in 1920 and went into business as president of Elliot and Huston real estate. Their building, pictured here, is next to the Farmers and Mechanics Bank on Eighth Street. (Courtesy of SAMCC.)

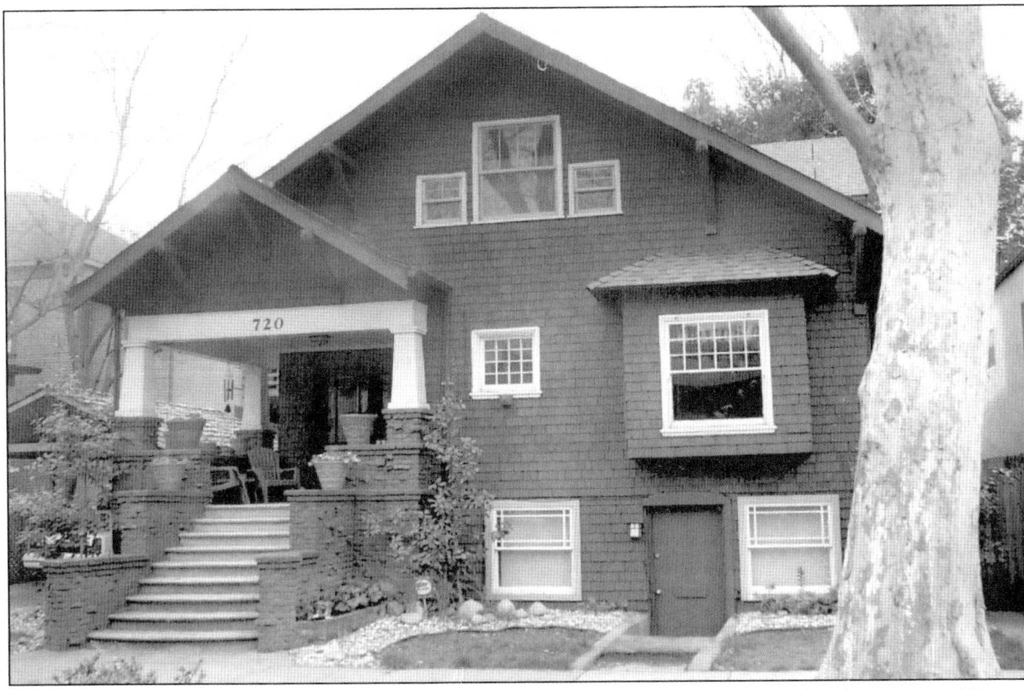

Vena and Edward P. Huston had the house at 720 Twenty-third Street built in 1914. He was chairman of the board at Fort Sutter Savings and Loan, president of the Sacramento Real Estate Board, honorary director of the California Real Estate Association, director of the YMCA for 35 years, and trustee of First Methodist Church for 30 years. (Photograph by Paula Boghosian.)

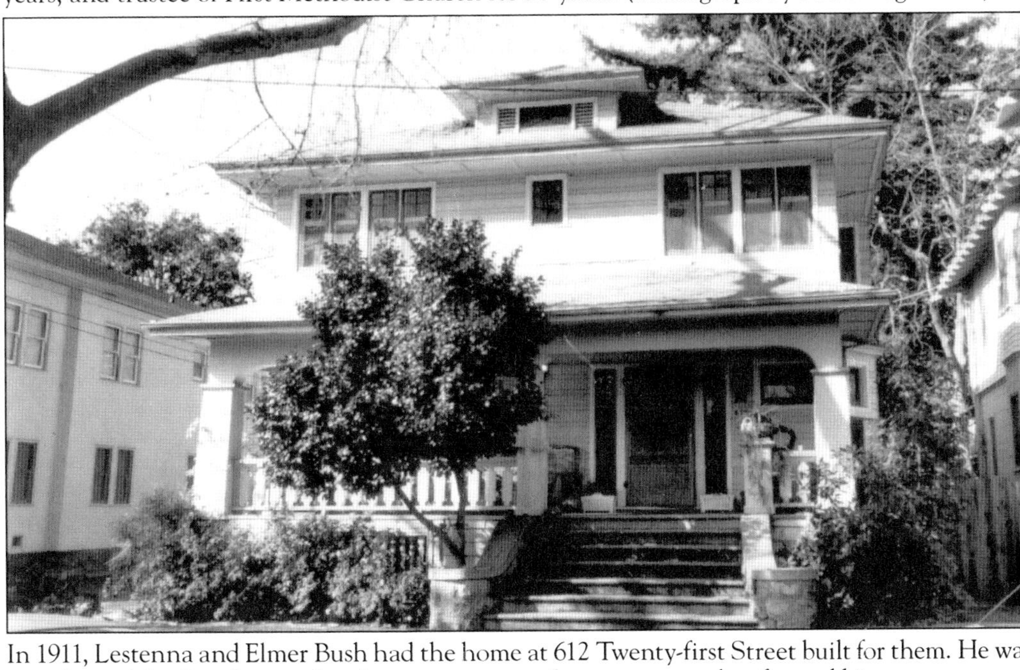

In 1911, Lestenna and Elmer Bush had the home at 612 Twenty-first Street built for them. He was president of the Ben Leonard real estate company for many years, but formed his own company, the Mortgage Realty Company, in 1935. Bush was a past president of the Sacramento Real Estate Board. (Photograph by Paula Boghosian.)

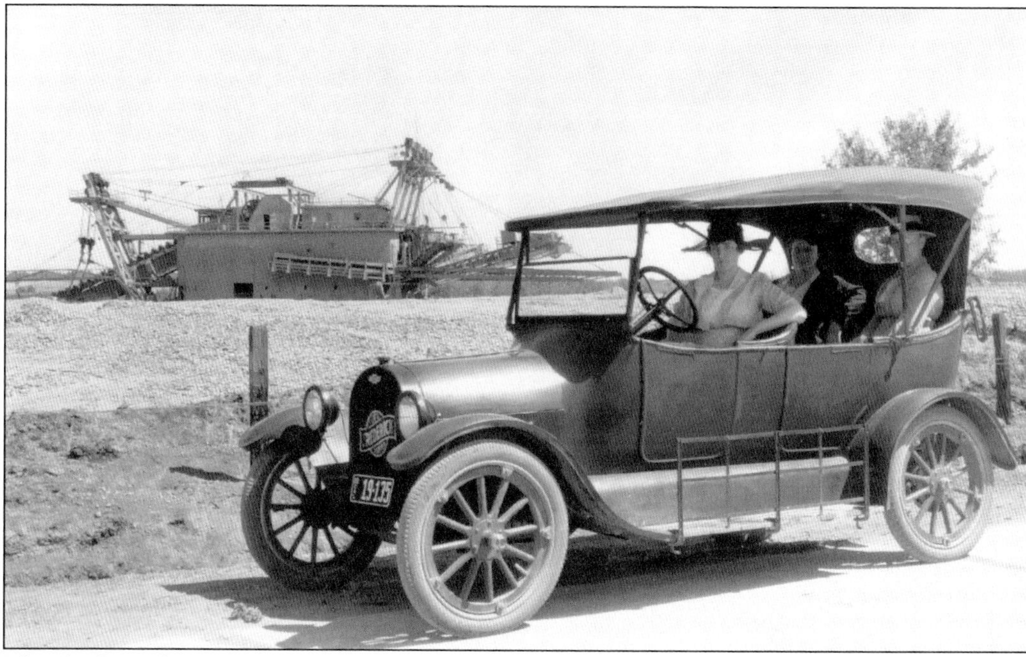

The dredge is busy reclaiming land by helping build levees in north Natomas. Boulevard Park had its own dredge captain, Charles Yeager, who lived at 500 Twenty-second Street. (Courtesy of SAMCC.)

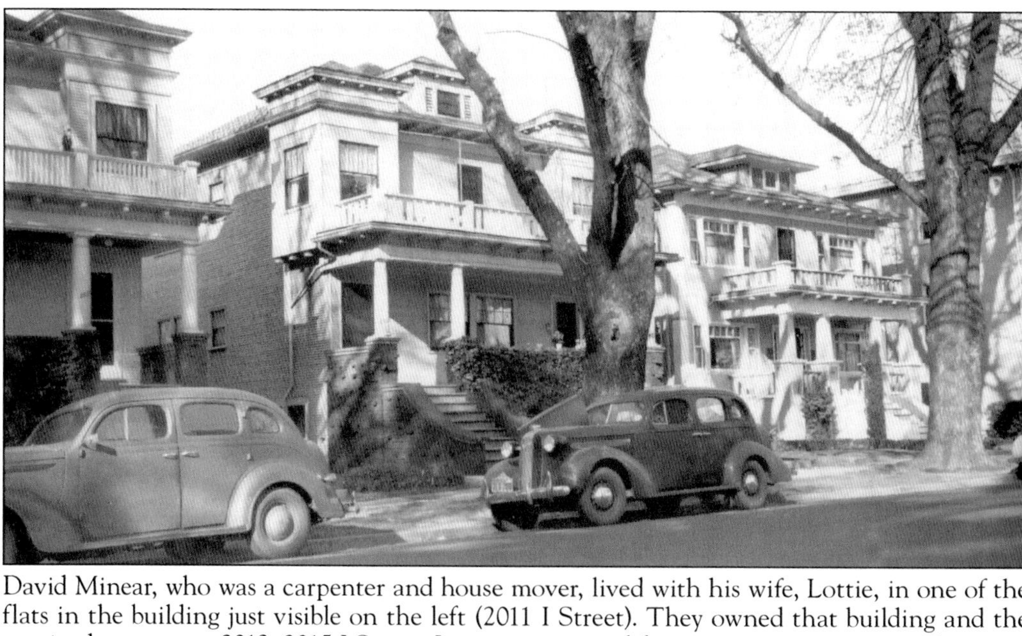

David Minear, who was a carpenter and house mover, lived with his wife, Lottie, in one of the flats in the building just visible on the left (2011 I Street). They owned that building and the one in the center at 2013–2015 I Street. It was not unusual for carpenters to own rental income property. (Courtesy of SAMCC.)

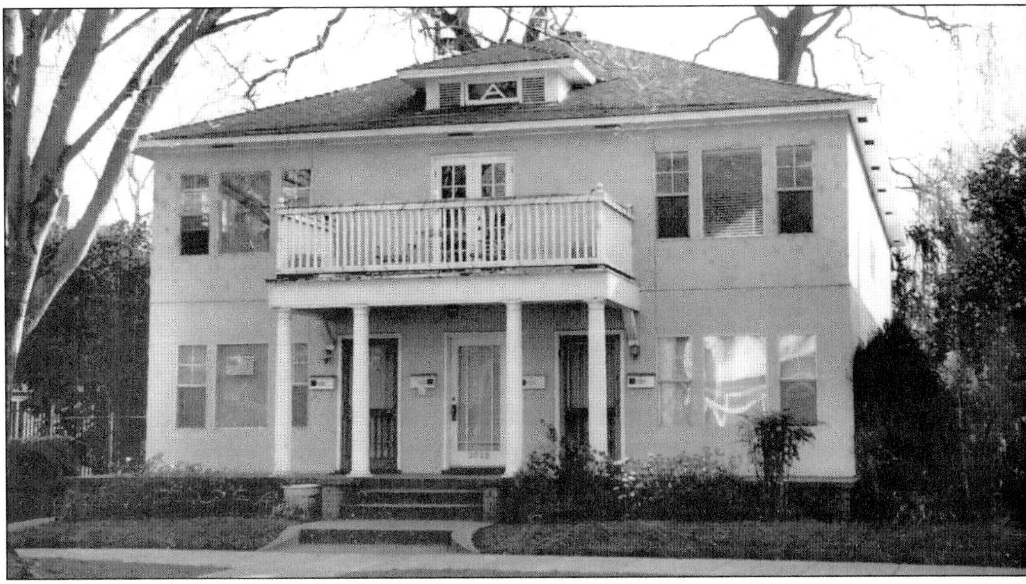

Rental income was an important aspect of real estate investment. There are only a handful of old apartment buildings in Boulevard Park and this one at 2201 I Street dates from the mid-1920s. (Courtesy of SAMCC.)

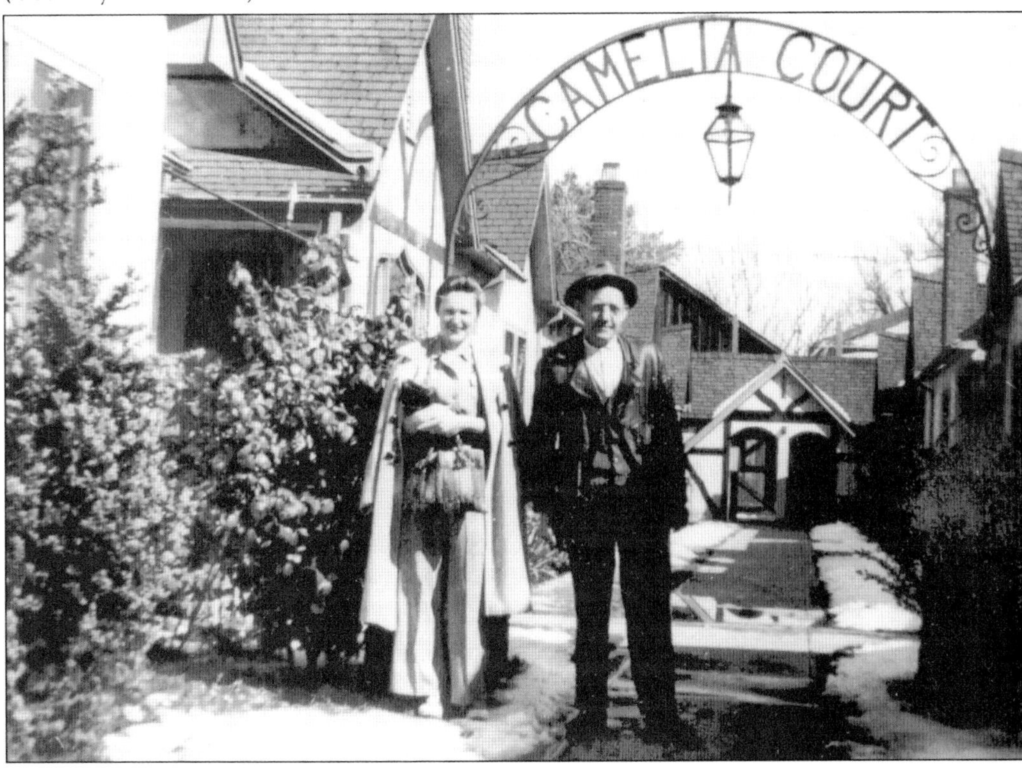

The Camellia Court Cottages, located at 2309–2315 H Street, are unique in Boulevard Park. Their small scale and English overtones in their design, add quaint charm to the neighborhood. The couple posed in front of the archway is Marie and Christian Madsen. They purchased the cottages in the late-1930s and lived in 2309B. (Courtesy of SAMCC.)

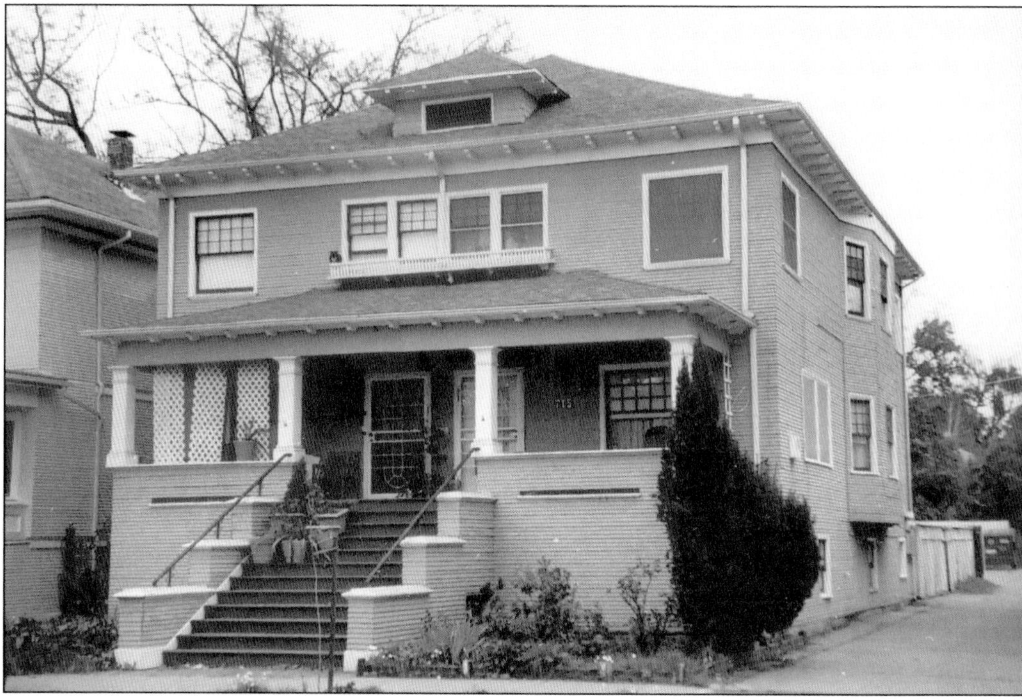

In 1906, this Colonial Revival duplex was built for James H. Brown, a department manager for the C. P. Nathan department store. He lived in one unit and rented out the other. One of his more interesting tenants in 1913 was Joseph J. Taffe, an officer in the SP police force.

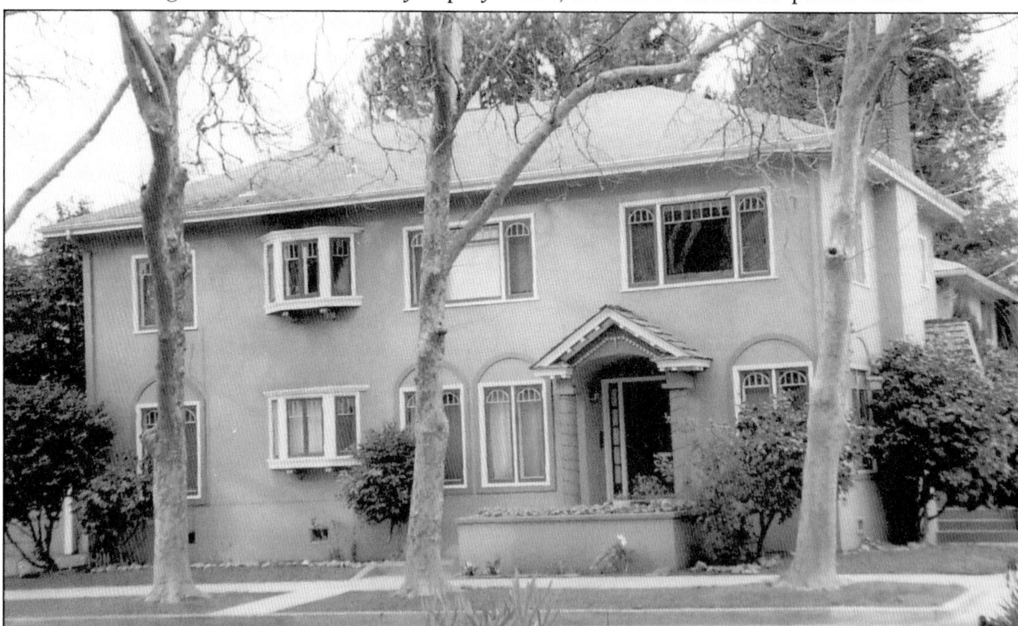

The son of a forty-niner, Edward P. Huston built this apartment building at 2231 G Street in 1906. He initially lived in it, and then in 1914 he moved to a house at 720 Twenty-third Street. He sold the building to George Morse in the mid-1920s, and Morse also lived in the building. Morse sold the building to Dr. Jacob and Emeline Abrogast. (Photograph by Don Cox.)

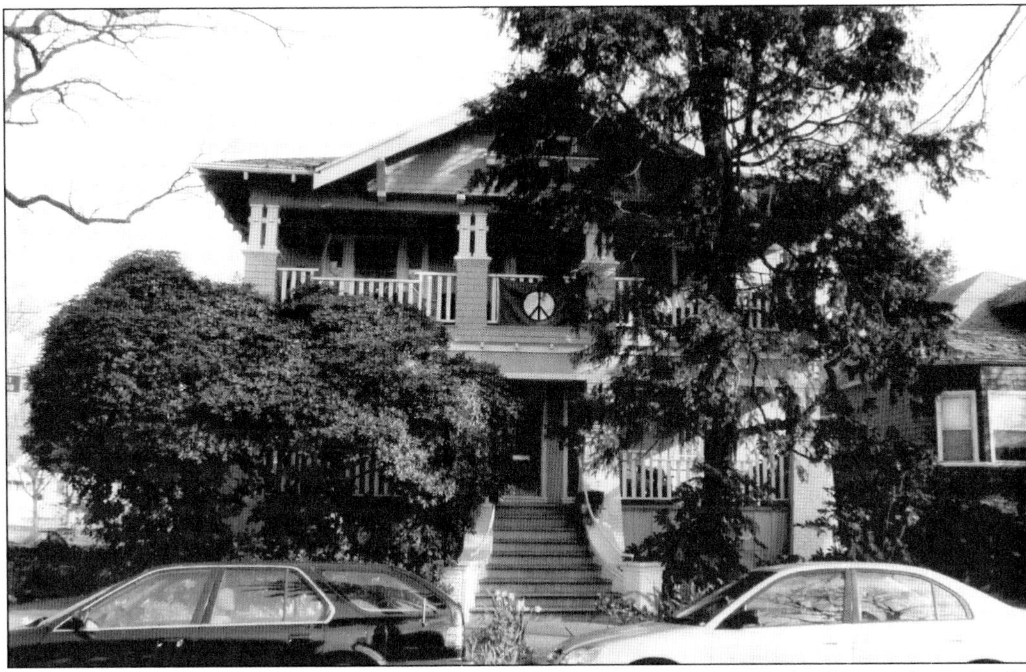

William I. Elliott was one of the first residents in these attractive 1916 Craftsman flats. At the time, he was a partner at the Skinner and Elliot automobile dealership at 1226 K Street (see page 119).

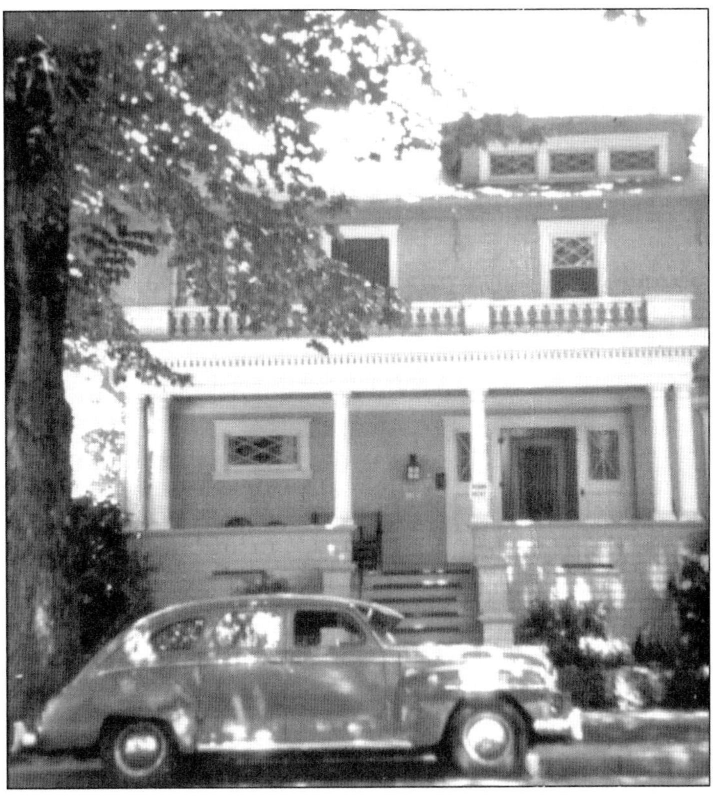

Mary Phlegar had the house at 2201 H Street built for her in 1908 and lived there about 30 years. In the 1960s and early 1970s, some of Boulevard Park's large houses were turned into boardinghouses or bed and breakfast facilities. Bessie and Noah Hughes owned this house in the 1960s and used it to board elderly women. (Courtesy of Vicky Valine.)

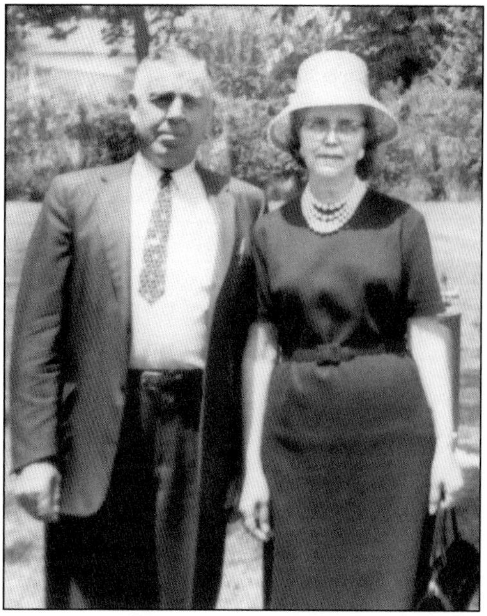

Posing for the camera during the 1960s are Noah and Bessie Hughes. Noah worked in the SP locomotive works. They did not own a car, and Noah walked to work every day. (Courtesy of Vicky Valine.)

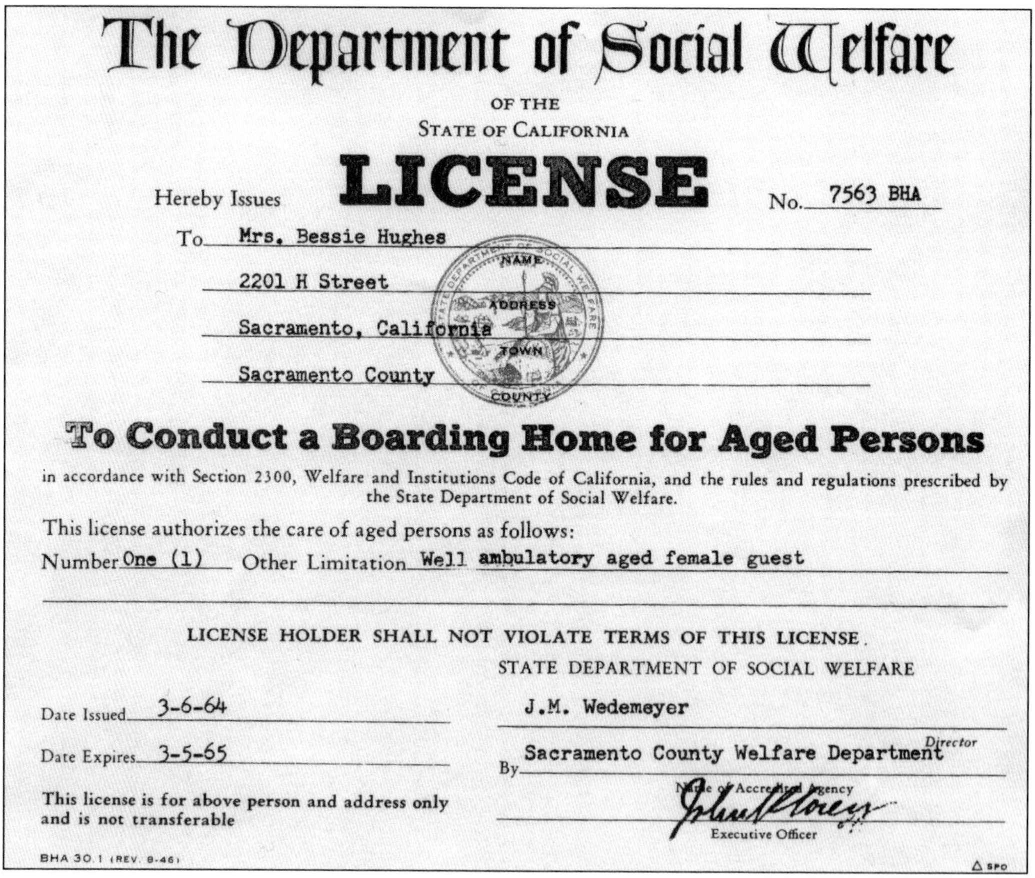

The Department of Social Welfare

OF THE

STATE OF CALIFORNIA

Hereby Issues **LICENSE** No. 7563 BHA

To Mrs. Bessie Hughes
NAME
2201 H Street
ADDRESS
Sacramento, California
TOWN
Sacramento County
COUNTY

To Conduct a Boarding Home for Aged Persons

in accordance with Section 2300, Welfare and Institutions Code of California, and the rules and regulations prescribed by the State Department of Social Welfare.

This license authorizes the care of aged persons as follows:

Number One (1) Other Limitation Well ambulatory aged female guest

LICENSE HOLDER SHALL NOT VIOLATE TERMS OF THIS LICENSE.

STATE DEPARTMENT OF SOCIAL WELFARE

Date Issued 3-6-64

J.M. Wedemeyer
Director

Date Expires 3-5-65

By Sacramento County Welfare Department
Name of Accredited Agency

This license is for above person and address only and is not transferable

Executive Officer

BHA 30.1 (REV. 8-46)

△ SPO

In 1964, Sacramento County issued this boardinghouse license to Bessie Hughes. The house has returned to single-family occupancy. (Courtesy of Vicky Valine.)

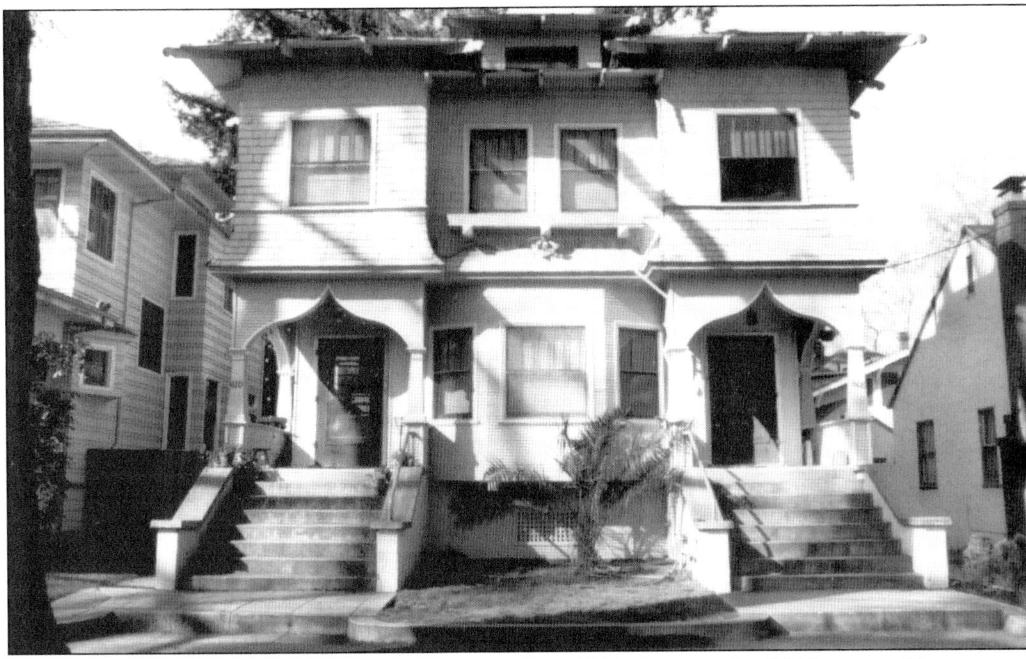

This Moorish Revival building was constructed in 1911. During the 1910s, one of its tenants, Herbert O. Williams, was a high school principal. In the 1920s, Williams went into the diplomatic service, and was employed by the American Consular Service in Belgium. In 1934, he was envoy to Mexico and, in 1935, he was consul to Gibralter. (Photograph by Paula Boghosian.)

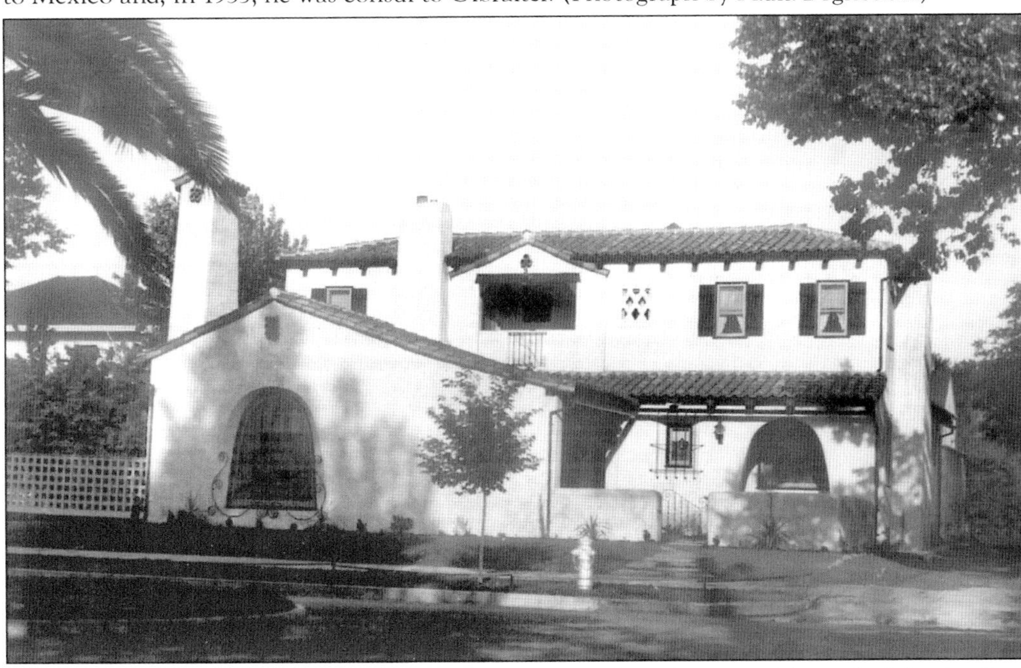

Clarence H. Smith built the income properties pictured on this page. He worked for the State Controller's office when he had this Spanish Colonial Revival duplex built in 1931. His niece Dorothy and her husband, Peter Actis, a lathe and plastering contractor, were the first tenants. Dorothy, who is in her 90s, still lives there at the present time. (Courtesy of Richard Borgquist.)

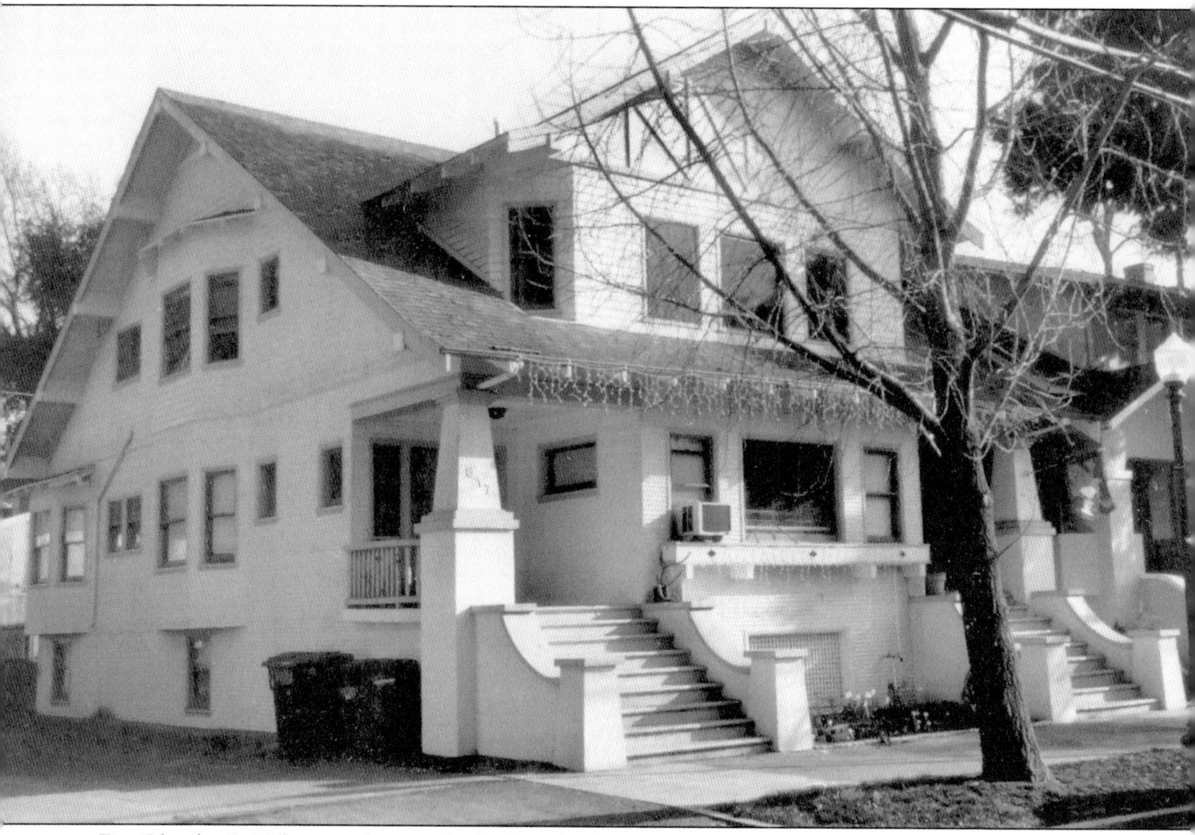

Dr. Charles J. Tolton, a dentist, built this duplex at 817–819 Twenty-second Street in 1913. He occupied one unit and rented the other to a physician and surgeon, Dr. Charles B. Jones.

Ten

Retail and Services

Retail sales and services cover a wide range of activities and products, and there were a number of Boulevard Park residents involved in a variety of them. While there were smaller retail hubs in Oak Park and North Sacramento, until the 1940s, most of these activities took place in downtown Sacramento. One would find a plumber's shop near a fine jewelry store and a department store containing a bakery adjacent to a very small key shop.

The earliest retail establishments on J Street outfitted miners for the northern mines and later shops, like Anthony Coolot's small five and dime store on J Street begun in the 1860s, helped make owners wealthy men. Two of the major department stores, Weinstock-Lubin and Hale's, were founded in 1878 and 1879, respectively. In Sacramento, Hale's was established by Marshall Hale. In different cities, each of his five stores was managed by one of his sons. By 1926, Hale's secretly bought the Weinstock-Lubin and Company but kept operating each store under its initial name. Over time and with good management, the Hale Brothers Company grew steadily, evolving into Broadway/Hale with Capwell's and ultimately owning the Neiman Marcus Company and Harrod's of London. Half brothers Harris Weinstock and David Lubin began their store in 1878, but later passed the presidency of the store to Samuel McKim of Boulevard Park, who held that position for 30 years.

Several businesses that began in the late 1800s or early 1900s, remained in business throughout most of the 20th century. The transition from horse and buggy travel to automobile changed some products and services substantially during the early 1900s, when Boulevard Park was being built. Carriage makers gave way to auto dealerships and services. Stables closed and gas stations appeared.

Emigh's Hardware, still in business on El Camino Avenue, began downtown as Emigh Winchell Hardware in 1910. C. H. Krebs and Company retailed art supplies, glass oils, paint, and wallpapers. The W. P. Fuller Company, selling paint, was established and went on to become nationally prominent. Moses Kimball established a sporting goods store in 1870, and his partner was L. Stuart Upson, a noted track athlete and one of the fastest cyclists on the Pacific Coast. His records were never broken because they were made on the high front-wheel cycle.

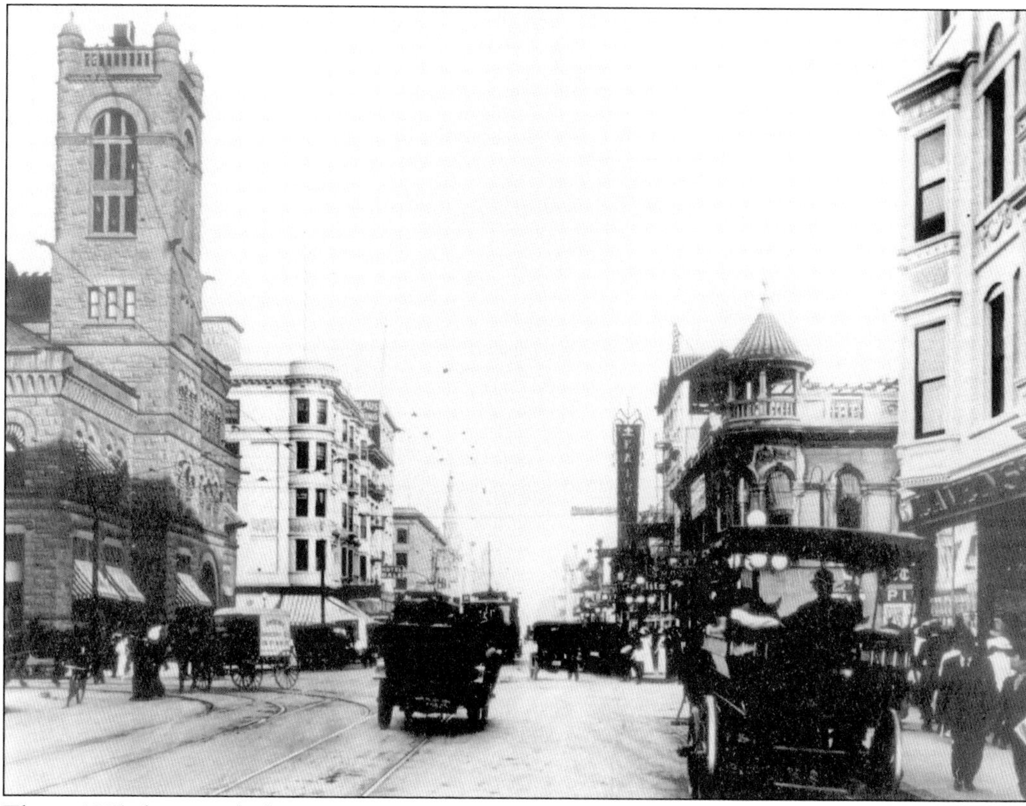

This *c.* 1915 photograph shows Seventh and K Streets looking east. Several Boulevard Park residents had businesses nearby The building just beyond the post office on the left was the property of John Ochsner. Alfred Braddock and his partner Charles O. DeLand had their shoe store across the street on the right, as was the Noack family's jewelry store. (Courtesy of SAMCC.)

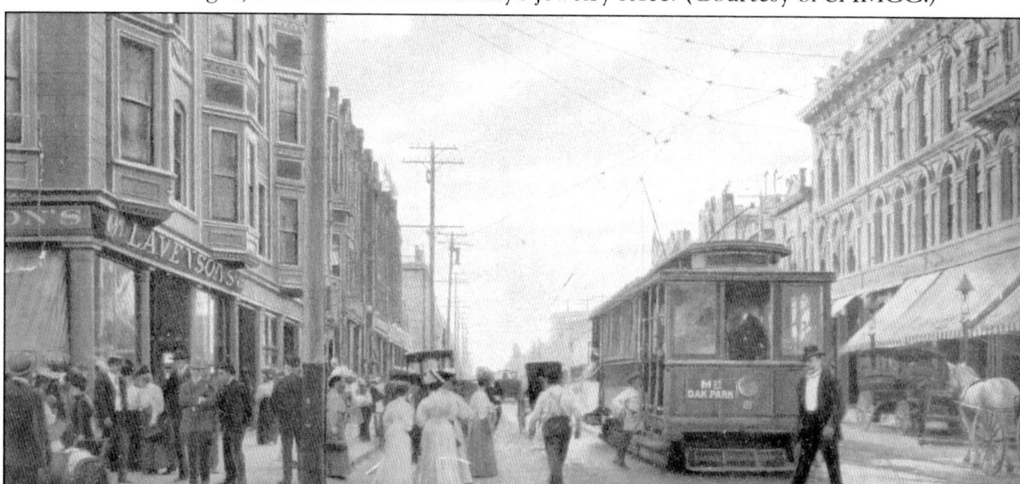

This *c.* 1900 postcard shows Seventh and K Streets looking west. Sarah and John Scott owned two houses in Boulevard Park at 710 and 714 Twenty-second Street. John was an employee of Lavenson's shoe store, which is on the ground floor on the left. (Courtesy of SAMCC.)

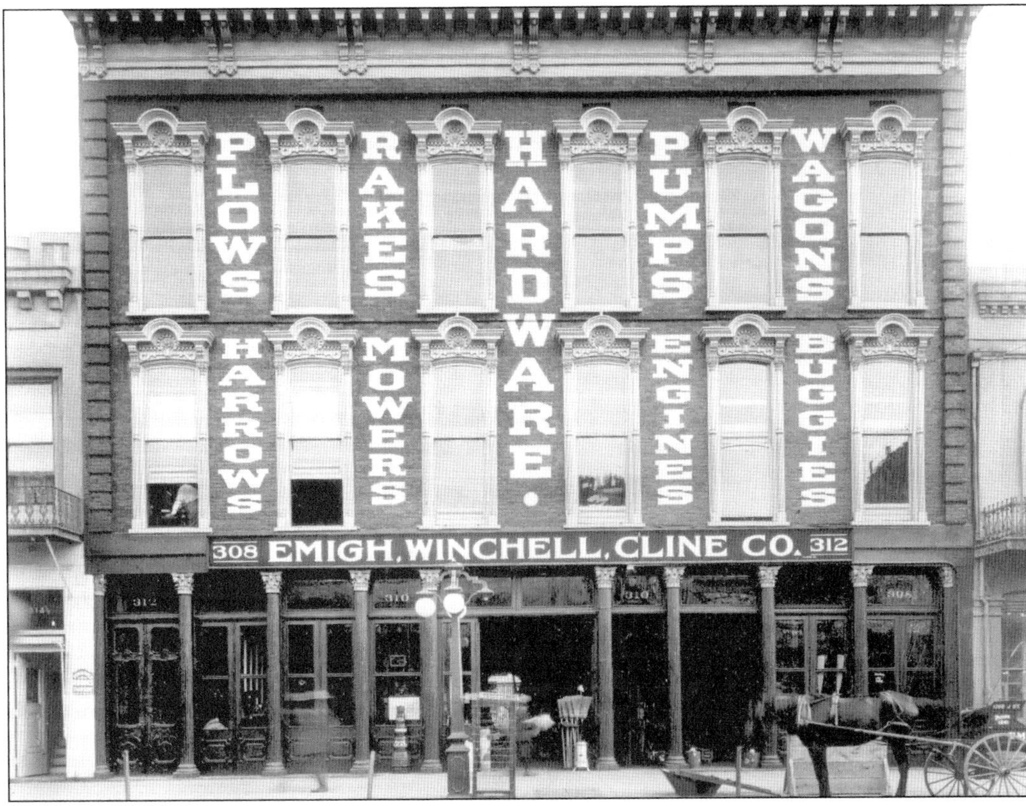

Emigh Hardware, still in business today on El Camino Avenue, was started in 1910 by James and Clay Emigh in this building at 308–312 J Street. In 1913, Harriet and James Emigh had their house built at 2406 H Street. The house was still occupied by their son Colby as late as the mid-1950s. (Courtesy of SAMCC.)

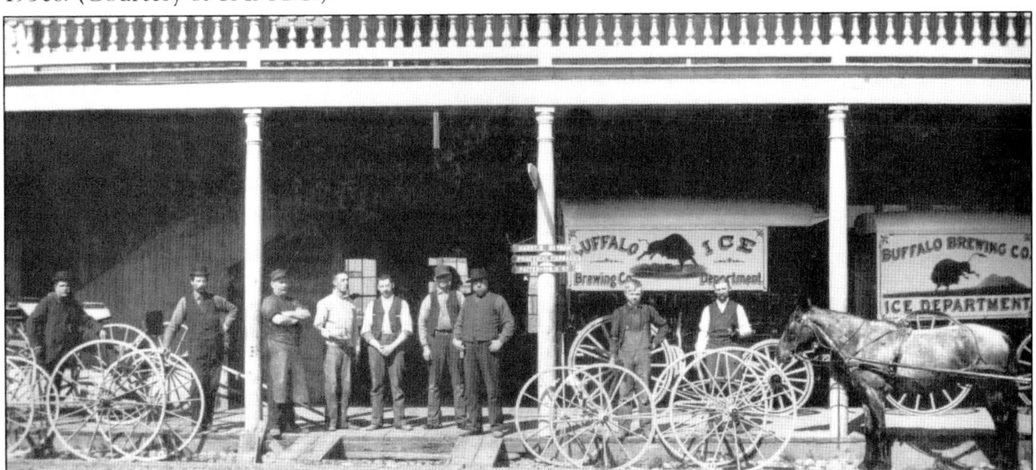

A good example of the sweeping changes that took part in society during the early years of Boulevard Park were the transformations in the occupations of Albert Derman (2022 D Street) and Henry O'Brien (2115 E Street), who both worked with Bowman's Carriage Works. Derman started as a blacksmith and O'Brien as a carriage painter. Later both were employed by Bowman's Hardware as mechanics. (Courtesy of SAMCC.)

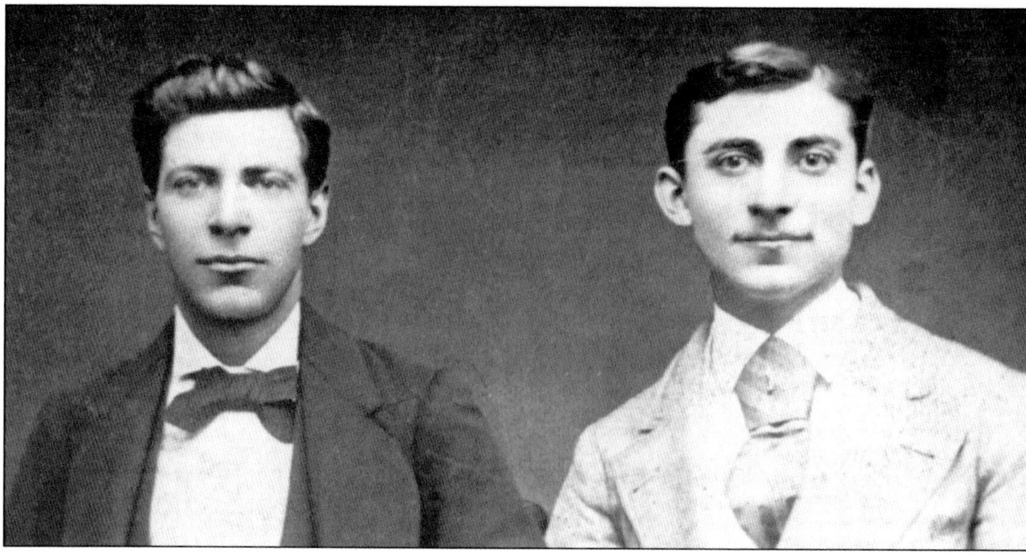

This photograph of half brothers Harris Weinstock (left) and David Lubin captures them as young men when they began their department store empire in Sacramento in the 1870s. Samuel W. McKim (2015 H Street) was president of the Weinstock-Lubin Company for 30 years. (Courtesy of SAMCC.)

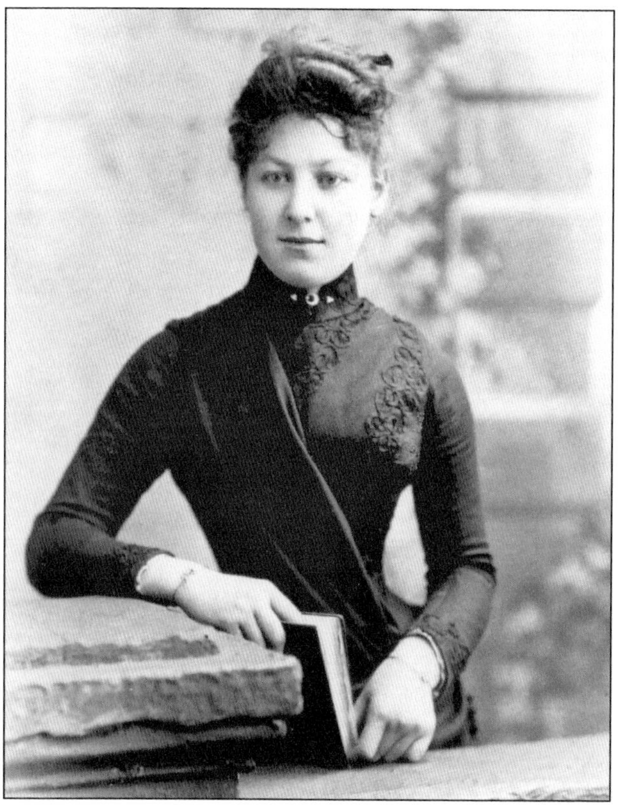

The pretty young woman pictured here is Florence (Platnauer) Lubin, David Lubin's second wife. Her brother was a local attorney and a resident of Boulevard Park (see page 81). (Courtesy of SAMCC.)

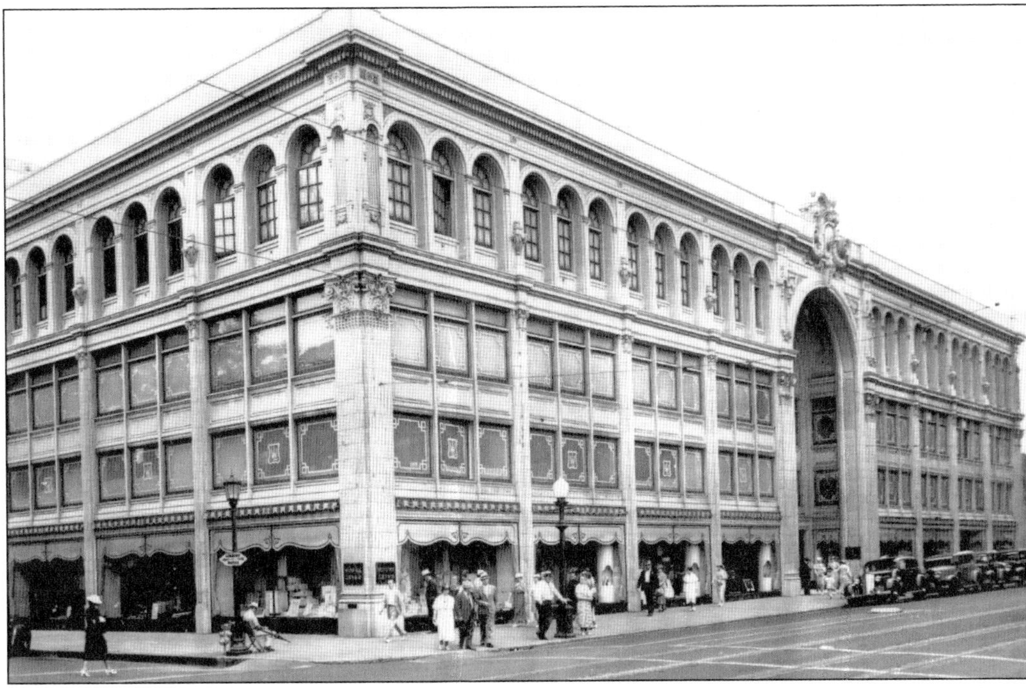

This landmark Sacramento building at Twelfth and K Street was built in 1923 by Weinstock and Lubin. (Courtesy of SAMCC.)

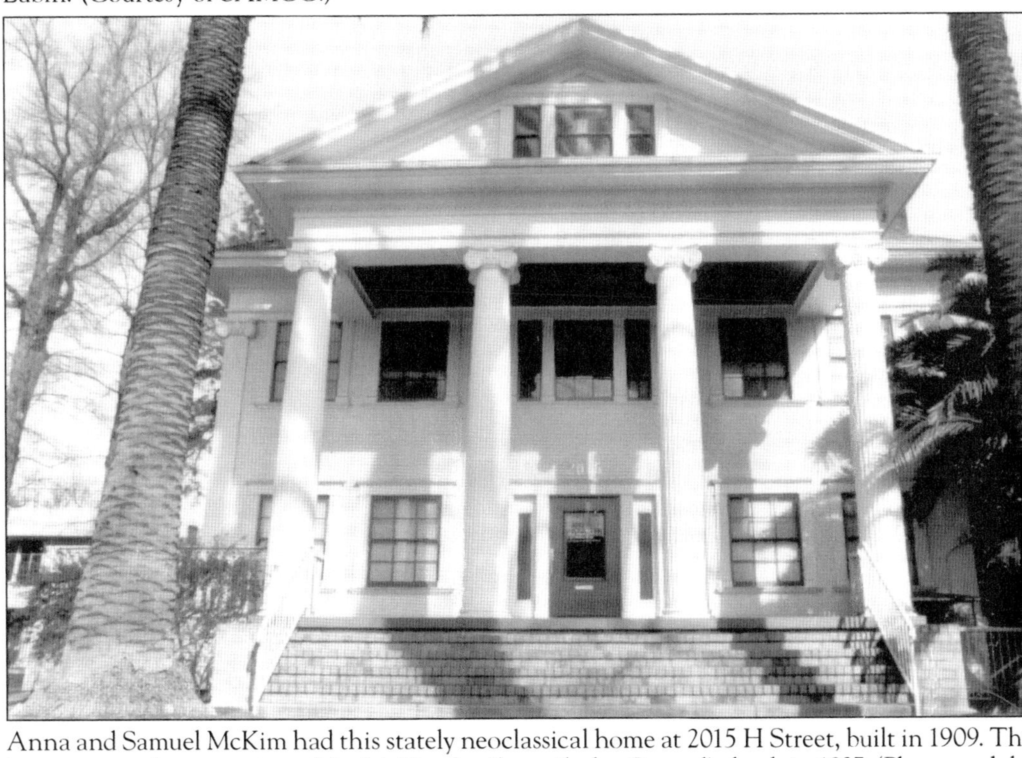

Anna and Samuel McKim had this stately neoclassical home at 2015 H Street, built in 1909. The house was in the possession of the McKim family until after Samuel's death in 1937. (Photograph by Paula Boghosian.)

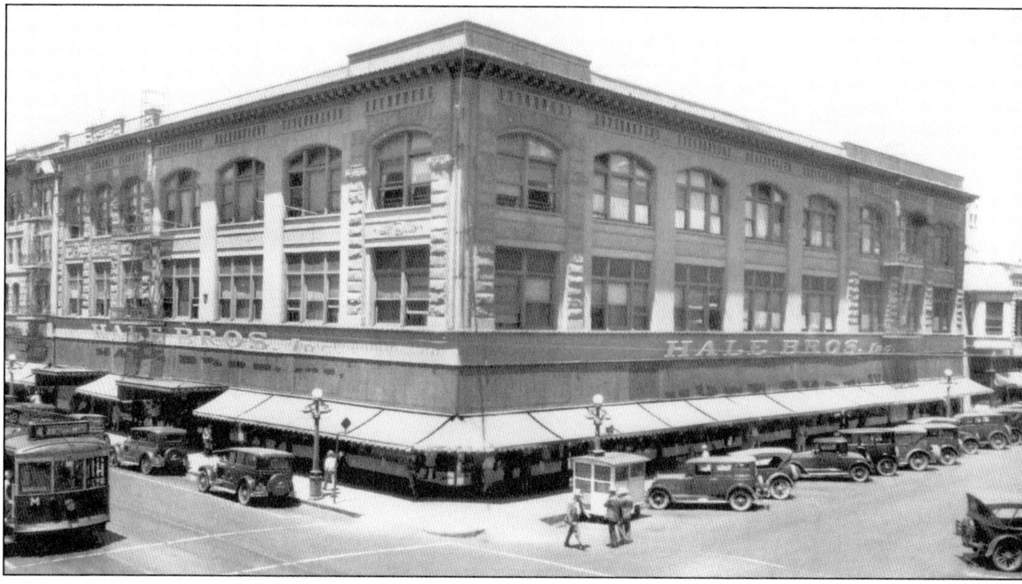

The Hale brothers building at Ninth and K Streets is another Sacramento landmark. It's restored current appearance dates from 1909, designed by Seadler and Hoen. For many years, it was not known that Hale's had secretly bought Weinstock and Lubin in the late 1920s. Forest May (2012 C Street), a buyer, and Charles W. Kuchman (617 Twenty-first Street), a department manager, worked in this building. (Courtesy of SAMCC.)

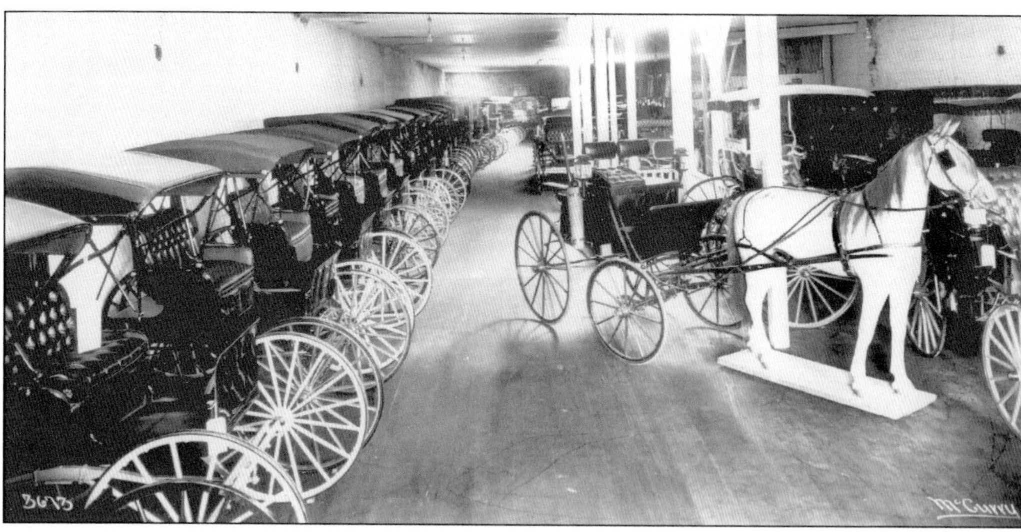

In 1909, most patrons would have parked their buggies at the curb on a dirt street. The carriages displayed for sale in this photograph were available from Bowman's. In less than 20 years, the hitching posts in front of many Boulevard Park homes went from a necessity to a quaint artifact. (Courtesy of SAMCC.)

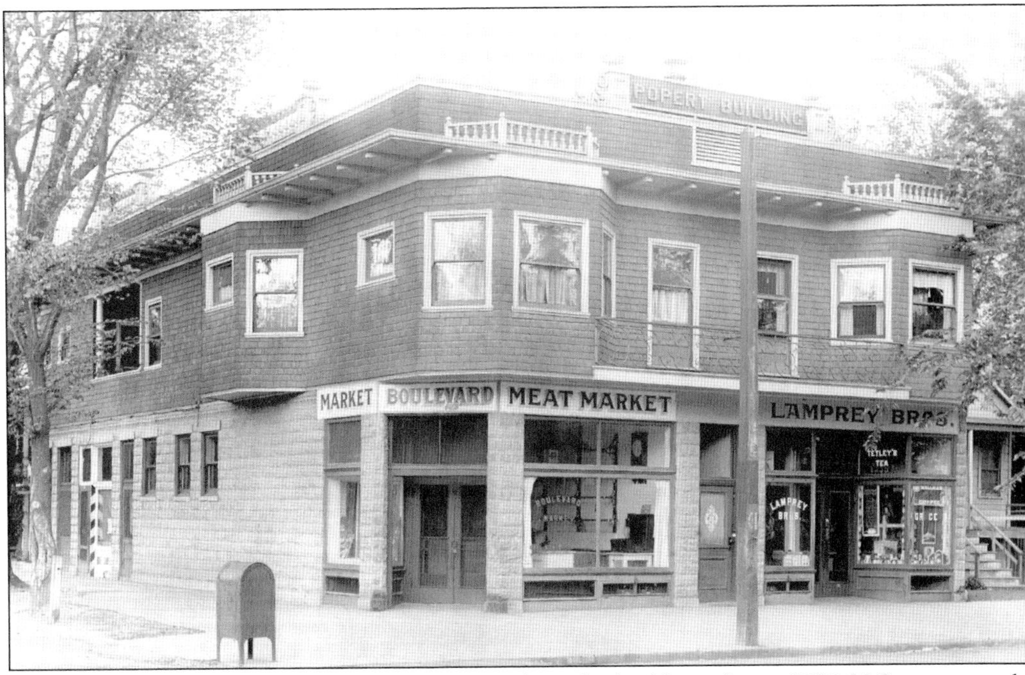

This photograph was taken in the mid-1930s when the building above, 2030 H Street, was the Boulevard Meat Market. Before that, it housed Cyrus Martin's (630 Twenty-first Street) pharmacy. (Courtesy of SAMCC.)

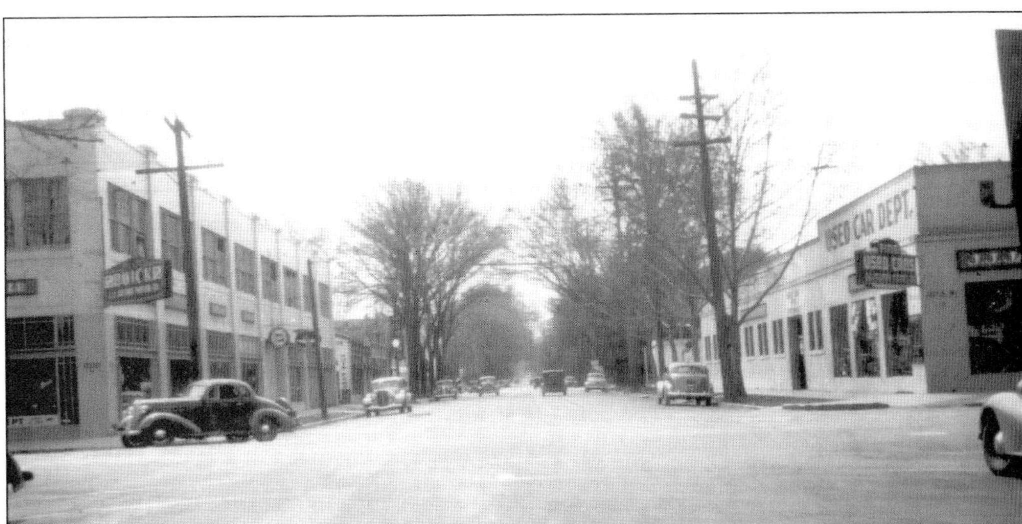

This c. 1940 Hepting photograph shows J. J. Jacobs's (620 Twenty-second Street) new and used automobile agency, with buildings lining both sides of Fifteenth Street. (Courtesy of SAMCC.)

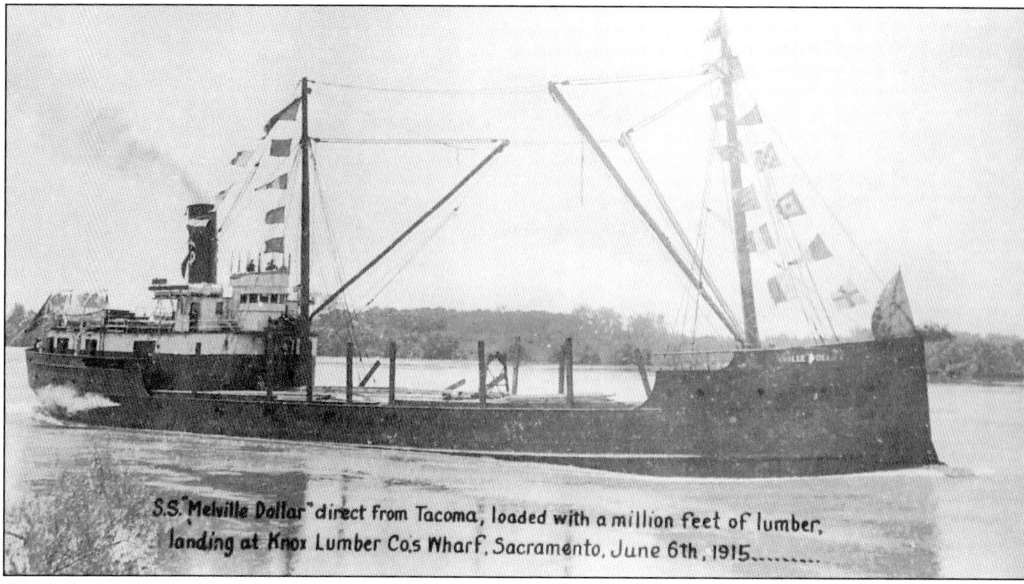

This ship is delivering lumber to the Knox Lumber Company. Oscar H. Miller (2001 I Street) was president and part owner of the Knox Lumber Company. He started as a bookkeeper for the firm in 1890 and retired 50 years later as its head. (Courtesy of SAMCC.)

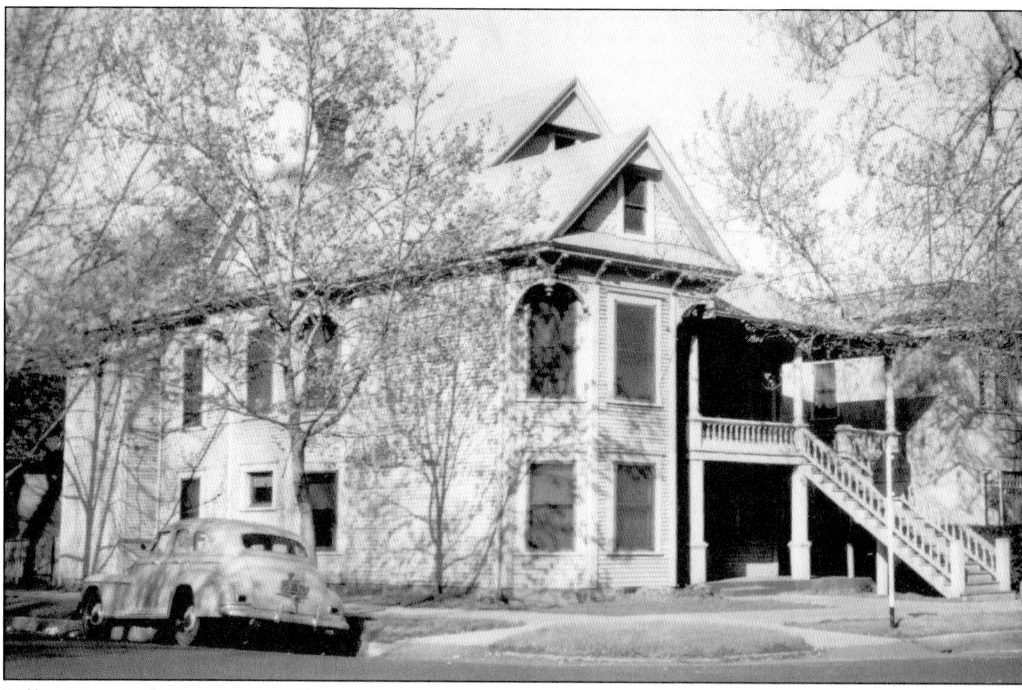

Lillie Mae and Oscar H. Miller lived at 2001 I Street for many years, beginning in at least 1905. As was often the custom of the time, since women lived longer than men, Lillie was the owner of the property. However, Oscar outlived both Lillie and their son Walter. The only one he could not outlive was their granddaughter Sandra Mae Miller. (Courtesy of SAMCC.)

This building on J Street was the headquarters of the C. H. Krebs and Company. Franklin Krebs, manager, was also a director at Fort Sutter Bank and a director of the Klamath Corporation. He was described by the *Sacramento Bee* as "prominent in the fraternal and financial circles of Sacramento." The stone storefront was designed by James Seadler in 1893. (Courtesy of SAMCC.)

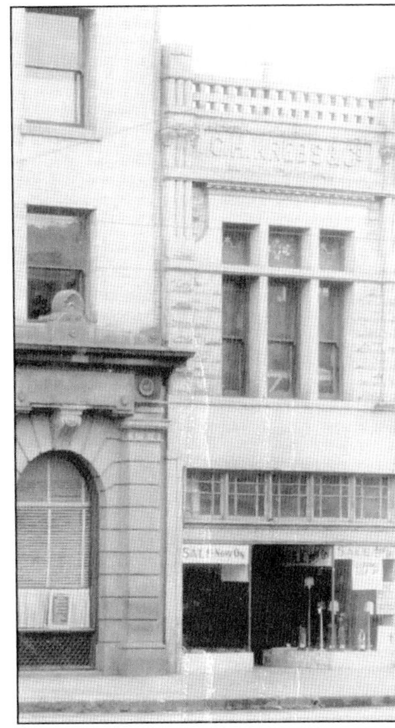

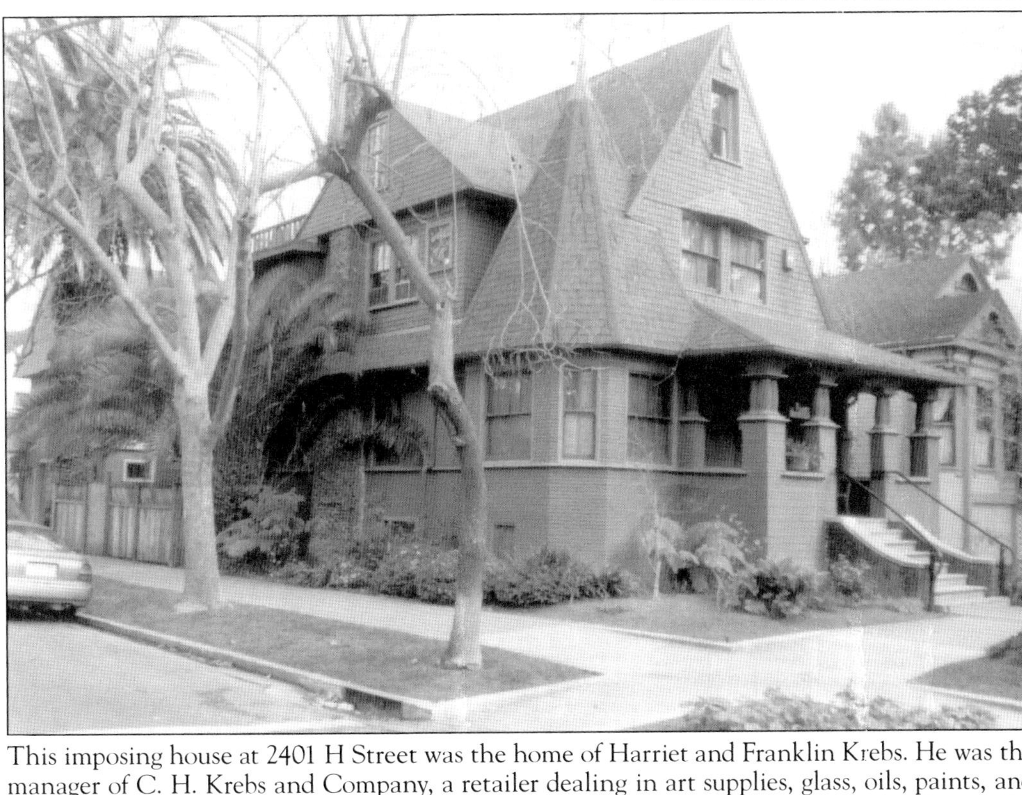

This imposing house at 2401 H Street was the home of Harriet and Franklin Krebs. He was the manager of C. H. Krebs and Company, a retailer dealing in art supplies, glass, oils, paints, and wallpapers. He died young at the age of 47 in 1913. Harriet, or Hattie, continued to live in the house until she passed away in 1938. (Photograph by Paula Boghosian.)

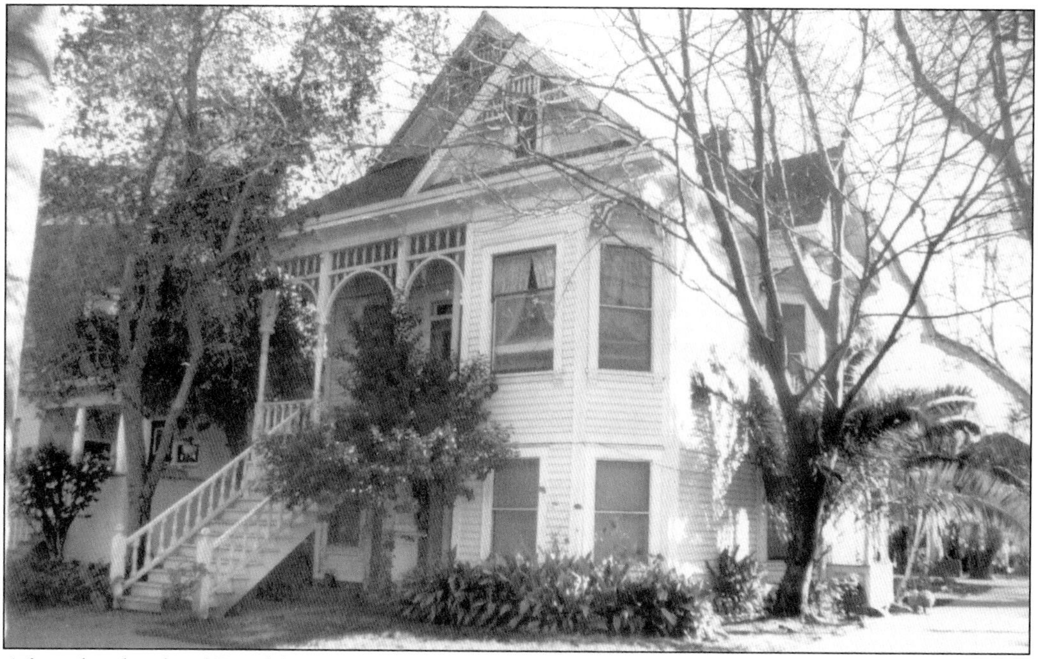

After the death of Franklin Krebs, Theodore Eder became the manager of C. H. Krebs and Company. He lived in this Queen Anne–style home at 2400 H Street, across the street from the Krebs House. Margaret and Theodore Eder lived in the house for a few years in the early 1910s and then used it as a rental until they sold it in 1938. (Photograph by Paula Boghosian.)

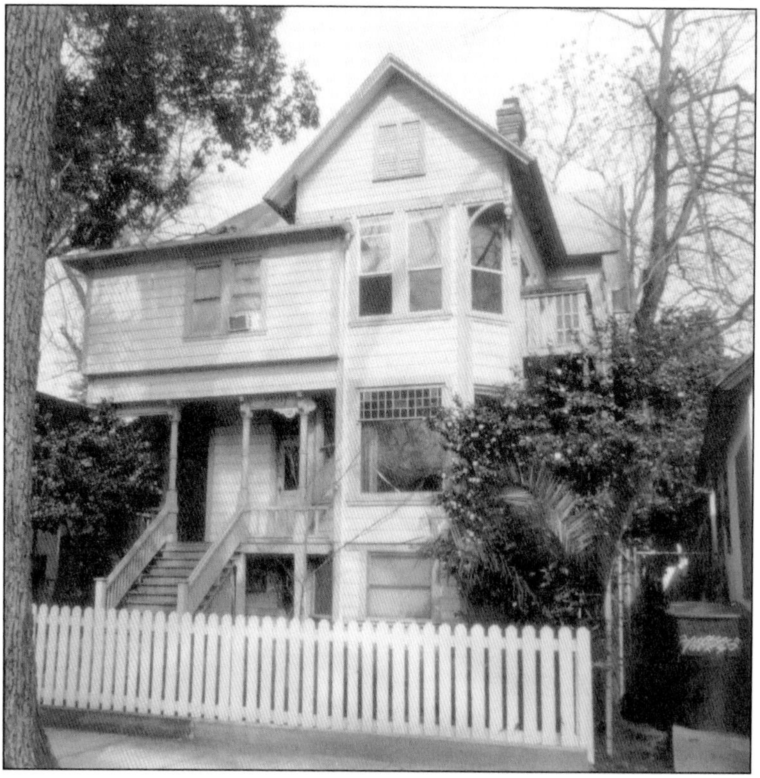

For 50 years, this house, just a block west of the Krebs and Eder houses, was the home of Alfred G. Labhard. In the 1920s, he was the superintendent of the paint department at C. H. Krebs and Company. His brother Theodore, who also lived in the house, was director of the local chapter of the American Bankers Association. (Photograph by Paula Boghosian.)

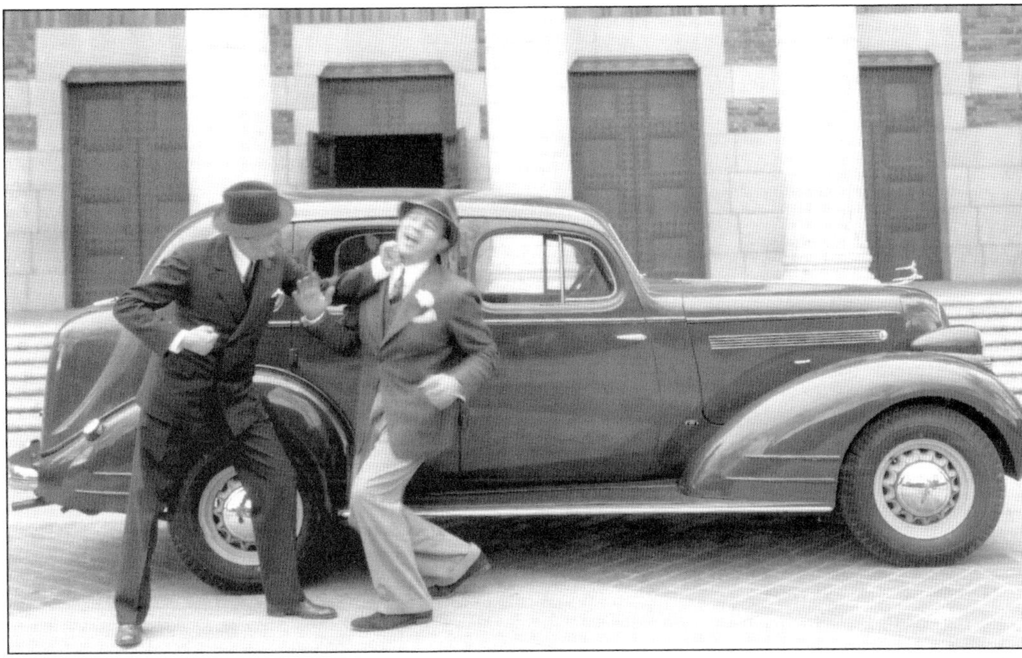

Auto dealer William Elliot (left) clowns around with heavyweight champion Max Baer before a Baer fight at Memorial Auditorium, probably a promotion for the 1934 Baer fight with Primo Carnera. Elliot lived in a flat at 401 Twenty-first Street for a few years. (Courtesy of SAMCC.)

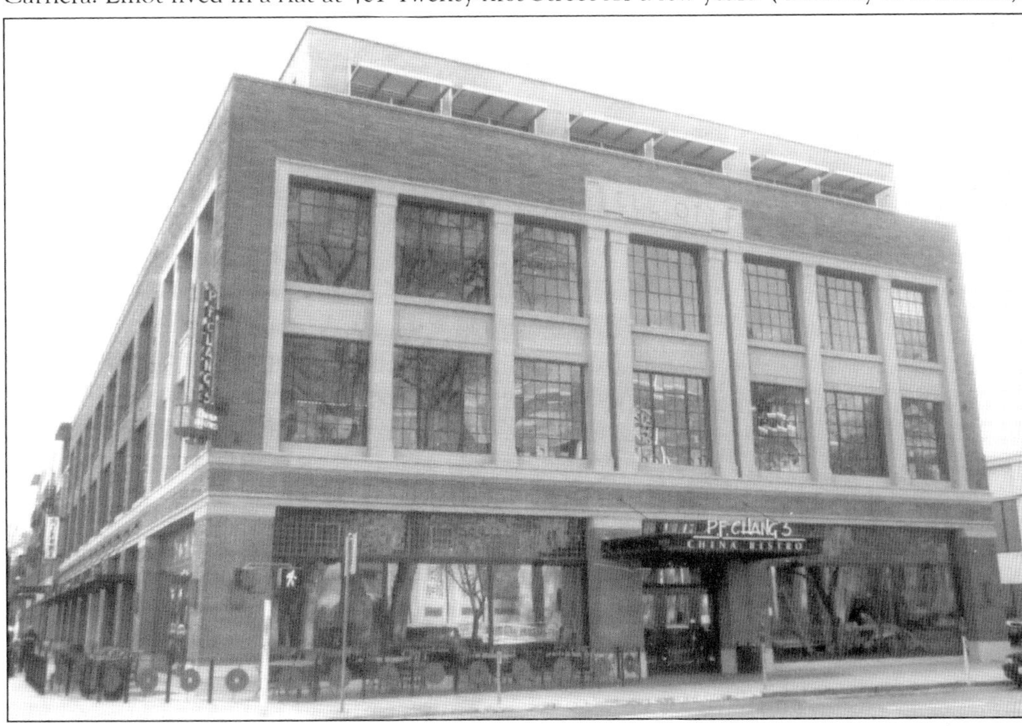

Elliot's auto agency was housed in this 1922 building across the street from Memorial Auditorium. It was recently renovated and is now occupied by two popular restaurants, offices, and loft apartments. (Photograph by Donald Cox.)

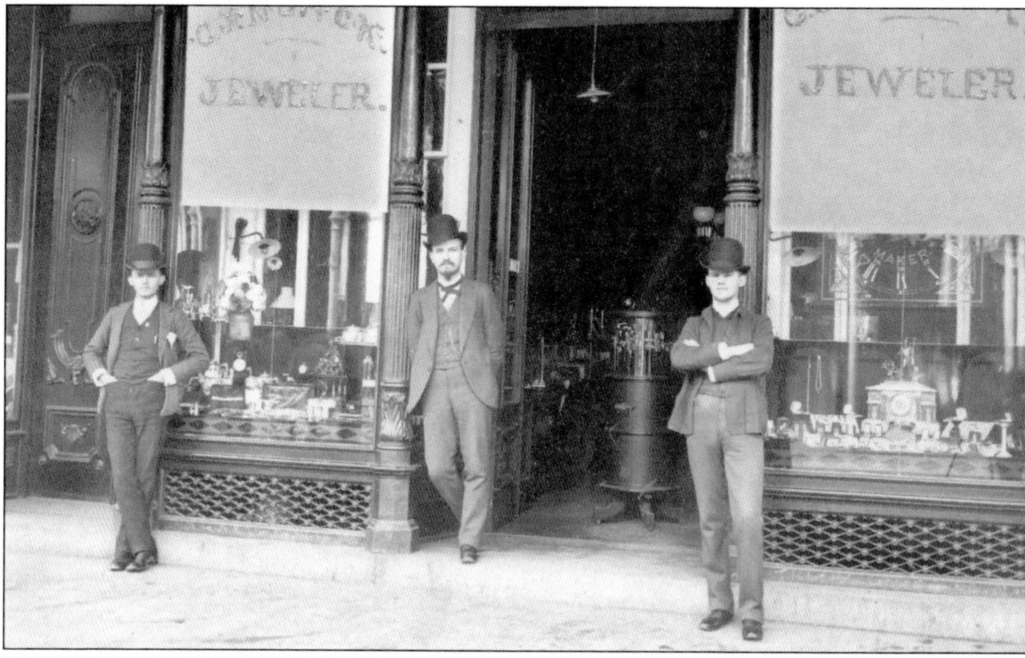

In 1870, Charles Noack established a jewelry store (614 J Street) in Sacramento and was joined in 1886 by his two younger brothers Otto (617 Twenty-first Street) and Alex (2119 G Street). In the photograph, the Noacks, from left to right, are Otto, Charles J., and Alex. (Courtesy of SAMCC.)

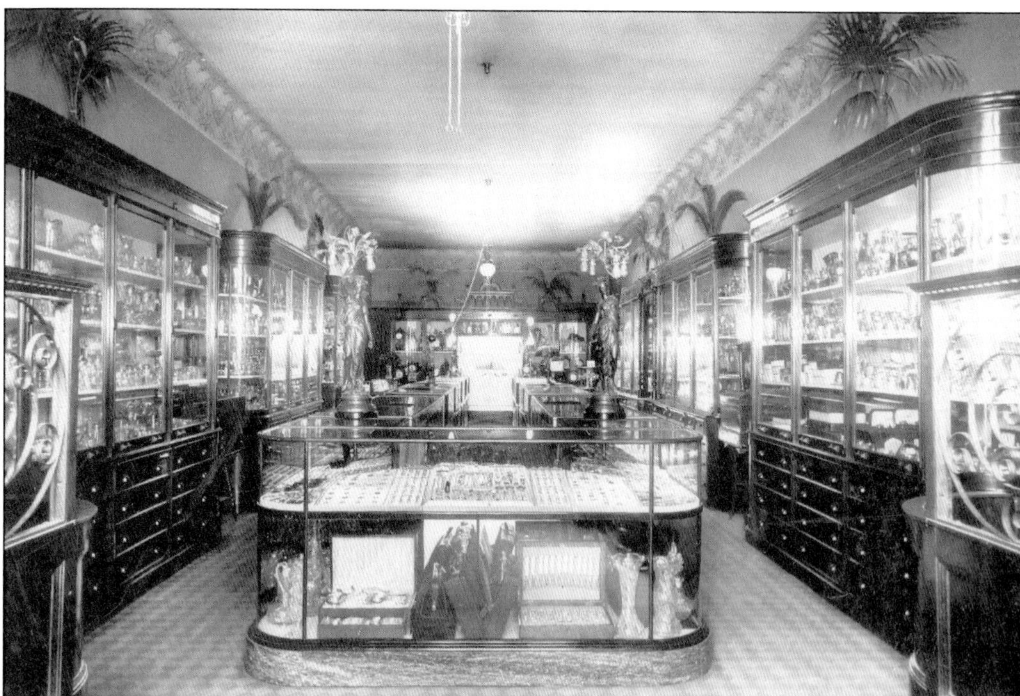

This photograph shows the interior of the 704 K Street Noack store in 1905. Although simple in design, it is elegantly appointed. Charles Noack died in 1905. (Courtesy of SAMCC.)

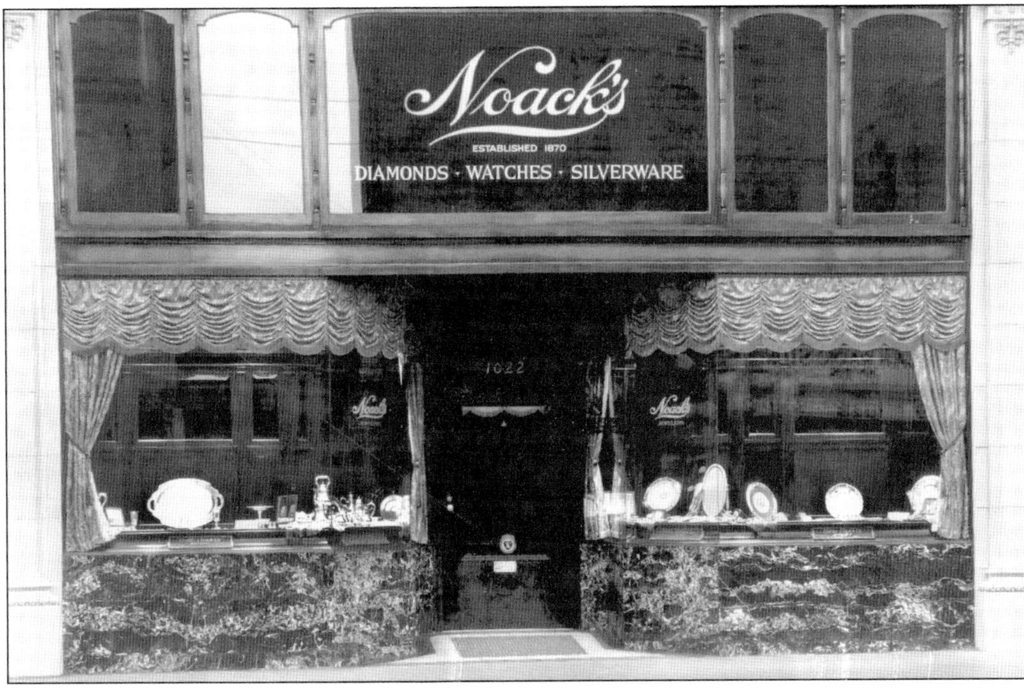

Noack's stores kept moving up K Street. Their next store, after 704 K Street, was 816 K Street and then this location at 1022 K Street. Prosperity led to larger stores and a more elaborate sense of style. (Courtesy of SAMCC.)

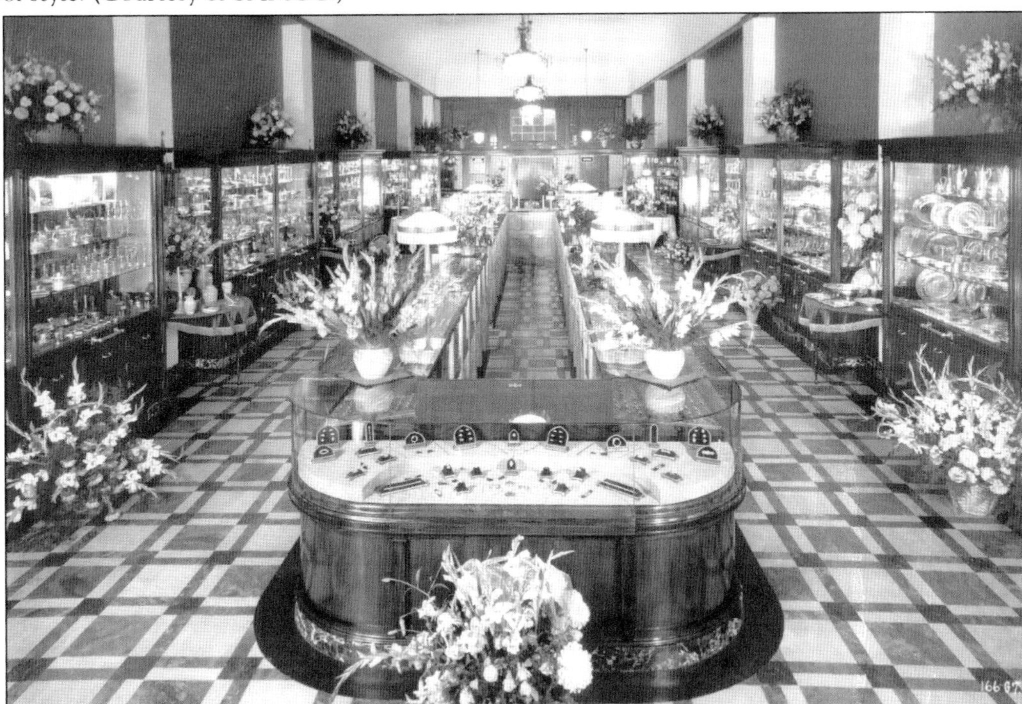

Compare the interior of this store at 1022 K Street to the one at 704 K Street. The elegance of this interior would rival any jewelry store today. (Courtesy of SAMCC.)

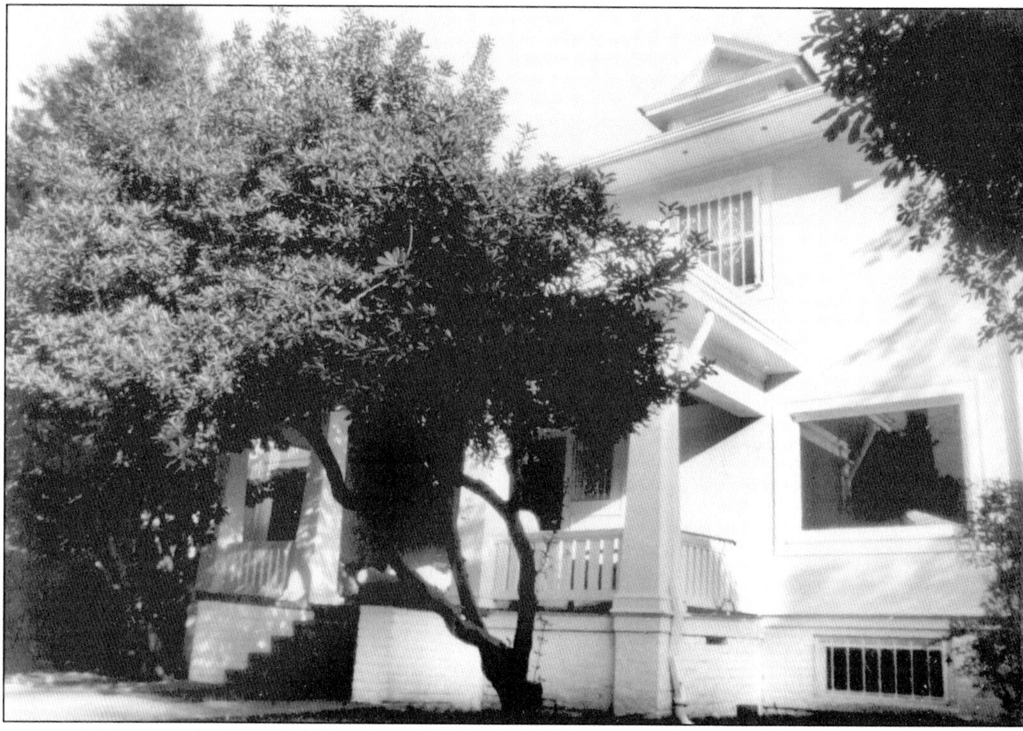

Around 1910, Catherine and Otto Noack built this house at 617 Twenty-first Street. Otto Noack was a musician. He had an orchestra that performed regularly at the Metropolitan Theater and he conducted a symphony orchestra for many years. By the time Otto died in 1943, the brothers had retired and sold the jewelry business. (Courtesy of SAMCC.)

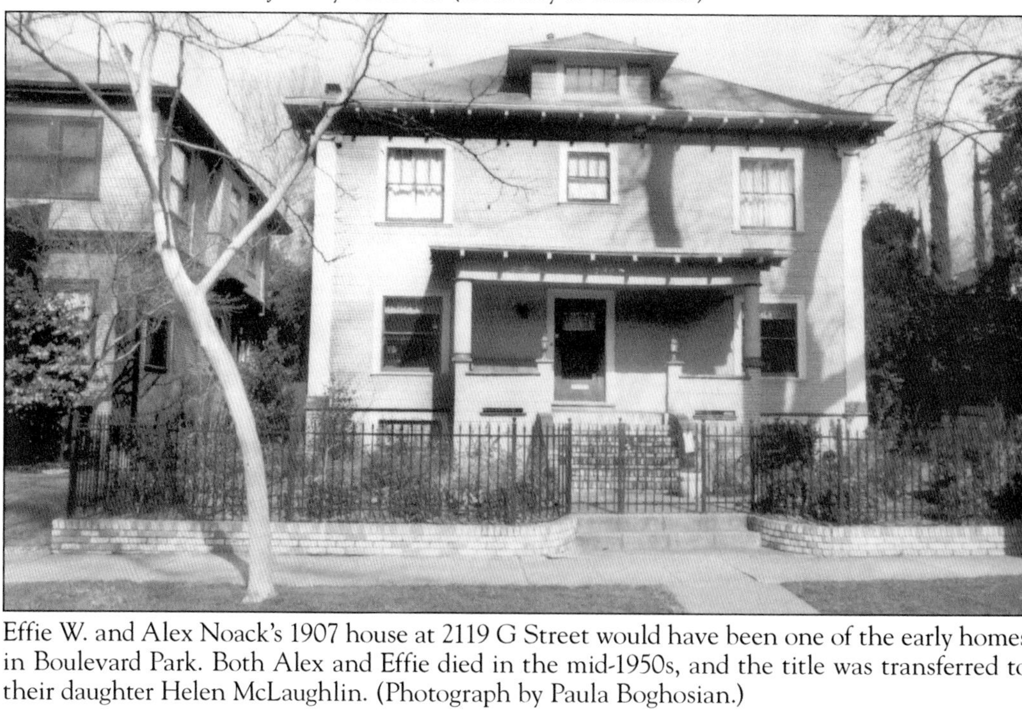

Effie W. and Alex Noack's 1907 house at 2119 G Street would have been one of the early homes in Boulevard Park. Both Alex and Effie died in the mid-1950s, and the title was transferred to their daughter Helen McLaughlin. (Photograph by Paula Boghosian.)

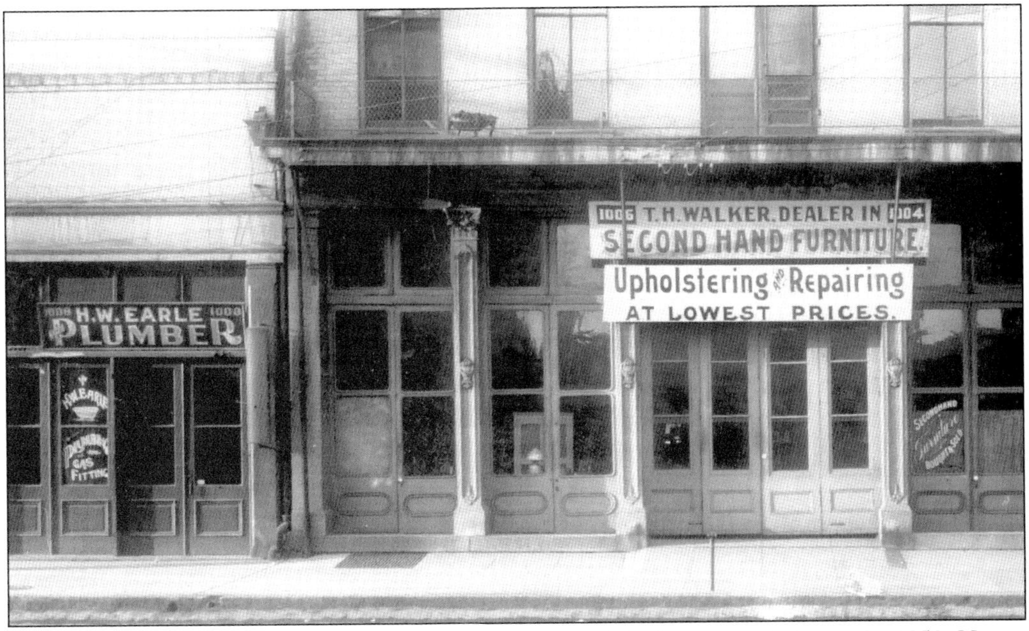

On the left in this photograph is the storefront of H. W. Earle at 1008 J Street. In 1858, Henry Earle founded a plumbing business. Henry's son Otis joined his older brothers in the business in 1908. While they focused mostly on residential plumbing, they did plumb the Sutter and Capitol Hotels. (Courtesy of SAMCC.)

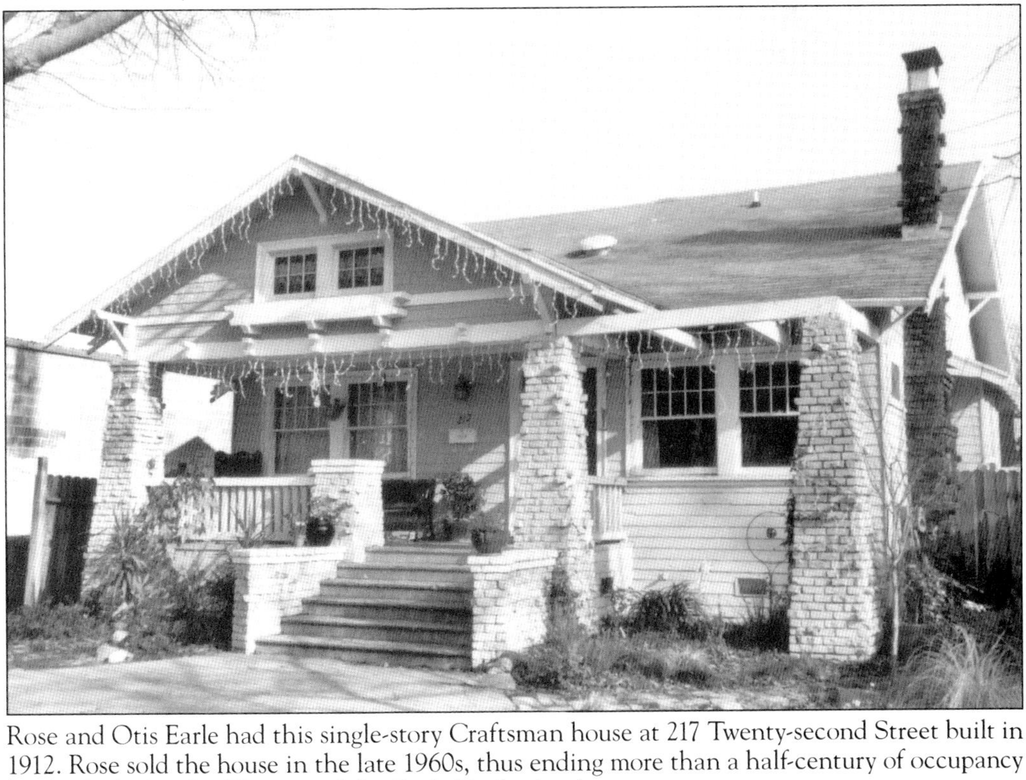

Rose and Otis Earle had this single-story Craftsman house at 217 Twenty-second Street built in 1912. Rose sold the house in the late 1960s, thus ending more than a half-century of occupancy by the Earle family. (Photograph by Paula Boghosian.)

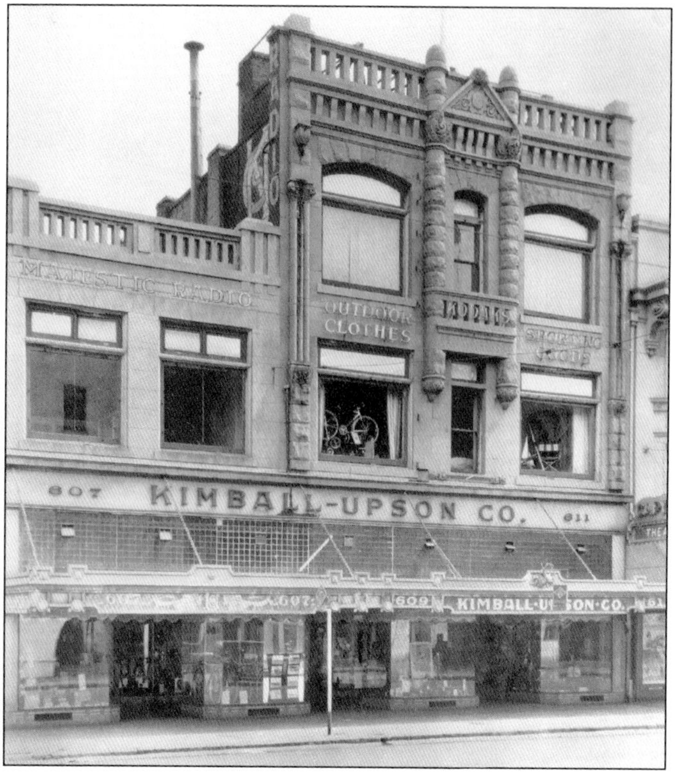

In 1870, Moses Kimball established a sporting goods store. In 1893, he took in L. Stuart Upson as a partner and they operated out of this store at 607–611 K Street for several decades. Upson was a noted track athlete and bicycle racer. In later years, the business transitioned into radios and auto parts. (Courtesy of SAMCC.)

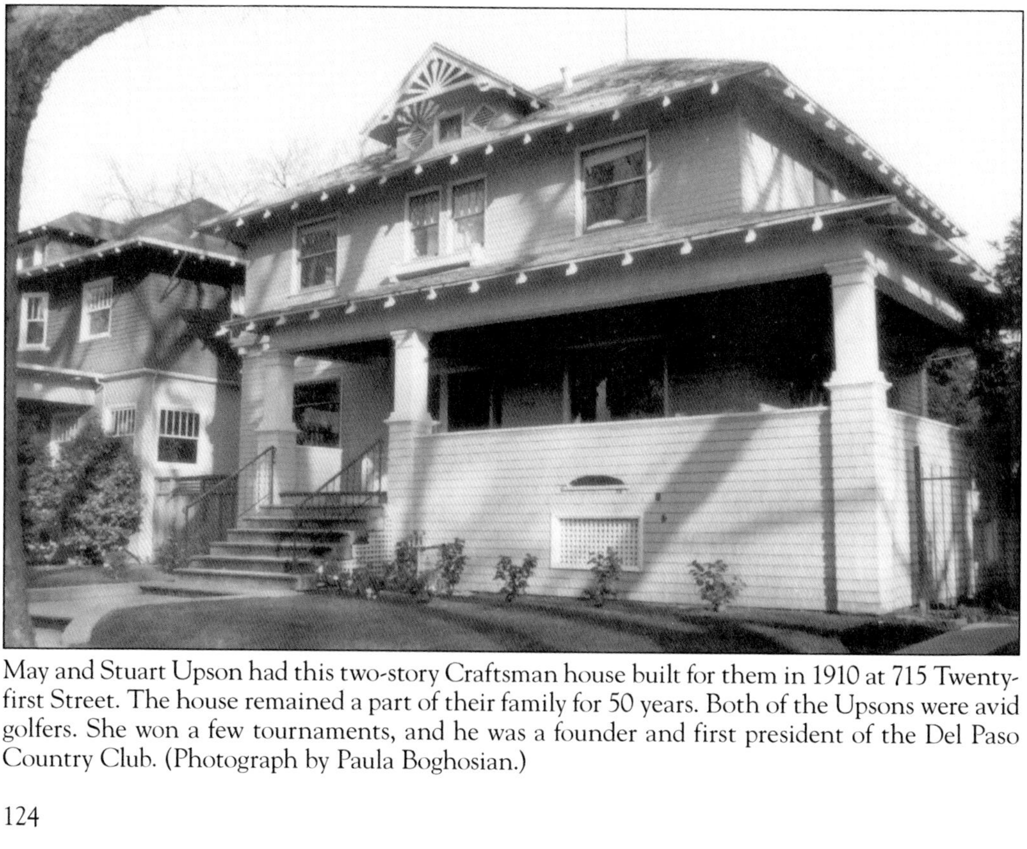

May and Stuart Upson had this two-story Craftsman house built for them in 1910 at 715 Twenty-first Street. The house remained a part of their family for 50 years. Both of the Upsons were avid golfers. She won a few tournaments, and he was a founder and first president of the Del Paso Country Club. (Photograph by Paula Boghosian.)

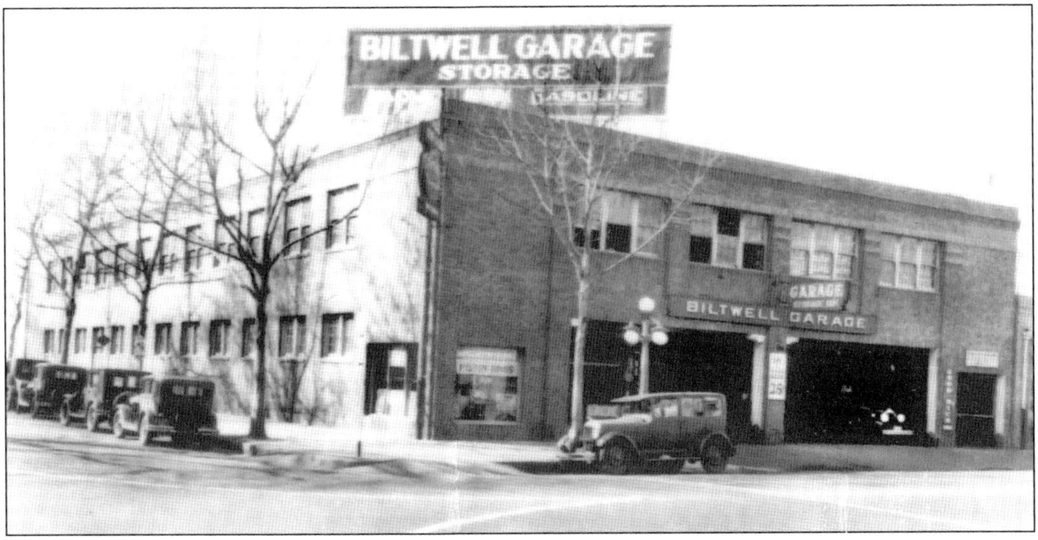

Louis Sposito (2000 E Street) originally made his money by establishing a freight and trucking company. He sold that business in 1923, which is about the time that his house was built. He invested some of his cash in the Biltwell Garage at 830 L Street. It is still used as a garage at the present time. (Courtesy of Paula Boghosian.)

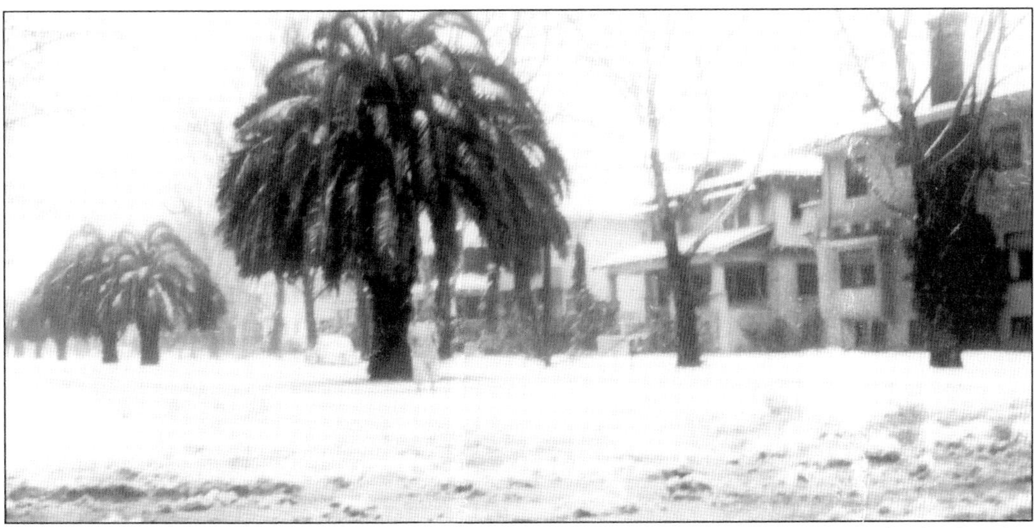

Hepting identified this woman in front of the palm tree as Louise Paahman, a cook who lived at 722 Twenty-fifth Street. This March 14, 1942, photograph was taken on H Street looking north to Twenty-first Street. (Courtesy of SAMCC.)

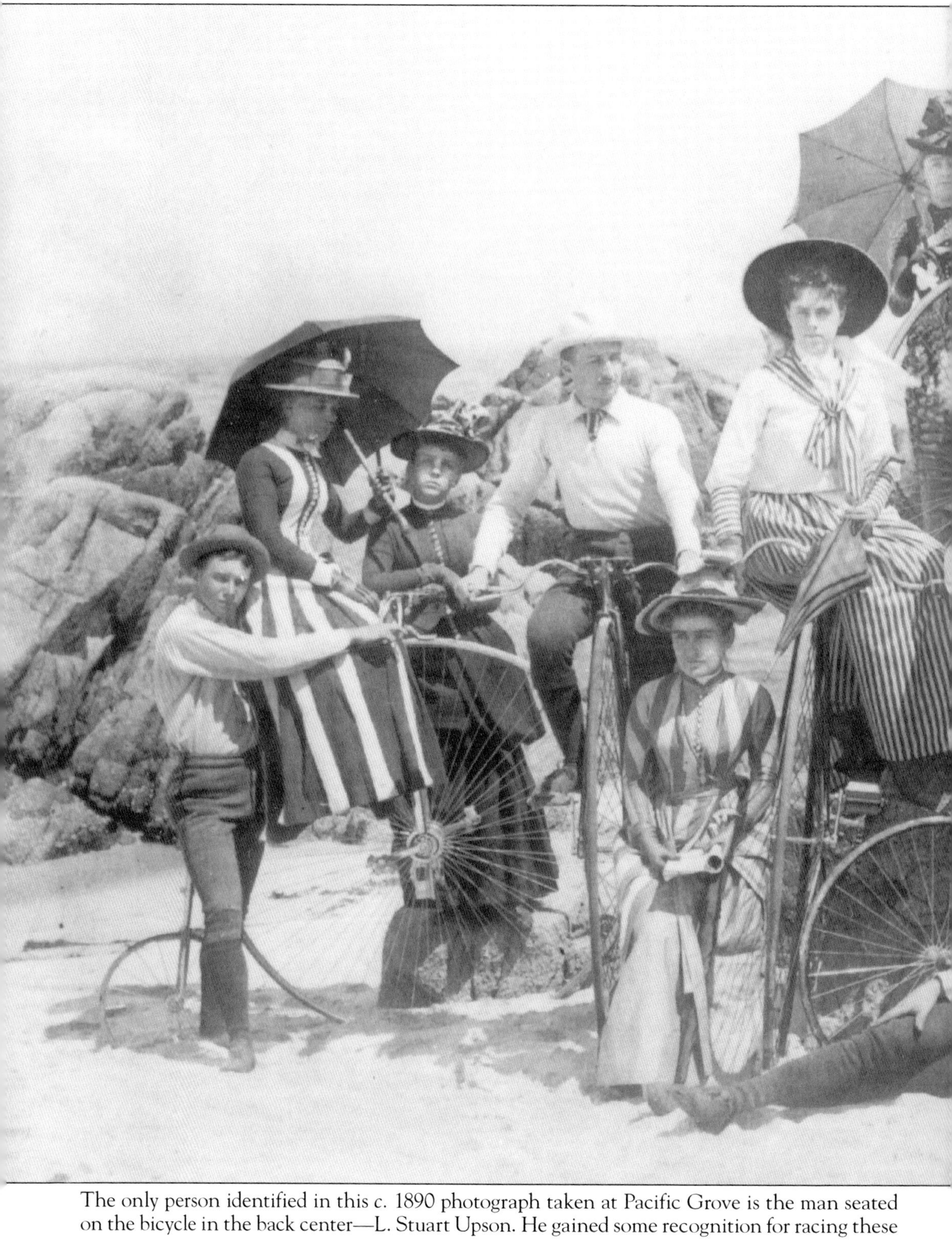

The only person identified in this c. 1890 photograph taken at Pacific Grove is the man seated on the bicycle in the back center—L. Stuart Upson. He gained some recognition for racing these

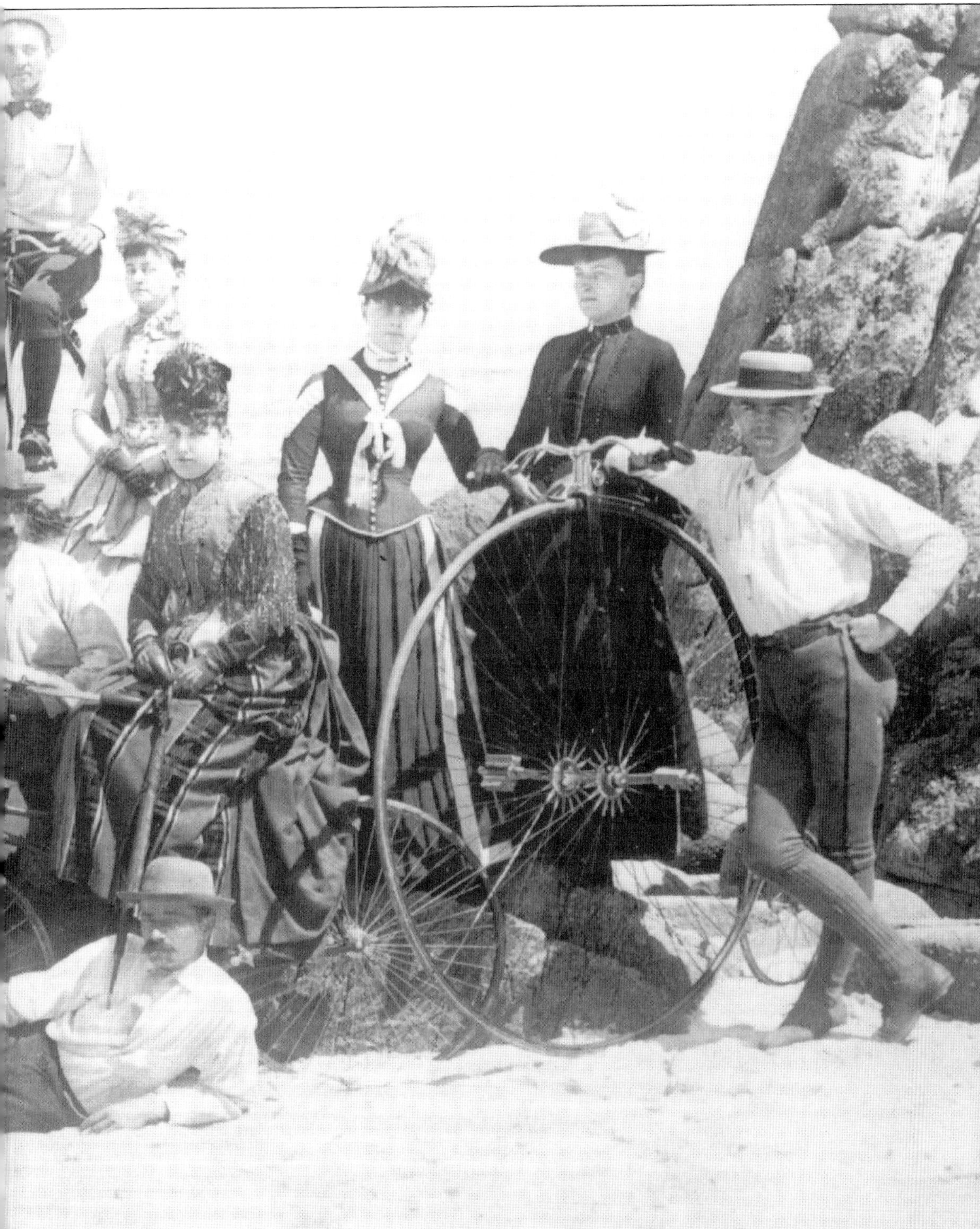

large-wheel bicycles, setting speed and distance records. The woman to the immediate left of him is probably his wife, Mae. (Courtesy of SAMCC.)